2

Tallulah Bankhead

Other titles by David Bret and published by Robson Books

The Piaf Legend
The Mistinguett Legend
Maurice Chevalier
Marlene, My Friend
Morrissey: Landscapes of the Mind
Gracie Fields: The Authorized Biography

Tallulah Bankhead

A Scandalous Life

David Bret

Robson Books

First published in Great Britain in 1996 by Robson
Books Ltd, Bolsover House, 5–6 Clipstone Street,
London W1P 8LE

British Library Cataloguing in Publication Data
A catalogue record for this title is available from the
British Library

ISBN 1 86105 015 1

Photoset in North Wales by Derek Doyle & Associates,
Mold, Flintshire. Printed in Great Britain by St Edmunds-
bury Press Ltd, Bury St Edmunds, Suffolk.

Contents

This book is dedicated to the memory of
Irene Bevan (1913–1996) and Les Enfants de Novembre

N'oublie pas …
La vie sans amis c'est comme
un jardin sans fleurs

Acknowledgements

Writing this book would not have been possible had it not been for the inspiration, criticisms and love of that select group of individuals whom I still regard as my true family and *autre coeur*: Barbara, Irene Bevan, René and Lucette Chevalier, Jacqueline Danno, Hélène Delavault, Marlene Dietrich, Tony Griffin, Roger Normand, Betty Paillard, Annick Roux, Monica Solash, Terry Sanderson, John and Anne Taylor, François and Madeleine Vals. God bless you all!

Special thanks to my tireless agent, David Bolt, and to the superb publishing team at Robson Books. Very many thanks too, to a select handful of Alabamans who each in his or her own way have helped to promote the name of Tallulah Bankhead throughout the world: Deborah and Rick Storey, the staff of the Carl Eliot Regional Library, Steve Cox, Donald Roxby, Gwen Parks, Donny H Grace, Velma and Kenneth Thomas, Mark Palmer and the staff of the Alabama Department of Archives and History. A huge, huge thank you to Nancy M Nilsson (the next time you visit Rock Hall, don't be afraid of using the lipstick – Tallulah would feel honoured!).

For their help and contribution to this book, I would like to thank the following journalists/columnists/writers, living and deceased: Zoë Akins, John Anderson, Cecil Beaton, Arnold Bennett, Alan Brien, John Mason Brown, John Cambridge, John Chapman, John Crosby, Bosley Crowther, Macdonald Daly, Gordon M Eby, Jerry Gehegan, Merv Griffin, Gladys Hall, Percy Hammond, Dora Jane Hamblin, Don Iddon, Clive James, Walter Kerr, Lane Lambert, H L McNally, Michael

Mok, Louella Parsons, Robert Lewis Shayon, Hannen Swaffer, J C Trewin, Richard Watts and Cecil Wilson.

For allowing me access to invaluable interviews, features and rare archive material, I thank the following publications past and present: In Great Britain: *Daily Mail, Daily Express,* London *Evening Standard, The Sketch, Theatre World, The Week-End Review, Motion Picture.*

In America: *Variety, New York Post, Daily Worker, New York Journal, New York Telegram, Time, Huntsville Times, Jasper Mountain Eagle, Hollywood Reporter, New York Herald Tribune, New York Times, Saturday Review, Picture Play, Evening Mail, New York Evening Post, Life, New Yorker, Philadelphia Daily News, Daily News.*

Most important of all I would like to express my undying love to my wife, Jeanne, still the keeper of my soul.

David Bret

Introduction

Tallulah is a wicked archangel, with her flaming ash-blonde hair and carven features. Her profile is perfectly Grecian. She is Medusa, very exotic, with glorious skull, high pumice-stone cheekbones and a broad brow. Her cheeks are huge acid peonies. Her eyelashes are built out with hot liquid paint to look like burnt matches. Her sullen, discontented rosebud of a mouth is painted the brightest scarlet and is as shiny as Tiptree's Strawberry Jam ...

This was how Cecil Beaton described Tallulah Bankhead, but no one better summed up this fascinating creature than Tallulah herself, in an endless succession of anecdotes and one-liners, peppered with the expletives that became her trademark.

TALLULAH LOVES TO SHOCK!

In August 1932, Hollywood's most feared scandalmonger, Hedda Hopper, wrote, 'We're in for an era of clean pictures which are unprecedented in the history of the motion picture industry.' She was referring to the Motion Picture Code which had recently been introduced by Will Hays who, on an annual salary of $100,000, had pulled together the Catholic Church and the Bank of America in his fight to cleanse to screen of its many forms of corruption: gratuitous violence, bad language, sex and any other subject likely to infringe upon public morality.

Hays and his handpicked team compiled a 'Doom Book' within which were written 130 names of 'unsafe and unsavoury persons'. Some had merely appeared stripped to the waist in adventure films. Others, such as Mae West and Jean Harlow, were accused of 'offending' the American nation by way of sexual innuendo. No star, however, incurred Hays's wrath quite so much as Tallulah, who was awarded a separate listing in the 'Doom Book' under the heading, 'Verbal Moral Turpitude'. In other words, she stood accused of corrupting her fans by telling them too much about her raunchy personal life.

Tallulah was warned by influential friends, such as Walter Wanger, not even to think of taking on the might of the Hays Office single-handed. As usual, she followed her natural instinct for causing trouble by arranging an interview with the equally fearless Gladys Hall of *Motion Picture* magazine. The published result of this meeting entered Hollywood lore as 'The Tallulah Bankhead I-Want-a-Man story' and, even in its heavily edited version, was said to have shocked Mae West. Hall explained the Bankhead phenomenon to her amazed readers:

> She disguises nothing. She gives to all the functions of loving and living, of body and soul, their rounded Rabelaisian biological names. She has a romantic interlude and discusses it with lurid detail and complete unreserve – his abilities and disabilities, his prowess or lack of prowess – with such consummate abandon that the unfortunate male can think of no recourse, except immediate suicide.

And if Will Hays's strait-laced disciples were shocked thus far, they blanched at the subsequent paragraph which contained just one of Tallulah's much-practised philosophies, this time not so censored:

> I am serious about my work. I am serious about marriage – too serious to indulge in it! I am the type who fattens on unrequited love, on the just beyond reach. The minute a man begins languishing over me, I stiffen and it's *finis*! I'm serious about love, *damned* serious about it now of all times, for I haven't had an affair for six months! That's *too* long! I am not promiscuous!

Promiscuity implies that attraction is not necessary! I may lay my eyes on a man, and have an affair with him the next hour! If there's anything *wrong* with me, it's certainly not Hollywood's state of mind! *I want a man! Six months is a long, long while! I want a man right now!*

TALLULAH LOVES BIG MEN

Her fascination for men who were 'well-blessed' began when that most distinguished of actors, John Barrymore, attempted to seduce her in his dressing-room. Universally revered as one of the handsomest but vainest men in the film world, Barrymore's mighty ego was given a thrashing by the teenage Tallulah not because she found him unattractive but because she was enjoying a secret liaison with a controversial actress. She later regretted her action when the actor sent her a nude photograph. Astonished by the size of the man's 'equipment', she made a pact never to sleep with any man who was not 'hung like Barrymore'. Equally astonishing is the fact that almost every man she had an affair with – she confessed to more than 500 and was probably not exaggerating – possessed this quality. She married just the once, to a man who divorced her a few years later citing mental cruelty and who was victim to one of her most cruel jokes. The occasion was a visit to her home by a *This Is Your Life* film crew in the days when the programme went out on live television. Her husband was asleep in bed after a heavy night of drinking. Tallulah whipped back the sheets and asked, in her most innocent voice, 'Darling, did you ever see a prick as big as that before?'

TALULLAH LOVES WOMEN

In her younger days, Tallulah boasted that she had slept with dozens of famous women and once threatened to give their names to the press after an argument with Louis B Mayer. At backstage parties she would invite female fans into her dressing-room and give them tips on clitoral stimulation, cross-dressing, lesbian sex and bondage. One of her great regrets, she said, was failing to seduce Greta Garbo, the woman she regarded as superior to every other being on earth.

The scriptwriter, Adela Rogers St Johns, had let the cat out of the bag by remarking how the Swedish lovely enjoyed parading around her garden stark naked and for weeks Tallulah and a friend loitered outside the star's walled Hollywood home, armed with an autograph book and telescope. Though she saw nothing, Tallulah did get to know Salka Viertel, Garbo's most intimate friend who had just begun scripting *Queen Christina* – she pestered her so much that after a great deal of deliberation, coded messages and secret telephone calls, a meeting was arranged at Salka's home.

Tallulah walked up to Garbo and tugged her eyelashes to see if they and their owner were real. She then 'swooned' on cue and had to be revived with half a bottle of brandy. Later, the Swedish beauty accepted an invitation to dine at Tallulah's place.

Dinner was prepared and the champagne put on ice but Garbo failed to turn up at the appointed time. Then, when Tallulah had almost given up hope, there was a knock on the door and her maid ushered in 'a Chinese woman complete with slanting eyes, a black wig, and an Oriental gown'. The woman announced in pidgin English, 'Miss Garbo unable to come – sent me instead!' Tallulah played along with Garbo's game all evening. When she was leaving, Garbo shook Tallulah's hand and said in her own sultry voice, 'Pleased to have met you, Miss. After Miss Bankhead you're the finest actress on the screen!' Years later, Tallulah wrote, 'Forget all the bilge about Garbo. She's excessively shy. When at ease with people who do not look upon her as something begat by the Sphinx and Frigg, a Norse goddess of the sky, she can be as much fun as the next gal!' The two women remained friends for many years, and Garbo was the only female star Tallulah never made fun of behind her back.

In fact, Tallulah developed a fanatical reverence for Garbo. The chair Garbo had used was placed in Tallulah's bathroom, next to the toilet, which she had also used, and for several months the room became a shrine which was always shown to reporters and friends. When another great star, Ethel Barrymore, dropped in for tea and asked if she might use the bathroom, she was sent next door.

TALLULAH LOVES HERSELF!

Her manic naracissism began at her convent. She developed a schoolgirl crush on one of the nuns and, when rejected and disciplined, she rebelled by turning cartwheels at Mass, by parading around the dormitory in the nude and by telling the other girls dirty jokes about monks and candles. Needless to say she was expelled. When she became a big star in London during the early twenties, she rented a flat in the centre of town and always removed her clothes before answering the door. When the neighbours complained about this, she always ensured that she was sitting on the toilet with the door open before visitors were shown in. This practice continued until she was well into her sixties and no longer a great beauty. Reporters would be told, 'Keep looking at my eyes, darling. My arse is like an accordion!'

TALLULAH IS DRINKING, DOPING AND SMOKING HERSELF TO DEATH!

The drinking began in New York, when she became the mascot of The Beautiful Young Things. She particularly liked bourbon, and though she abstained from alcohol altogether during the final years of the war – 'Until the English have evacuated Dunkirk!' she declared – by 1950, when she was at the height of her fame, she was getting through two bottles of Old Grandad a day and 100 cigarettes. When her doctors warned her that she was slowly killing herself, she added ginger ale to the bourbon and substituted her usual brand of cigarettes for 150 cork-tipped ones. She compromised again when emphysema was diagnosed, buying a portable oxygen cylinder which she used between puffs.

Tallulah took pills to help her sleep, pills to keep her awake, and pills to help her cope with pills. She dabbled with every opiate and barbiturate known to man but preferred what she called the working-class simplicity of cocaine. When warned of its perils, she responded, 'Cocaine isn't habit-forming, darling. I should know, I've been taking it for years!'

TALLULAH IS AN AUTHORITY ON THE HUMAN CONDITION!

If there was always someone close at hand to record her every indiscretion, Tallulah's good deeds by and large went unnoticed. She regretted never having had children of her own and, if she was sometimes stingy even with her best friends, she was unable to resist the innocent gaze of a child. She raised vast amounts of money for children's hospitals in Britain and America – once, when she encountered a group of scruffy urchins in a downtown backstreet, she emptied the contents of her purse for them all to share and ordered her secretary to supply each youngster with a brand new bicycle.

Tallulah hated racial and sexual prejudice and, as an avowed anti-Communist, delivered stringent speeches in her semi-official capacity as daughter of the late Speaker of the House, throughout America on the eve of the McCarthy witch-hunt. During the early years of the war, recovering from a serious illness, she worked tirelessly for Finnish refugees and, urging her country to augment the war, petitioned the Senate and addressed 50 million people on radio stations across the United States with her pamphlet, 'Human Suffering Has Nothing To Do with Creed, Race or Politics'. Some years later she was instrumental in getting both Harry S Truman and John F Kennedy into the White House. Saddened by the latter's death, she told her family, 'Jack's murder was one of the two most horrid moments of my life. The other was when I found out there was no Santa Claus.'

TALLULAH LOVES TO SING!

When asked by the *chanteuse*, Hildegarde, to fill the guest spot in her *Raleigh Room* radio show, Tallulah led everyone to believe that she would be enacting a scene from one of her plays, or reading a Dorothy Parker poem. She stunned thousands of listeners by announcing, 'I'm not sure that America is quite ready for this, my darlings, but your Tallulah is going to sing. You've been warned!' She then crooned 'I'll Be Seeing You', in an almost toneless basso-profundo voice with her old rival, Clifton Webb, to which Hildegarde replied, 'Not if I see you first, darling!' Even so, the radio station switchboard was jammed for two hours by fans asking for more of the same. Tallulah later claimed, 'They weren't asking for more. They were making sure I would never sing again because I'd set off every cat howling in America!'

This was untrue. There was a heartfelt quality within the Bankhead *sprechtsinger* voice not readily found in legitimate crooners. Though in no sense a torch-singer in the Piaf/Holman tradition, the sincerity within the handful of songs she did get around to recording is breathtaking.

TALLULAH APPEARS IN SOME OF THE WORST PLAYS EVER WRITTEN!

She was the most demanding of actresses: exorbitant salaries, large percentages of box-office takings, unconditional expenses for herself and her entourage. If the script was good, she improvised lewd asides and changed whole lines to satisfy the cravings of her largely homosexual audiences. A line from *A Streetcar Named Desire* – 'The girls are out tonight!' became *the* gay pass-word in late-fifties America and caused near riots in theatres whenever she uttered it.

Tallulah received some of the worst reviews ever penned by theatre critics, but always used these to her advantage. When she appeared in Shakespeare's *Antony and Cleopatra*, the play was closed by a single line in a newspaper: 'Tallulah Bankhead barged down the Nile last night – and sank!' This line and other criticisms were met with hilarity when she read them out during her cabaret act.

An anonymous critic attempted to fathom her out by writing, 'Tallulah brings a certain majesty that even a playwright could not hope to create with mere words.' She was, however, best summed up by Walter Kerr of the *Herald Times*, who said, 'It's difficult to remain honestly appalled by Tallulah while you are rapt in admiration. A blithe spirit with a rusty voice is at work here! Hail to her!'

Tallulah Bankhead
Born: Alabama, January 1903
Died: New York, December 1968

1

The Sunset Fraternity

William Brockman Bankhead was born in Moscow, Alabama, in 1874, the son of a cotton-miller, who later became a congressman and senator. Obsessed with politics and unashamedly racist, Will studied law at Georgetown and, failing to secure a position in the much sought after Indian Territory, he finally moved to Huntsville. Here, in the autumn of 1899, he met Adelaide Eugenia Sledge, a Virginian belle who had been visiting the town to buy her trousseau. For Will and Ada, as she was always called, it was love at first sight. Breaking off her engagement and outraging her family, she rushed off to Memphis with Will, where they were married on 31 January 1900.

Ada's and Will's first daughter, Eugenia, was born 24 January 1901 and, according to an entry in the journal of Marie Owen, Will's sister, – 'Tallulah Brockman Bankhead was born around 12 February 1902.' Her actual date of birth, written clearly on birth certificate and other official documents, reads 31 January 1903 – her parents' third wedding anniversary – and the event took place in their second-floor apartment in the Schiffman Building on Huntsville's opulent Courthouse Square. Throughout her life, Marie Owen remained Tallulah's confidante but Tallulah never forgave her this one mistake.

Her Christian name, though somewhat unusual, was by no means rare in a society whose offpsring were frequently named after local beauty spots and landmarks. Will's mother had been baptized Tallulah because her parents claimed that she had been conceived during a stop-over at Tallulah Falls, Georgia. It was an Indian name, Choctaw for 'delightful sound' – though appropriately, perhaps, it also translated as 'terrible waters' in another dialect. Both these meanings would apply to Tallulah Bankhead later in life, when she would say, 'Well, darling. We were the only two scenic wonders in all America!' her preferred 'theory', however, came from an anonymous Irish poet who wrote her several lengthy, articulate fan letters. 'He said Tallulah was derived from the name of a sixth-century Irish saint,' she recorded in her autobiography. 'He swore that fugitive Hibernians fled to Georgia long before Button Gwinnett signed the Declaration. My Irish bard said Tallulah was Gaelic for 'colleen', and had charts to prove it!'

Immediately after Tallulah's birth, Ada became ill with blood-poisoning and, on 23 February 1903, she died, aged just 21. The baby was actually christened next to Ada's open casket, and later inherited her Bible which Ada had inscribed, while she lay dying, 'As a spiritual source at the end of each exacting day, may I recommend to you your little mother's favourite, the 103rd Psalm?' Though she hardly ever went to church, save to attend the occasional wedding or funeral, Tallulah learned Psalm 103 while very small, and was still quoting it, verbatim, in her stage show 50 years later.

At the time of his wife's death, Will Bankhead was still only 28. Blond, handsome, muscular through intensive workouts at Georgetown where he had captained the university football team and received several medals for his prowess in other sports, Will was regarded as one of Huntsville's most eligible bachelors. Only days after Ada's funeral, his family urged him to go out and find himself a suitable companion if only for his daughters' sakes. Instead, he took to drink, became a manic depressive, finding living with his children an unbearable burden. For a while he tried to cope, but in his blackest moments he put the fear of God into everyone by sleeping with a loaded pistol under his pillow, threatening to shoot himself on numerous occasions. He also got into scrapes with the local rednecks, usually over women, and often returned home black and blue after some drunken brawl. There seems little doubt, too, that his overt affection for Eugenia, while completely ignoring Tallulah, meant that he blamed her for her mother's death. Subsequently the girls were farmed out to relatives in Fayette, then to Will's parents' home in the small mining community of Jasper, 70 miles or so from Birmingham, Alabama. The house, 'Sunset', which at that time was home to four generations of Bankheads, stood on a low hill just outside the town.

Captain John Bankhead and his wife Tallulah were rich – only recently they had sold their controlling interest in Coca-Cola, and two coal mines – which was probably just as well, for Will did not contribute one cent towards his daughters' upkeep. What little money he had went on women and drink. He did visit them most weekends, however, and always at holiday times, though according to Tallulah he was never there for her birthday – because Eugenia's was seven days before hers, Tallulah had to make do with 'celebrating' hers a week in advance, or not at all.

This apparent neglect during her formative years – though Will more than made up for his failure later on – was certainly a contributory factor towards Tallulah's reckless behaviour as a child, and may have had much to do with her waywardness as an adult. She was also made to feel inferior to her sister – the fact that she was plump, unattractive, tomboyish and prone to every ailment did not help. She listed these in *Tallulah*, her racy autobiography, published in 1952, as: measles, pneumonia, mumps, whooping cough, erysipelas, smallpox and tonsillitis. She frequently told the story of how, on a childhood picnic with her father, she was bitten 'above the pantie-line' by a rattlesnake. Accordingly, Will is alleged to have snatched off her panties and sucked the poisoned blood from the wound, becoming himself violently ill as a result. Some sources, including an account by Eugenia, claimed the malady to have been a carbuncle on her bottom which had had to be lanced. True or not, when Tallulah filled in her passport application form many years later she wrote 'snakebite' in the box intended for 'distinguishing marks'. Worst of all her childhood illnesses were the innumerable bouts of croup which required the then necessary application of mustard plasters, a horrendous treatment – before cigarettes 'completed' the cure – which led to her acquiring her famous throaty voice and laugh.

Tallulah's single redeeming feature in her childhood was seen to be her beautiful blonde hair, which accentuated her deep-set blue eyes. This enabled her to be selected to play the Moon in her first school play, where she wore a costume of brown crêpe paper. Even so, Eugenia got to wear the brightest garb – she played the Rainbow – though the event was a scorching success for Tallulah because she received an all-too-rare hug from Will.

Tallulah had always been bad-tempered, but her tantrums grew worse as she took to bullying her sister and most of the rest of her class at school. At home, whenever she got out of control she would be dragged out into the yard by Grandmother Tallulah and doused with a bucket of water. Only Captain John, a towering, large-framed Confederate veteran, whose very stare terrified just about everyone who got on the wrong side of him, could exercise any kind of authority over her – or so he liked his wife and Will to believe. In fact, Tallulah was the only one capable of outstaring him and making him crease with laughter.

Tallulah loved nothing more than to accompany Captain John on his electoral campaigns, travelling through many parts of northern Alabama. She also got to know the predominantly Negro district of Jasper, partly founded by the descendants of slaves brought back from South Carolina by her paternal great-grandmother. She got on well with these people, proving that in this respect at least she was very different from her father.

However, when in 1910 both her grandparents left Jasper for the Congressional sessions in Washington, Will Bankhead once again found himself unable to cope with two hyperactive young girls, and the pair were sent to live with his sister, Marie Owen, in Montgomery.

Marie was Tallulah's favourite aunt, mainly because she pampered her and allowed her to have much of her own way.

The state archivist, Marie subsequently compiled a mammoth eight-volume history of Alabama and, in her late seventies, published several novels and a play. It was Aunt Marie who enrolled her nieces at the Gussie Woodruff School, where they excelled in deportment, and where for a while Tallulah's behaviour seemed to improve. They returned to Jasper during the summer holidays and this time Tallulah really did try Will's patience and shot-through nerves. One afternoon she found a trunk of old clothes in the attic and persuaded Eugenia to dress up in their mother's favourite green taffeta riding outfit. Will was so badly shocked by what he saw that he opted to send his daughters as far away as possible – to the Convent of the Sacred heart, in Manhattanville, New York. Though none of the Bankhead fraternity was Catholic – Eugenia and Tallulah had been brought up in the Episcopal faith of their mother, for Will's mother was as anti-Catholic as he was anti-Black – this was the only establishment at the time which would admit girls as young as nine and ten as boarders.

For the over-spirited Tallulah, the Spartan discipline of the Sacred Heart was too much to bear. The building was large, cold, and shut off from civilization by a high wall. She quickly became the butt of the other girls' jokes because of her name, which one of the sisters had branded 'a pagan sound' in front of the whole school. She also detested the habit of being forced to bathe in a nightshirt – overweight or not, she had never been ashamed of her body, and she was punished many times for shedding her clothes and preening herself stark naked in front of her bedroom mirror, setting a precedent for her often quite shameless behaviour in later years. At the end of the first term, when all the girls who had done well in class paraded in front of their parents in the school chapel, wearing white veils and carrying a lily, for Tallulah there was no flower and the veil was black.

Will visited the girls that Christmas, having been summoned by the Mother Superior and, in his limited capacity as a parent, assumed that Tallulah's problem lay in her being closeted for lengthy periods of time. He effected a 'remedy' by taking both daughters to the theatre, though his choice of play – *The Whip*, a hugely successful British import, which was playing at the Manhattan Opera House – could hardly have been deemed appropriate entertainment for two impressionable young girls. The no-holds-barred production featured mob scenes, a hunt with real hounds and a train crash, a tableau set in the Chamber of Horrors, and a recreation of the Newmarket Gold Cup on a treadmill. Tallulah remembered, 'The curtain hadn't been up for five minutes before Sister and I were on the verge of hysterics. By the end of the first act both of us had wet our pants … at the final curtain I was a wreck, frantic, red-eyed and dishevelled. I didn't sleep for two nights running. I've *never* recovered!' Soon afterwards, still refusing to accept any form of correction, in a fit of hot-headedness, Tallulah threw an inkpot at the Mother Superior – she had been caught 'flashing' at the gardener, and her actions got her expelled and sent back to Jasper. As a matter of course, her sister returned with her.

By this time, Will Bankhead had recovered sufficiently from his various indispositions to have become actively engaged in his first congressional election campaign. He therefore had an excuse for not wishing to be encumbered with his daughters. Aunt Marie could not take them in, either, as she was nursing her husband through a serious illness, and Captain John was away with Summer Congress. Thus, in September 1913, Tallulah and Eugenia were enrolled at the Mary Baldwin Seminary, in Staunton, Virginia – a suitable distance for them to be out of their father's hair for the time being, but close enough to Captain John and Grandmother Tallulah, in Washington.

At the Seminary, Eugenia again proved the favourite, a fact painfully exhibited by her being offered a part in the school play, as Tallulah was grounded for contracting teenage spots. Even so, Tallulah stole the show by talking loudly throughout the performance and getting tipsy on rough cider afterwards – putting on a show of her own, dancing vulgarly and turning cartwheels.

Tallulah was particularly affected by two events of varying significance. Firstly, Will lost his congressional election, a bitter campaign which he had endured under the inglorious and humiliating nickname of 'Little Willy' – alleged to have had nothing to do with his stature, but with his failure to stand the pace with some of his lady friends between drunken binges. He had also been severely criticized for not being a real family man, in that he had purposely raised his daughters outside Alabama.

The second 'event' could have proved more serious, had the facts been more widely broadcast. At the age of 12 Tallulah fell in love for the first time – with one of the nuns from the Seminary. Her name was Sister Ignatius, and this schoolgirl crush is said to have developed after the nun had defended Tallulah during a playground brawl. The 'affair', which fortunately never materialized, gave way to some of Tallulah's more ribald jokes later in life, jokes which the Catholic church never took kindly to.

In 1914, Will Bankhead remarried, against his mother's wishes and without telling his daughters. The bride was Florence McGuire, the 25-year-old daughter of a lawyer friend whom he had been courting off and on for several years. Exactly why Grandmother Tallulah disliked Florence so much is not known, though it may have had something to do with her being his secretary in an age when fraternization with the lower ranks was not *comme il faut*.

Initially, Tallulah got on famously with Florence, grateful that she had brought her father to his senses, and because Florence had been the one to persuade Will into buying his first car – a Hudson, with 'modern' isinglass windows. She also grew suddenly and quite incredibly fond of Will, now that he was being more of a father to his family. Several years after his death, she eulogized, 'To me, he was a fusion of Santa Clause, Galahad, D'Artagnan and Demosthenes. He was the gallant, the romantic, the poet, above all the actor.'

With Will and Florence there were trips to local beauty spots, and a memorable outing to Myrtle Beach in South Carolina, where Tallulah vividly remembered the onset of 'the curse' – her first period. In this year too there was her first encounter with royalty when the family's visit to Washington coincided with that of the Prince of Wales, later King Edward VIII. The Prince's arm was in a sling – the result of a sporting mishap –

though Tallulah always maintained that his indisposition was due to too much handshaking. And, while Florence refused to curtsy to a 'mere boy', it was left to Grandmother Tallulah to teach everyone a lesson in protocol. 'Grandmother, enslaved by the Cinderella story, made a curtsy that brought her nose to the rug,' she wrote. 'She seemed to be submitting her head to the axe. Her overlong salute blocked the traffic for three minutes.'

Sadly, this idyllic sojourn came to an abrupt end early in 1915 when Will, acting solely in his daughters' interests, thought it might be prudent to separate them for a while. Eugenia was sent to the Margaret Booth School for Young Ladies, in Montgomery, where Will hoped she would learn Latin, English Literature and become well versed in the arts. Tallulah was so envious of her sister – and irked by Will's promise that if Eugenia did well she would be sent to finish her studies abroad in Florence – that she later claimed to have attended the school herself. In fact, she was enrolled at the Dunbar Holy Cross Academy, near Washington, where, virtually overnight, she developed into one of the most delinquent pupils the establishment had ever encountered. Without Eugenia, and with few friends of her own, Tallulah got into all kinds of mischief – even more so once she had set her sights on showbusiness.

One evening, Tallulah sneaked out of Dunbar to witness a performance by Alla Nazimova, the stunning Crimean-born actress, in *War Brides*, developing a crush on the star which, if nonconformist was at least harmless because there seemed no chance of ever meeting her in the flesh. What Tallulah may not have known was that this temperamental, alluring woman was renowned if not reviled as the doyenne of the Hollywood lesbian clique and that her Bohemian evenings at The Garden of Allah, her estate on Sunset Boulevard, were the source of many raised eyebrows. Tallulah was so enraptured by Nazimova's camp, over-the-top acting style that she at once began emulating her by drooping her heavy-lidded eyes and fainting on cue whenever she felt emotional, which was often. This renewed period of recklessness may have been short-lived but it served its purpose. Within weeks she was joined at the Academy by Eugenia, dispatched by Will to keep an eye on her.

Eugenia was now 15 and sufficiently pretty – in spite of an eye deformity – to date any of the respectable young men who were allowed into Dunbar whenever there was a dance or social function. Tallulah was not so fortunate. Her face was still covered in pimples, and though she measured just over five feet, she tipped the scales at 9st 4lb. This did not bother her too much, for now that she had been reunited with her sister she had decided to do something about it.

In 1916 the Bankhead girls left Dunbar. Will had just been elected to Congress from the Tenth District of Alabama – surprising everyone, including himself – and the time had come for his daughters to prepare for their débuts in Washington society. For this they were enrolled at the prestigious Fairmount Seminary, where Tallulah studied classical music: after just a few weeks she was able to play some of the more basic Chopin *études* on the piano, and had even tackled the classical violin, though the latter was soon dispensed with when Captain John bought her a fiddle. Then, quite suddenly, at a time when she had decided to let her hair grow long in keeping with the Southern belle tradition, she went on a diet and shed more than 20 pounds of unwanted puppy fat. Her spots cleared up too and, though her family frowned upon such things, she went out and bought her first make-up kit and began painting her lips bright red, à la Nazimova.

The transformation was astonishing, and photographs taken at the time show her looking considerably more alluring than any of her idols, and a good deal older than 15.

When Tallulah fell ill with a virus, Will Bankhead dispatched another of his sisters, Aunt Louise, to Fairmount, and a few days later she and Tallulah set off for Atlantic City, where it was hoped the sea air would effect a cure. Aunt Louise, a formidable woman, widow of B F Perry, the former governor of South Carolina, bought Tallulah an ankle-length sealskin coat for the trip and, naturally, they stayed at the best hotel in town.

When Tallulah discovered that Nora Bayes – billed as 'The Greatest Single Woman Singing Comedienne in the World' – was appearing in Atlantic City in vaudeville, on the huge salary of $5,000 a week, she insisted upon seeing Bayes' performance seven times in succession. When she realized that the singer was staying in the very same hotel as Aunt Louise and herself, she was beside herself with joy and refused to budge from the foyer until she had met her idol and secured her autograph. Henceforth, Tallulah's exhibitionism and self-confidence, never less than overpowering, became almost manic. Tallulah Bankhead would become a major star simply because she had convinced herself that she would never be otherwise.

In June 1917 one of her photographs – a profile, in huge fur collar and broad-brimmed hat – was sent to *Picture Play* magazine, who were running a competition for twelve cinema hopefuls. The prize was an all-expenses-paid trip to New York and a promised featured role in a film to be produced by Frank Powell of the Powell Producing Corporation, which had launched Blanche Sweet and Theda Bara. Tallulah entered the Screen Opportunity Contest with customary good humour, not expecting anything to come of it. The results were published in the September issue of *Picture Play* and the list included such instantly forgettable names as Henrietta L Grant, Lela Sue Campbell and Myrtle Owen Anderson. Tallulah's picture *was* there, with the caption, 'Who is she?' Her application form had been lost among those of the other 50,000 entrants.

Dozens of girls contacted *Picture Play*, claiming to be the mysterious Number Twelve – many going to great lengths to find identical hats and furs. Fortunately for Tallulah, Captain John had retained a duplicate photograph, and an official letter in his capacity as senator cleared the matter up once and for all.

In 1917, Captain John was riding high on the crest of a decidedly popular political wave, for his most recent legislation had resulted in the development and construction of two federally financed transcontinental road systems. These were the Bankhead Highway, stretching southwards from the Capitol, then west to the Golden Gate Bridge and the north-heading Lincoln Highway. This powerful man was all for his granddaughter taking the trip to New York and, if nothing else, getting the 'acting bug' out of her system. He was supported by Tallulah's stepmother Florence, though for different reasons. Since Will Bankhead's elevation to Congress, the entire family had moved to an apartment at 1868 Columbia Road, an opulent district of Washington, and for some reason Tallulah and Florence had begun falling out. Rather than move in with her parents in their rooms on the seventh floor, Tallulah had elected to live with her grandparents on the sixth. Added to this, Florence welcomed the opportunity of having Will to herself for a little while. Grandmother Tallulah, however was opposed to the New York trip. She thought her granddaughter far too young to leave home and was pleased that her son was getting to know his daughters for the first time in his life. Tallulah attempted to rectify the situation by going on a hunger-strike. Then a compromise was reached: Captain John, whose word was law, announced that Tallulah *would* go to New York but that she would be chaperoned by Aunt Louise, who at that time was in mourning after the death of her 18-year-old son, William. Widowed from her first husband and separated from her second, Aunt Louise was living with William's fiancée, Ola Davis, an amateur singer who also aspired to make the big time in New York. Aunt Louise's only condition was that Ola should accompany them. Captain John did not object. The girl was close to Tallulah's age and he hoped she might keep her out of trouble. He also decided that, rather than rely on the dubious finances of the Powell Producing Corporation, he would pay for the threesome to stay in reputable lodgings.

Before the trip to New York, the Bankheads had another problem to sort out. Eugenia, now conscious of the fact that Tallulah would be regarded as the family belle and having courted dozens of boys since arriving on Columbia Road, had met and fallen in love with Morton Hoyt, the son of the late Solicitor-General of the United States – marrying him just hours after their first meeting. However, because Will Bankhead had been forewarned of the event, he reached his daughter before the union was consummated, the marriage was annulled, and Hoyt was sent packing. This would not deter Eugenia, however, who went on to marry her beau twice more!

In New York, Aunt Louise rented rooms on the fashionable

West 45th Street. The promoter contracted by *Picture Play* had either disappeared or run short of funds. In any case, when he gave an indication that he was not about to honour the deal with the twelve motion-picture hopefuls, Captain John alerted his New York representative, Knox Julian, who began acting on Tallulah's behalf. She and her 'colleagues' thus spent three weeks working in a Brooklyn studio, and were each paid $75. The finished film, of which no complete print survives, was *The Wishful Girl*, directed by Del Henderson and John B O'Brien, and starred another *Picture Play* winner, François du Barry.

Anticipating that Tallulah would be satisfied now that she had collected her prize, Aunt Louise set off on her own personal crusade, visiting scores of spiritualists in an attempt to get in touch with her dead son, and more or less leaving her charges to look after themselves. Tallulah spent much of her time with Knox Julian, who wrote her letters of introduction to a number of theatrical magnates. One of these was Benjamin Hampton, the vice-president of the American Tobacco Company who had recently acquired massive shares at Goldwyn and Rex Beach Pictures. Another was the legendary impresario David Belasco of Famous Players. It was in his office that Tallulah learned that he had found her sufficiently interesting to consider her for a small part, only to turn her down after being warned of her 'reputation' by Aunt Louise. Tallulah was so furious that she at once reported the incident to Captain John. What happened next remains obscure, but was probably the result of the combined efforts of Hampton, Belasco and Captain John himself.

In February 1918 Aunt Louise and her charges moved to the Algonquin Hotel on West 44th Street, arguably the most famous meeting place in New York for actors, artists, writers and intellectuals – though Aunt Louise was apparently unaware of the fact and only chose the Algonquin because someone had told her that it was the in-town residence of Commander Evangeline Booth of the Salvation Army. It was here that Tallulah received a telephone call from a representative of the Shubert Brothers, at that time the most important agents in New York.

Lee and Jake Shubert were the archetypal showmen, very much in the Ziegfeld tradition, who believed in the maxim, 'One must speculate to accumulate'. In many ways their productions were forerunners of the great American stage musical. In New York, people still remembered their phenomenally successful *Vera Violetta* which, in 1911, had made household names of Al Jolson, Harry Pilcer and Gaby Deslys. One of their principles was that potential Broadway hits should not be launched there but on the much tougher provincial circuit. It was on this understanding that Tallulah successfully auditioned for a walk-on part in *The Squab Farm*.

Tallulah was thrilled, though *The Squab Farm* was not quite the great vehicle that she had anticipated, and its première in March 1918 at the Bijou Theatre on 45th Street was savaged by the critics. Singling out the walk-ons, one wrote, 'There are four young girls who might be better in the care of their mothers.' The *New York Times* dismissed the play as 'a garish travesty of life in the movies, all in bad taste.' Such remarks, however, were remedied by Knox Julian, who paid to have an entire column inserted in the *Evening Telegraph* praising not just Tallulah's acting abilities, but extolling the virtues of Captain John and the whole Bankhead clan. Alma Tell and Gladys Sinclair, the stars of the show, were allotted just two lines.

The Squab Farm ran for just three weeks, after which Tallulah was approached by Ivan Abramson, the Russian-born independent film director, who offered her a more substantial role in *When Men Betray*. The film was a flop – Tallulah denounced it 'as trifling as it was silent' – but when an anonymous reviewer described her as 'exquisite of feature, dainty of form, and deliciously feminine', this did not go unnoticed by some of the distinguished guests at the Algonquin. These included the musical-comedy star Elsie Janis, Douglas Fairbanks Jr, Anita Loos and all three Barrymores, Ethel, John and Lionel. Her most rewarding friendship was with Estelle Winwood, a fine British actress sixteen years her senior, who would stick by her through thick and thin for the rest of her life. Estelle was currently enjoying enormous success on Broadway in *Why Marry Me?*, which only recently had been awarded the very first Pulitzer Prize. Another close friend was the flagrantly bisexual actress, Jobyna Howland, a six-foot blonde bombshell hailed by Dorothy Parker as 'The Spirit of the Ages', and whose fondness for foul language was legendary. Tallulah also befriended, initially in a small way, Ethel Barrymore – calling her 'The Virgin Mary', though never to her face. She was not amused, however, when Barrymore, who hated her Christian name, urged her to change hers ... to Barbara!

In spite of the many recommendations put forward by these new friends on her behalf, however, parts were not forthcoming and Tallulah was only allowed to stay on at the Algonquin – and receive a generous allowance from Captain John of $50 a week, of which almost half was spent on her modest hall-bedroom with bath – because she continually led him to believe that some producer or other had promised her a part after seeing her on the screen. Astonishingly, she was believed by everyone but Aunt Louise, who was growing tired of her niece's fickle ways and tantrums and was more than ready to relinquish all responsibility for her.

For Aunt Louise, the last straw came during the summer of 1919 when, in order to earn a little spare cash to buy clothes with which to impress the Algonquinites, as they were called, Tallulah spent an afternoon, unchaperoned, in the private rooms of a young male photographer, posing semi-nude for a series of publicity shots. Although Tallulah almost certainly did not have sex with the man – she always maintained that she had been a 'technical' virgin until the age of 20, alluding to her much-repeated statement that her first lover had been another woman – this did not prevent her from fabricating an anatomically detailed account of the visit to her aunt, who immediately threw in the towel and enlisted with the Red Cross! A few weeks later, having informed Will of his daughter's latest peccadillo, Louise sailed to join her unit in France.

Aunt Louise was replaced as Tallulah's chaperone by her more preferred aunt, Marie Owen, who was impervious to the fact that her stage-struck charge was running dangerously short of funds. She was nevertheless concerned about Tallulah's sudden acquisition of bad language and about the amount of interest being shown in her by Jobyna Howland. Thus, when her niece started becoming too much of a handful – which was remarkably soon – Marie Owen also gave up on her and returned to Montgomery.

Acting on the orders of Captain John, desperately worried that a girl of Tallulah's fiery disposition and age, not constantly supervised, might resort to prostitution, Knox Julian visited the Algonquin. Its manager, Frank Case, was offered a substantial fee to keep an eye on her. Case's response was a curt, 'No, thank you. I can run the busiest hotel in New York or I can look after Tallulah Bankhead, but I sure as hell can't do both!' A tricky situation was saved by Aunt Louise. By the time she arrived in Paris to join her Red Cross unit, the war was over and, probably for the first time in her life, Tallulah was genuinely pleased to see her on her return.

Despite the failure of *When Men Betray*, Tallulah had managed to capture the attention of a former glove salesman named Samuel Goldfish, then just beginning to make a name for himself in the film industry – within a few years, as Samuel Goldwyn, he would become the most feared and respected mogul in Hollywood. Goldfish cast her opposite the dashing Tom Moore in *Thirty a Week*, which was completed in November 1918. Like its predecessor, it was not a success.

Returning to Washington for the winter, Tallulah attended her sister's coming-out party, and had a 'sexless fling' with a young man named Robert Carrère who introduced her to another of her idols, the actress Helen Hayes, then appearing in J M Barrie's *Dear Brutus*. Robert also took her to one of that season's most popular plays: Rachel Crothers's *39 East*, starring Constance Binney, and staged and produced by Mary Kirkpatrick, one of Captain John's closest friends. Tallulah was so disappointed by what she considered a paltry performance that she demanded to be introduced to Binney that she might tell her so to her face. Fortunately, the meeting did not take place, though the remarks did get back to Constance Binney. Through Mary Kirkpatrick she met an entrepreneur named Lyman Brown who had seen her in *Thirty a Week*. Brown hired her to join his summer-stock company in Somerville, Massachusetts – rehearsing one production during the daytime and appearing in another six evenings a week. Astonished by Tallulah's capacity for learning an entire script after reading it aloud just three or four times, he asked her to stay with the company and move with them to Baltimore, the next stop on the road. Tallulah turned him down – declaring that for her it would be the New York stage and the big time, or nothing at all.

2

The Darling of the Algonquinites

Tallula's big chance came when she returned to the Algonquin: one of her fellow guests, Frank Crowninshield, the publisher of *Vanity Fair* and the much-respected host of the famous Condé Nast parties, informed her that Rachel Crothers was on the look-out for a 'dramatic' actress to understudy Constance Binney in the New York production of *39 East*. Crothers, one of the greatest playwrights of her day who always supervised the productions of her work, announced that her current cast were due to take a vacation and that when they returned, the understudy cast would take a second production on a nationwide tour.

Tallulah contacted Mary Kirkpatrick immediately, and attended the auditions at the Broadhurst Theater. Constance Binney, who had heard of Tallulah's acid comments only a short time before, was asked to sit in on the proceedings. Tallulah marched up to her and stunned her by saying, 'Miss Binney. All those horrible things I said about your performance in Washington ... I just wanted you to know that I meant every word!' In spite of this she got not just the part, but an amazing deal from the playwright – $100 a week, the services of a part-time maid, and a generous clothing allowance which exceeded her wildest dreams.

Tallulah spent much of her free time with Rachel Crothers and Frank Crowninshield at the Coffee House Club on West

45th Street – another artistes' meeting-place, it had been recently founded by the 50-year-old bachelor. Under Crothers's tutelage, and the watchful eye of Crowninshield who was reporting back to Captain John, Tallulah took lessons in French, speech, ballet and deportment. Because of her brash outspokenness, she became the playwright's favourite, often rehearsing at her apartment, and sometimes staying over. Her co-star, understudying Henry Hull in *39 East*, was Sidney Blackmer, a 23-year-old hopeful who had just served in Europe with the American Expeditionary Forces. He did not like Tallulah and she could not stand him. Over the next few weeks she did not miss one single Binney performance: standing in the wings, she memorized every gesture. Away from the theatre she socialized rarely, save for her nightly visits to the lounge and lobby of the Algonquin.

Tallulah's first performance in *39 East* took place in July 1919 when she was only 16, and her family were there to share in the great moment. Only Captain John and Grandmother Tallulah failed to turn up because of illness, though when the senator was informed of her success he agreed to her staying on in New York, with or without a chaperone. Like everyone else he believed that she had grown out of her tantrums, and that she would be perfectly capable of standing on her own two feet. To a certain extent he had nothing to worry about, though Tallulah's erratic behaviour did cause a multitude of backstage rows, particularly with the strait-laced Sidney Blackmer, who disapproved of her friendship with Jobyna Howland and her saucy offsides to the stagehands. She also had the habit, before curtain-up, of standing directly in front of the lights so that her dress looked transparent. The adage, 'If you've got it, darling, why not flaunt it?' had already begun to serve her remarkably well.

The storyline of *East 39* was uncomplicated. Rachel Crothers's plays were aimed at pleasing the masses, their working-class simplicity an essential ingredient that enhanced their appeal and swelled the box-office coffers. The plot revolved around the Binney/Bankhead character Penelope Penn, a minister's daughter who is staying at the lodging-house that gives the play its title. Penelope is kidnapped by a hoodlum when walking through Central Park but she is saved by her lover (Blackmer) who finds her hat on a park bench and instinctively realizes that all is not as it should be. At first, Tallulah began misplacing the hat because she found it difficult to co-ordinate movement with script but, when she realized that her actions were getting on her co-star's nerves, she would purposely fling it anywhere; it was reported variously as landing in the stalls, the pit, and once around the neck of a mechanical swan!

During the run of the Crothers play, Tallulah was accepted into that section of the New York theatrical set known as the 'kid flappers', a movement said to have been developed by Margalo Gillmore. The kid flappers were radical young things, very much like the *demi-mondaines* of turn-of-the century Paris. They lived life to the full, drank neat bourbon and smoked cigars or cigarettes, insulted their peers, and used 'in-words' like 'crazy', 'divine', 'shit' and 'darling' – Bankhead essentials that would remain in her vocabulary for the rest of her life. They shocked their mothers, guardians and maiden aunts by shedding their inhibitions and their corsets, and by broadcasting this to all and sundry: any young woman who wore stays to a tea dance was referred to as 'Old Ironsides'. And like their early French counterparts, the kid flappers accepted jewellery and other expensive gifts from wealthy patrons and lovers of both sexes with whom they had usually spent the night – few of them actually did 'turns' for hard cash. One incident is recorded where, at one of the Condé Nast parties attended by a large number of kid flappers, Frank Crowninshield learned of Tallu-lah's deadly accurate, deadpan impersonation of Ethel Barry-more and actually got her to enact this in front of the great lady herself – not that she would have taken much persuading. Tallulah had perfected her impersonation by going to see Barrymore 15 times in Zoë Akins's *Déclassée*, and the actress's only complaint, it seems, was that Tallulah had made her appear too fat, to which the youngster retorted, 'But Ethel, darling, you *are* too fat!' Her reward, which she appreciated only as an acknowledgement of her talent, was a resounding crack across the face!

Offended or not, Ethel Barrymore soon became a valued
friend, though not a close one. The ageing star also supported
the cast of *39 East* during the autumn of 1919 when they and
the companies of six other productions, who were members of
the Actors' Equity union, went on strike after their respective
producers had ignored their demands for better working
conditions and more equitable contracts. Tallulah had taken
her grandfather's advice to join the union, though in those days
this was not obligatory, and she personally invited the
Barrymores – Ethel, Lionel and John – to a rally at the Old
Lennox Opera House where she engaged herself as usherette,
showing the public to their seats while relieving them of their
entrance fee, which she insisted should be as much as everyone
could afford. The organizers of the rally had set themselves a
target of $100,000, but actually raised less than half this
amount. They would not have achieved even this had it not
been for Tallulah who, in the heat of the moment rushed on to
the stage and pledged $100 on behalf of her grandfather,
reminding the audience that if a United States senator could dip
his hand in his pocket and set an example, then so could
everyone else. Captain John was so proud of her that he
reimbursed her the $100 in a package which contained her very
first evening dress. However, Tallulah had an almighty bust-up
with her patron-of-sorts, Knox Julian, who had criticized her
for involving herself in the strike in the first place; she was
about to ditch him once and for all when she collapsed in the
lobby of the Algonquin with excruciating stomach pains.

Tallulah was rushed to St Elizabeth's Hospital, where a
surgeon performed an emergency appendectomy. Only when
they opened her up did they discover gangrene and, when
peritonitis set in, she very nearly died. Six weeks later, on her
release, the Actors' Equity strike was over and she was sent
home to recuperate – and to shock her relatives with tales of her
exploits amongst *hoi polloi* of the New York acting fraternity.
She was surprised to find that the Eugenia–Morton Hoyt
romance was still going strong and that the couple were now
formally engaged – they would marry for the second time a
year later.

Tallulah had been contracted by Jake Shubert to take *39 East* on the road, a gruelling nine-month stint which, in her current state of health, would have been most unwise. Thus with considerable nerve, considering the importance of the Shuberts and the fact that she was a mere novice, she informed them that she would not be returning to the play. Then, no doubt because she was afraid of being sued for leaving them in the lurch, she forwarded a doctor's certificate. Once certain that this had done the trick, she returned to New York and immediately booked back into the Algonquin.

Having learned that Tallulah had fallen on hard times, so to speak, John Barrymore began taking an active interest in her welfare. The great actor, who was approaching the height of his fame, and at the same time just starting out on a 20-year trail of self-destruction, only had to make a chance remark to his sister Ethel – 'Just who *is* that beautiful girl?' – when all the time he knew perfectly well who she was, and Tallulah was expected to feel flattered. Though regarded by many as even more handsome than Valentino, there was something about the man which she did not like: she later said that his much practised animal magnetism had cut no ice with a girl who had already decided to pursue life as the huntress and not become the victim. Even so, when one of the Algonquinites told her that Barrymore was thinking of asking her to star in one of his films, she was in such a hurry to get to their rendezvous at the Plymouth Theater, where he and his brother Lionel were appearing in *The Jest*, that she wore a dress which she had had on for days. When a friend reminded her of this, she quipped, 'Who cares? He'll only be interested in seeing my knickers!'

Barrymore stunned Tallulah by asking her to be his leading lady in *Dr Jekyll and Mr Hyde* ... and, as she had predicted, he began 'making little animal noises' and asked her to have sex with him, there and then, on his dressing-room couch. Most women would have given their eye-teeth for such an opportunity, and so too would Tallulah, under differing conditions. 'I had no prejudices against informal alliances,' she later reflected, after rejecting the role. 'But I felt no good should come of trying to blend business with pleasure.' There was a photograph doing the rounds at that time, depicting the actor gazing seaward from the deck of his sloop – tanned, long-limbed, athletic-looking and stark naked (the 'loincloth' he wears in some prints was added after the Hays office seized the negatives). What impressed Tallulah, invariably setting a vital precedent so far as *she* was concerned, was the size of the actor's penis. Henceforth whenever possible, her men would have to be 'hung like Barrymore', and she always made a point of telling absolutely everyone she met, from royalty to the man in the street, just how 'hung' most of them were.

Shortly after this episode, Captain John died suddenly, leaving a void in Tallulah's life which would never be filled. She was playing Rose de Brissac in Zoë Akins's *Footloose* at the Greenwich Theater at the time, barely able to conceal her grief and impressing Burns Mantle of the *Evening Mail*, who wrote, 'Tallulah is a promising young ingénue ... able to inject a telling realism in a difficult role.'

Towards the end of 1920, Tallulah went to see Pauline Frederick – another great star who always preferred the legitimate stage to films – in the most successful role of her career, *Madame X*. The effect was the same as it had been with Nazimova and, when one of the Algonquinites arranged a meeting, Tallulah rushed off with one thought in mind – to begin a friendship with her childhood idol which might she hoped progress beyond the platonic. Pauline Frederick was not interested in this, so Tallulah decided that if she could not have the still attractive but boyish-looking wife, then perhaps her handsome, rugged, bisexual husband, actor-playwright Willard Mack, would suffice. She wrote of Mack, 'Any man who could qualify for *her* favours must have had gifts over and above those visible to the eye!' Again it was a remark aimed at Mack's alleged endowment, and his prowess in the bedroom.

During the course of the next few evenings, Willard Mack offered Tallulah several good roles in his plays, and even went as far as suggesting that he would write something especially for her. What he did not offer, however, was himself – the most Tallulah got was a sumptuous dinner at a Chinese restaurant, accompanied by a lengthy account of how he had always adored his wife and followed by a respectable goodnight peck on the cheek. Tallulah was so incensed that she never saw him again.

But through Willard Mack she was introduced to Alexander Woollcott, arguably the most read and respected critic of his day. Fat and extremely effeminate and almost always seen wearing a red silk-lined opera cloak and bottle-bottomed spectacles, Woollcott had the reputation of being able to close or prolong a play with a few well-chosen words in his column in the *New York Times*. He later appeared as a radio reviewer under the pseudonym 'The Town Cryer' and, later still, he became the model for Kaufman and Hart's *The Man Who Came To Dinner*, a role which he successfully interpreted on Broadway. According to his biographer, Woollcott was 'a "turnip" – an asexual due to a hormonal imbalance who had once wept on Anita Loos's shoulder because he had never become a mother.' Edna Ferber said of him, 'He's just a New Jersey Nero who has mistaken his pinafore for a toga.' Others, including Tallulah, referred to him as Louisa May Woollcott, a pun on the authoress of *Little Women*. Though Tallulah never really liked him, she respected his friendly attitude towards her and recognized its value, and was often seen being escorted by him to some theatrical première or other.

It was through Alexander Woollcott that Tallulah became recognized as an up-and-coming wit, something in the Louella Parsons/Dorothy Parker mould. It was considered *très chic*, during the early Twenties, to see the plays of the Belgian dramatist and poet Maurice Maeterlinck, the creator of *The Bluebird*. Tallulah had sat through *Aglavaine and Selysette*, coming away from the theatre wondering what all the fuss had been about. Consequently, when Woollcott invited her as his special guest to the opening night of the little-performed *The Burgomaster of Stilemonde*, she was truly confused. Turning to her companion, she said loudly, 'There's less to this than meets the eye!' In fact, she had meant to say that there had been *more* to the play than had met the eye but, when Woollcott repeated the statement in his column, all of a sudden there were thousands of Americans clamouring for 'more of the Bankhead girl's wit'. Over the next 40-odd years, she would not disappoint them.

Woollcott's article revived the interest previously shown in Tallulah by Rachel Crothers, who now contracted her to play Hallie Livingston in *Nice People*, which began a 20-week run at the Klaw Theater early in 1921. The cast was predominantly gay and included Henry Hull, Rod la Roque (of whom more later), and the Berlin-born actress Katherine Cornell, whom Tallulah always admired. The fact that Cornell stayed married to the openly homosexual producer, Guthrie McClintick, for 40 years never ceased to amaze her.

'No great shakes' was how Tallulah described the play that caused a minor sensation among New York theatregoers in which the butch-looking Francine Larrimore appeared wearing workman's overalls. Tallulah played her flapper self, smoking a lot, and sipping genuine bourbon as opposed to the usual coloured water, even though she still was legally a minor. It also featured a moral ending to a potentially offensive situation: when the heroine spends the night with a male friend, an independent witness is produced to prove that nothing 'untoward' has happened. The première was attended by Eugenia and Morton Hoyt, who had recently rented an apartment next door to the Scott Fitzgeralds and, later on in the run, the celebrated couple themselves turned up backstage to congratulate her. Tallulah was particularly fond of F Scott Fitzgerald's wife, or Zelda Sayre as she remembered her from her youth in Montgomery when Zelda, two years her senior, had gone around shocking the community with her daring antics.

Tallulah was also seen by a 21-year-old Noël Coward, visiting New York on a shoestring budget and having to decide which, if any, Broadway shows he would be able to afford. He remembered the occasion in *Present Indicative*.

> I thought the production and the acting good, and the play poor, but what interested me most was the tempo. Bred in the tradition of gentle English comedy with its inevitable maids, butlers, flower vases and tea tables, it took me a good ten

minutes of the first act to understand what anyone was saying. They all seemed to be talking at once. Presently I learned my first lesson in American acting ... the technique of realizing first which lines in the script are superfluous, and second knowing when and how to throw them away.

Halfway through the run of *Nice People*, Tallulah moved into the West 57th Street apartment of Bijou Martin, wealthy actress daughter of the opera star, Ricardo. With Bijou she got drunk for the first time, and became involved with the sect known as The Beautiful People, spear-headed by the likes of Noël Coward and Geoffrey Holmesdale, the Earl of Amherst. The latter was on the staff of the *Morning World*, and extremely influential on the social circuit. It was probably Amherst who coined the motto of The Beautiful People – 'Will You Come To My Snow Ball?' – nothing less than an open invitation to their binges of heavy drinking, drug-taking and overt bisexual activity. Journalists and photographers were also asked along to these gatherings, not to participate in any way but to make them more exciting by bringing them to the public's attention. Tallulah and three of her female friends very quickly earned the honour of becoming known as 'The Four Horsewomen of the Algonquin', after she had been described in Alexander Woollcott's column as 'comely, competent, and luxuriating in her feline role'. She reacted to this with her usual lightning retort, 'My father always warned me about men, but he never said anything about women! And I don't give a fuck what people say about me so long as they say something!' Henceforth her constant, deliberate shocking would always give the critics something to say.

Tallulah still had a crush on Pauline Frederick, though she was not too bothered about engaging in any pursuit. Although her close friendship with Bijou Martin remained platonic, she still consorted with Jobyna Howland and there were any number of one-night stands with young women whom she plied with chocolates and flowers and, on one occasion, with her only fur coat. Sex, or the quest for it, was accompanied by the more than occasional snort of cocaine, or 'snow', which could be purchased from the dealers who touted for trade outside the tearooms on West 40th Street. Sometimes, if the prim and proper Estelle Winwood was with her, her supply – usually hidden in a knotted handkerchief at the bottom of her handbag – would end up being rooted out and flushed down the lavatory. When high, Tallulah would hitch up her skirt and do handstands or cartwheels and it is reported that she never wore underwear when she did this. Dorothy Parker, present at one of these displays, baptized her 'Whistler's Mother'. In her autobiography, Tallulah was surprisingly frank when discussing her initiation into 'snow':

> My host led me into the bathroom and handed me a paper of glistening crystals. I was shaking in my boots. He took some on the end of a nail-file and sniffed it up either nostril. My brow clammy, my knees rattling, I followed suit. I was sure I would take off like a rocket. To my surprise I experienced no sensation save that born of another achievement. For weeks I confused my friends by saying at every opportunity, 'My dear, cocaine is simply divine!'

Later in life, one of her favourite one-liners would be, 'Cocaine *isn't* habit-forming … I should know that, darling, I've been taking it for years!'

Tallulah also entered into a brief period of mysticism, urged by Bijou Martin and Estelle Winwood. Seer to the famous in those days was the Scots-born Evangeline Adams, who lived in great style on Riverside Drive. Adams's methods were not altogether authentic, but when Estelle Winwood informed Tallulah that her life had been suitably enriched by a prediction which had come true, Tallulah agreed to a visit. Sometimes the seer merely repeated what she had read in that morning's newspaper horoscope column. Sometimes she used Tarot cards; more often than not she simply opened the Bible and prodded it willy-nilly with a pin. Typically perhaps, Tallulah's first 'key-word' was 'Jezebel' and, when Estelle explained that the Jezebel in the Bible had ended up being thrown to the dogs, she quipped, 'Yes, darling, but before that happened she got to *ride* with a couple of kings.' In retrospect, Evangeline Adams did offer Tallulah some sound advice, even if she only was stabbing in the dark when she told her, 'Your future is in England, dear. You must go there at once – even if you have to swim.' Tallulah's response was that she would think about it.

Spurred on by cocaine binges and the occult, at a party hosted by Geoffrey Amherst, Tallulah was introduced to his new lover whom Amherst affectionately addressed as Naps. Naps was Napier George Henry Sturt, the 3rd baron Alington whose family seat was at Crichel, in Dorset. He was 24 years of age when he met Tallulah and, though he became the greatest love of her life, even she could not work him out properly:

> Napier touched off conflicting emotions in me. With him, I was irked by his nonchalance, his cynicism, his flashes of cruelty. Away from him, I found these flaws attracted me. It's awkward to explain Napier's effect on me. He wasn't good-looking, he had an almost repulsive mouth, but he lived recklessly. He scorned the conventions, loved to gamble, and when it pleased him had great wit and charm. But my love for him was mixed with resentment. He was a riddle I could not solve.

In relation to his physical attributes, Tallulah was probably selling Napier Alington short. Most contemporary sources have described him as 'typically tall, dark and handsome', and his portrait reveals him to be something of a Dorian Gray type – like the Oscar Wilde character, he was unbelievably vain, selfish and on a narcissistic par with Tallulah herself. When, suitably impressed by her fruity vocabulary, he insisted that she had impeccable class, this prompted her to utter, 'I can say shit, darling, because I'm a lady!' – a phrase which was almost always expected of her whenever she attended some important society function. Cecil Beaton, a close friend of Alington's, who was later to become a friend to Tallulah, said that Alington was, 'a tired boy in appearance, essentially young, with the willowy figure of a bantamweight champion, a neat head covered with a cap of silken hair, pale, far-seeing eyes and full Negroid lips.' He was in fact in the early stages of tuberculosis and had arrived in New York a short time before both for the benefit of his health and to study the American banking system.

Refusing to submit to the impersonal environment of a New York hotel, he was staying with Mrs Cornelius Vanderbilt, the acknowledged queen of New York society. Here, he proceeded to make a nuisance of himself. When Mrs Vanderbilt organized a dinner party in his honour and to introduce him to New York's in-crowd, Napier decided to meet the only New York he was interested in. Having already seduced Mrs Vanderbilt's footman, he feigned a headache and the pair went off to explore the nocturnal delights of Greenwich Village. Here he met the former partner of Gaby Deslys, the enigmatic Hungarian-born dancer Harry Pilcer.

Recently returned from a sensational season in Paris, where he had appeared in a revue with the awesome Mistinguett – it was he who had inspired her biggest hit, *My Man* – Pilcer had moved in with the revue star Teddie Gerrard, said to have been more neurotic than anyone else in American vaudeville. Napier took turns to sleep with the two stars – sometimes sleeping between them – and always delighted Tallulah with his word-for-word account of what had transpired during the night. He further offended Mrs Vanderbilt by standing her up for an important opera date and by turning up during the interval flanked by two drunken sailors. In spite of these humiliating incidents, his hostess is said to have continually forgiven him, saying, 'One sentimental smile from Naps would have charmed the ducks off any pond.'

When Tallulah fell in love with Napier, she again claimed that she was a 'technical' virgin but boasted that, in spite of his homosexual leanings, he was a good lover. She also added, 'And he was big where it mattered. Forget the experts and take it from me – which would be a good deal more comfortable than taking it from Naps, size *does* matter, darling!' And though she was only about 18 at the time, and with no connections that would have mattered to a member of the British aristocracy, she had little difficulty wooing him away from his male lovers, for the time being, at least. More than this, for a while Napier's intentions seemed *so* honourable that he proposed marriage, hoping that this would induce her into sleeping with him more often. It did, of course, and for several weeks the pair were inseparable – almost, for sometimes Napier would get up in the middle of the night and, without a by your leave, rush off to Greenwich Village to catch up with Harry Pilcer and pick up some of the rough trade he had come to appreciate. He was an aficionado of sado-masochism and often could only maintain an erection when bonded, beaten, or whipped. Tallulah once said that she had enjoyed sex with him most of all only when he had spanked her and she had been able to claw him with her fingernails.

Tallulah's next few plays were hacked to pieces by the New York critics. Only one did her any good – *The Exciters*, a poor comedy which she called 'the unfunniest thing I ever did'. It opened in September 1922 and only Burns Mantle tried to make her feel despondent by describing her as 'looking tired and fed-up'. She had good reason to, for Napier Alington had left for England. There had been no warning, not even the slightest difference of opinion and he had not even bothered to say goodbye. He had tucked his favourite photograph of her inside his wallet and she did not realize what had happened until he had been absent from their love-nest for three days.

The initial success of *The Exciters* compensated Tallulah for her disappointment. Frank Crowninshield wrote in *Vanity Fair* that she was 'this world's most subtly amusing imitator of Ethel Barrymore', and this time the actress was impressed because she was no longer made to look fat. Then, quite unexpectedly, her performances began attracting one section of the public which the critics hated unanimously – the Gallery Girls, who invariably greeted her with a rapturous, whooping applause each time she walked on to the stage, before she had uttered a single word of dialogue – not an acceptable thing to do in the New York of the early twenties.

Most of these girls were, like Tallulah and her character in the play, flappers. Most were lesbians, or were certainly confused by their sexuality and as many as possible were allowed into the star's dressing-room after the performances to be addressed as 'darling' and to offer her tiny posies of flowers which were either 'divine' or 'simply wonderful'. The 'touching' craze began too, an essentially European custom where

Tallulah would lay her hand on the listener's while offering
some sound or impractical advice, such as what lipstick to
wear, how to make the best of the colour of one's eyes and how
best to masturbate. The talk was of liberation, of what 'useless
shits' men were, and of the rapidly spreading trend of shedding
one's inhibitions with one's corsets.

It was not Tallulah's outrageous offstage behaviour and racy
comments that got her noticed by the legendary British
impresario, Charles B Cochran, but Burns Mantle's witty
article describing her impersonation of Ethel Barrymore.
Cochran, talent scouting for the equally eminent Sir Gerald du
Maurier, was on an annual trip to New York. Initially, his
mission had been to secure the rights to two Broadway hits –
The Seventh Heaven and Somerset Maugham's *Rain*. As a
matter of course, Burns Mantle pointed him in the direction of
the Algonquin, where he was reunited with his friend Estelle
Winwood and introduced by her to Tallulah. The effect on him
is said to have been electrifying. Even when informed that he
would not be able to stage the two plays, Cochran was
determined that he would make her a star in *something* in
London. Tallulah, who had tried just about everything sexually
and otherwise, was more than ready to admit that she was now
in search of new horizons and, added to this the fact that her
much-loved Napier Alington was in England – albeit living
with another man – she did not take much persuading. Before
leaving New York, Cochran financed an expensive photo-
graphic session in the studio of Ira Hill. This time, however, her
beautiful hair and eyes were the centre of attention and, when
Cochran tucked the photographs into his portfolio, he
promised that he would stay in touch.

Tallulah had probably dismissed Cochran's enthusiasm as
just another unfulfilled promise. However, on 10 December
1922, she was handed a cable: POSSIBILITY ENGAGEMENT
WITH GERALD DU MAURIER IN ABOUT EIGHT WEEKS.
WRITING FULLY. CABLE IF FREE. The play was *The
Dancers*, which Gerald du Maurier had co-written with Viola
Tree. Tallulah began doing her homework and found out that it
had been du Maurier who had been largely responsible for

launching the career of the stophisticated British actress Gladys Cooper. Even so, she waited until she had received Cochran's further instructions before making her final commitment. This came in the form of a lengthy letter, explaining that du Maurier's play contained two parts, one English and the other American, and that in his opinion the latter would be better suited for her. The letter also suggested that though travelling all the way to London was risky, she would at least be reimbursed with her fare and en-route expenses – in short, she had absolutely nothing to lose. On the negative side, she was told to expect only half her regular New York salary but that the chances of being offered more substantial roles after *The Dancers* were very good.

Tallulah was two weeks off her nineteenth birthday, still a minor, independent of her father though not financially so, and unable to raise the steamer fare to England. Will Bankhead, if compelled to accept and support her career, would not lend her the money because he believed that a man of Cochran's standing should have paid up front. He was also financing Eugenia's first divorce from Morton Hoyt – Tallulah's sister had already left for Reno, where it was easier to obtain a divorce. Not to be outdone, she booked a berth on the *Majestic* and then set about finding the money. Having decided that she needed a minimum of $1,000, she approached her friends at the Algonquin. All admitted that going to England would be an incalculable risk – despite the fact that she had been provisionally hired because of her looks and the fact that *The Exciters* would not have been nearly so successful had it not been for Tallulah's legion of lesbian aficionados. There were further doubts when, upon receiving Tallulah's cable stating that she was free, Cochran wired back: TERRIBLY SORRY. DU MAURIER'S CHANGED PLANS. At the time she told a journalist, 'A summons from du Maurier was like a bugle call from Olympus.'

Charles Cochran had asked her the secret of her ravishingly beautiful hair and she shocked him with the truth: for years she had only washed it in Energine dry-cleaning fluid. Estelle Winwood assured her that her gorgeous hair would find her work anywhere, even if *The Dancers* failed to materialize. Thus her excitable spirit told her that there would be no backing out. She cabled Cochran again: I'M COMING ANYHOW! and he returned the message: DON'T: THERE'S A DEPRESSION HERE. IT'S VERY BAD. By this time, however, Tallulah had collected her travel documents and her $1,000 from a General Coleman du Pont, a wealthy, eccentric friend of her late grandfather's.

In New York Harbour, Tallulah was given a roistering, noisy send-off by her flapper friends and there was a tearful, but no doubt relieved, farewell from Estelle Winwood, who asked her at the last moment if she had remembered to pack a coat. Tallulah could have explained that since her benevolent act of several months ago she did not even possess a coat, though her friends at the Algonquin had collected to buy her an evening dress. In any event, Estelle removed her own mink and draped it across Tallulah's shoulders, for good luck. Then, minutes before the *Majestic* set sail, she craved just one more favour – she asked Estelle to cable London and book her into the Ritz.

3

Queen of the Gallery Girls

Throughout the long, arduous sea journey, Tallulah danced, had fun and no doubt tried to forget that she could have been on a hiding to nothing. She sent Cochran another message and his reply was that he would meet her. He did, at Paddington – she had travelled up from Southampton alone – and he escorted her to the Ritz, apparently the only London hotel she had ever heard of. She spent the next day with Cochran and his wife and between them they formulated a plan: Tallulah would state that she had never received the second cable calling off the London engagement and Cochran would negotiate with Gerald du Maurier on her behalf.

Gerald du Maurier's 'kingdom' was Wyndham's Theatre and, as resident actor-producer-manager, he exercised his right to star in every production there. Currently he was appearing in *Bulldog Drummond* and Tallulah insisted that she should be introduced to him that very evening. She found his performance exhilarating. Though 50 years of age, he was able to portray the hero with suavity and charm. His acting was very much in the style later perfected by Leslie Howard and George Sanders – sophisticated, mockingly supercilious, perfectly English and, though the word had yet to be invented, camp. Du Maurier was also very much of a philanderer and, though like John Barrymore, he was given the cold shoulder when he attempted to seduce Tallulah, she did not give a good impression of herself when she barged into his dressing-room, without knocking, and announced, 'Well, here I am!'

Politely, du Maurier explained the predicament Tallulah had put him in, not believing for one moment the ruse about the cable because he had seen all the subsequent ones. He told her that *The Dancers* was the first play he had ever written and that the risk in staging it had been so great that he and his co-author Viola Tree had decided to stage it under the pseudonym Hubert Parsons – thus, in the event of a flop, du Maurier would not suffer a blot on his impeccable career. He then explained that he had contracted another actress for the part of the American flapper, Maxine. Tallulah simply shrugged her shoulders and returned to the Ritz as though she had been doing this sort of thing all her life.

Charles Cochran, who now held himself responsible for what looked like becoming a costly mistake – ostensibly to be paid for out of his own pocket – did not give up on her. Meeting her the next day for lunch, he advised her to tart herself up and visit du Maurier alone ... and hatless. The change in the man's attitude was nothing short of astonishing. He introduced her to his daughter Daphne, soon to become renowned as one of the world's best-selling romantic novelists and, when she blurted out, 'Daddy, this is quite the most beautiful girl I've seen in my life!' Tallulah's future was secured. Du Maurier questioned her about her family background and asked how she had come by such an exotic name, all the while staring at her beautiful hair. Within an hour he was convinced that she *was* Maxine and, early the next day she signed the contract for £30 a week – £15 a week *less* than the original actress was getting, for her own contract stipulated that as she had been replaced at the very last minute, she would be retained on full salary during the run of the play, just in case Tallulah did not come up to scratch. The arrangement worked well – the actress had recently give birth to a baby and appreciated the rest. Even so, Tallulah had to work doubly hard perfecting the role of Maxine, for when she signed the contract for *The Dancers*, the première was just two weeks off.

A few days after booking herself in at the Ritz, Tallulah

renewed her relationship with Napier Alington. Since rushing out of New York he had not contacted her once. Now he breezed into her room as though nothing had happened and dumped a tiny Pekingese puppy into her lap. The dog was called Napoleon and, while he was making little puddles all over the carpet and the plush upholstery, his new mistress romped on the bed with her errant lover. The rest of the day they spent reminiscing over the respective gaps in their lives, and a little later Tallulah was introduced to Napier's latest boyfriend Lord Edward Latham, a theatrical dilettante and designer. He was a key member of The Bright Young Things, the London counterpart of the crowd she had mixed with at the Algonquin, who had their own meeting place at a place known as The Ivy. The Bright Young Things were even more controversial than anyone Tallulah had ever met. Sex was permissible and more acceptable with complete strangers, usually of the same sex, and in daring, unusual locations, such as in the backs of cars, or up against a tree in Hyde Park while being watched by one's friends. It was considered *de rigueur* to drink cocktails from dusk to dawn, to see the sun come up through a drug-induced haze and to invite a member of the clergy to each and every orgy, not just to shock, but to debate the existence of God and offer 'alternative' versions of the Scriptures ... the only part of the deal not accepted by Tallulah.

At one of these shindigs, Tallulah met Olga Lynn, a social-singer who had acquired a following, not to mention a veritable fortune, performing at tea dances and aristocratic soirées in and around London, besides appearing in *Louise* during a brief season at Covent Garden. She was also befriended by Lady Diana Manners, the actress daughter of the Duke of Rutland, an effete and much-respected woman, who boasted to everyone that she was a close friend of the French singer, Mistinguett, whom Charles Cochran had tried and failed to tempt across the Channel to appear in a du Maurier revue. Olga officially introduced her to London society at The Bright Young Things Costume Ball, in February 1923. Tallulah and Napier dressed as twin brothers from the Versailles court of Louis XIV, both wearing powder-blue satin breeches which

Tallulah called 'ball-crushers' and which led her to bawl, at a
strategic moment when everyone was looking at her escort, 'It's
all right for Naps, darlings – but what do I do if I want to pee?'
The remark made her an instant hit and she became the
coqueluche, or 'darling', of The Bright Young Things.

The Costume Ball was Tallulah's last public engagement
before the opening night of *The Dancers*. The next day, nursing
an almighty hangover, she began rehearsals. For an entire week
she stopped smoking, after Cochran had warned her that she
might run out of breath halfway through her opening dance.
She also moved out of the Ritz into a temporary flat provided
by Napier around the corner from the theatre. Gerald du
Maurier then told her that she would benefit considerably by
extending her limited dancing abilities and she was sent on a
crash course to a ballet school in Bloomsbury. Her teacher was
Léonide Massine, then aged 26, flamboyantly bisexual and not
renowned for offering compliments. He suggested to Tallulah
that she could have made the grade as a ballerina but that she
was a decade too late. Some years later, she said of him, 'Away
from the bar, young Léo was just another musclebound,
rhythmless clod.' All the same she became passionately
interested in ballet and at one first night – overhearing two
refined ladies stating that the male dancers' 'ding-dongs' only
appeared large on account of the elasticity of their tights – she
filled everyone's ears by bellowing, 'If you've got to talk about
men's cocks, darlings, then at least call them cocks. I won't
have the most beautiful part of the male anatomy dismissed as a
ding-dong!'

The Dancers, billed as 'a melodrama in four acts', opened on
15 February 1923 and was sufficiently important to attract the
likes of the Duke of York (later George VI), the Marquess of
Salisbury, Gladys Cooper and most of The Bright Young
Things, headed by Napier Alington and Edward Latham. The
plot was so contrived that most critics did not bother trying to
work any of it out and put it down as being 'far-fetched'. Had it
not been for Tallulah's presence – she told du Maurier to his
face that the production was second-rate – the Hubert Parsons
effort almost certainly would have been another 'also-ran'. It

told of two girls who are so infatuated with the Charleston – condemned by the *Daily Mail* as 'almost rivalling the antics of a tribe of savages' – that they allow the craze to rule their lives. However, while Maxine lets the dance enhance her fame and her aspirations to become a famous ballerina, the English girl, Una (played by Audrey Carten) falls in love with her dance partner, gets pregnant and commits suicide. Tallulah opened and closed the show and Audrey Carten occupied the middle two acts.

For some reason known only to Gerald du Maurier, Tallulah appeared on stage wearing a white buckskin dress and ridiculous headdress of white feathers, from which her hair cascaded down to the small of her back. The scene was a Wild West saloon, to which she was escorted by the Earl of Chevely (du Maurier), who served her with a cocktail before asking her to execute a frenetic Indian Charleston. The first time she did this there was a deathly silence in the theatre, though by the end of the first act there was such a stamping of feet and yelling that she fled in a panic to her dressing-room and spent the next 40 minutes crying her eyes out. When, however, she heard Audrey Carten getting the same treatment during the second and third acts, she realized that this was a British audience's way of showing their profound admiration. Then, as she walked on to the stage to take her curtain call with the rest of the cast, several young women threw flowers from the gallery. After several years as a hit-and-miss on the New York stage, London had turned her into an overnight sensation! Writing in the *Daily Sketch*, Anton Dolin enthused, 'She could have gone through any modern ballet and not even been out of breath at the end.'

The usually waspish-tongued Hannen Swaffer, who turned up for the première wearing his black cloak and wide-brimmed hat – Tallulah said he looked 'like Aristide Bruant gone wrong', though they became lifelong friends – wrote in the *Daily Express*, 'Tallulah is the essence of sophistication ... she gives electric shocks! Sex oozes from her eyes! She is daring and friendly and rude and nice, and all at once!' The eminent theatre historian, J C Trevin, who was given a ticket in the stalls, where he sat among The Bright Young Things, called her, 'A smouldering, pouting young woman, with a voice like hot honey and milk and a face like an angry flower', and concluded, 'The play could not have mattered *less*. She had acted herself into a cult.'

Tallulah *did* rapidly become a cult but not just among The Bright Young Things. As with her later appearances in New York, her much-publicized nonconformist antics got her noticed by the British equivalent of her Broadway Gallery Girls. This time the fans were mostly Cockney and they went one step ahead of their American counterparts by not just burning their corsets, but by emulating Tallulah's every gesture. Pub singers in the East End announced music-hall songs in a quaint, rough-edged 'Tula' drawl and addressed indifferent audiences as 'darlings'. Fans who could afford to do so bravely ventured out alone and stood at bars, sipping whisky and smoking cigarettes. Others rushed out of the theatre after Act One to watch Tallulah leaving on her lover's arm for some dinner engagement – as she was not appearing in the middle of the play, she saw no point in hanging around backstage. When she returned to the theatre, usually one minute before the last act, so did the fans, stomping back to their seats with as much noise as was humanly possible.

One evening, between acts, Tallulah did not dash off to her favourite restaurant with Napier. Borrowing Audrey Carten's nail scissors, she hacked off her hair, bobbing it to just below the nape of the neck. Charles Cochran almost had a fit and Gerald du Maurier was so furious with her – bearing in mind he had only hired her in the first place because of her hair – that he threatened to fire her. Tallulah told him to go ahead; she did not care. When she walked on to the stage there was a glacial silence which genuinely frightened her. Then all of a sudden the Gallery Girls began shrieking their approval. Tallulah later remarked that had she dashed on to the stage and begun devouring the props, her girls would have followed suit. Their subsequent actions, however, surprised even her. The news of what she had done spread across London like wildfire and, over the next few evenings the Gallery Girls began sawing through their own locks in the theatre while she was performing. Instead of picking up flowers for her curtain call she found herself side-stepping over hanks of hair, in varying stages of cleanliness.

A contemporary report on Tallulah and her Gallery Girls was penned by Arnold Bennett, part of which reads:

> At 2 pm you see girls, girls, girls in seated queues at the pit and gallery doors of the theatre. They are a mysterious lot, these stalwarts of the cult. They seem to belong to the clerk class, but they cannot be clerks, typists, shop-assistants, *trottins*: for such people don't – and can't – take a day and a half off whenever their 'Tallulah' opens. What manner of girls are they, then? Only a statistical individual enquiry could answer the question. All one can say is that they are bright, youthful, challenging, proud of themselves and apparently happy. It is certain that they boast afterwards to their friends about the number of hours they waited for the thrill of beholding their idol, and that those who have waited the longest become heroines to their envious acquaintances.

Two months into the run of *The Dancers*, Gerald du Maurier took a two-week holiday and Viola Tree brought in an understudy. This had no effect whatsoever on the play's popularity – most of the time when Tallulah was not on stage, the audience chatted loudly or engaged in a singsong. However, when he returned and Tallulah asked for two weeks off, du Maurier refused – to lose her now, albeit temporarily, would have a crippling effect on the box office, he said, particularly as he had just got away with doubling ticket prices. Tallulah insisted. Du Maurier then offered to increase her salary – to what it should have been in the first place – only to be told, quite bluntly, where to shove his money. He finally gave way when Viola Tree told him that she had arranged to travel to Venice with Olga Lynn and that they would be taking Tallulah along whether he approved or not.

At the very last moment, the trio were joined by Olga Lynn's friend, Sir Guy Francis Laking, a 19-year-old alcoholic of whom she said, 'That poor darling looks so frail, an ejaculation would blow him off the face of the earth!' Francis – his family and friends hardly ever used his first name – had been the first child to have been born in St James's Palace since James II, one fact which Tallulah always found fascinating, for the times were many when she declared that he should never have been born at all. By all accounts he was not very nice to know. She started off calling him 'witty and cloudy-gendered', eventually dismissed him as 'ass-sniffing loathsome' and once said in an interview that she and Lady Diana Manners were the only ones in London who would speak to him. Francis was also full of his own importance, but without the magnetism of an Alington, and spoke with a speech deficiency which Tallulah often mocked. He was also bisexual, which of course in her circle was a must.

In Venice, the four friends were put up by Cole Porter and his wife, and at once walked into a domestic drama which Francis and Tallulah only aggravated. Although Porter's wife had turned their home into a miniature Louisville, welcoming just about every American who set foot in the town, her husband was in the middle of a violently passionate affair with one of his ex-undergraduate pals from Yale, the bearded actor Monty Woolley. Even Tallulah caught her breath when Porter introduced Woolley as 'my old fuck-buddy'. The pair's antics, however, only fascinated her. As a musician, Porter was an undisputed genius but he was also an insufferable snob. He sneered at the servants, he was deliberately rude to the locals who only revered him. Both men had a penchant, when they began to grow tired of each other's company, to 'send out' for black studs and, if these were not readily available, they solicited rough trade the way Napier Alington had in New York.

Tallulah behaved herself at the Porters, preferring boating with Francis Laking to partying, and it was on such an excursion that she collapsed and had to be brought ashore and admitted to a clinic. The diagnosis was not too serious – because she had walked around hatless, treating the Italians to too many sightings of her hair, she had gone down with sunstroke and developed a temperature of 106. The indisposition laid her low for a few days, but the fun soon resumed. En route to England she stopped off in Paris, where Olga Lynn and Viola Tree took her to Chez Molyneux to purchase several dresses and pairs of expensive silk pyjamas. She also heeded Olga's suggestion that, in the event of her being 'menaced' by some of her more fervent Gallery Girls, Tallulah would be better giving up her London flat and moving in with her, to her house in Catherine Street. Tallulah did this at once and the parties here were wilder than anyone could have imagined. Olga supplied Tallulah with her own personal maid but when the maid did not turn up for work one morning and someone knocked on the front door, Tallulah answered the call without a stitch on, setting a precedent that would continue right into her old age. The caller was Gerald du Maurier, there to welcome her back to London – only to be demanded the doubled salary that he had offered to keep her there in the first place. The man was so embarrassed by what he saw that he agreed, then turned on his heels without entering the house.

Far from suffering because of Tallulah's absence, *The Dancers* took off again, reaching unprecedented success and finally closing in a blaze of publicity after 344 performances, the second-longest run of Tallulah's career. She received dozens of offers but, because none of them came up to the standard of the du Maurier play, rather than turn them down she asked for a minimum salary of £200 a week, anticipating that by this means she would increase her 'property value'. The ruse backfired on her and she accepted the lead in *Conchita* – the first time her name appeared on billboards above the name of the play – only because she found the playwright's name, Edward Knoblock, such a hoot and more than typical of the company she was keeping.

Conchita opened at the Queen's Theatre on 19 March 1924 and was an absolute horror. Tallulah played a rough-and-ready Lupe-Velez-type vixen who runs a hotel somewhere in Cuba for a slippery politician. She refused to attempt a Spanish accent – not that her girls would have tolerated anything other than the voice they were used to – and absolutely hated her co-star in the second act, a tiny monkey, which bit her several times during rehearsals. On the night of the première, the animal jumped into her arms, whipped off her black wig and tossed it into the orchestra pit. The audience began laughing and Tallulah decided to give them something to laugh at. Flinging the monkey aside like a rag, she turned a series of cartwheels. The Gallery Girls went wild – henceforth, even in the most serious of plays, she would hardly ever get away without acting the fool.

In her autobiography, Tallulah refers to *Conchita* as 'one of the all-time clinkers' and, short of walking out on the production, she did all she could to ensure that it had as brief a run as possible. She and her maid put on disguises and mingled with the crowds outside the theatre, vociferating about 'that godawful play and that awful Bankhead woman'. Her efforts seem to have worked – the boos, she said, would have rocked the walls of Jericho – and its closure was celebrated with Francis Laking and Olga Lynn at Ciro's, one of London's top eating establishments. Here, there was a minor drama when Tallulah bumped into Gladys Cooper who, after seeing a performance of *Conchita*, had dismissed it as 'crap'. Tallulah thanked Cooper for her opinion by ordering a pint of best bitter … and pouring it over the actress's head.

She was in more distinguished company in her next play, *This Marriage*, starring opposite Herbert Marshall and the genteel Cathleen Nesbitt. The play opened at the Comedy Theatre in May and ran for 53 performances. Again, the plot was uncomplicated: a wife, insisting on an open marriage, is informed by her doting husband that he has a pretty mistress (Tallulah, naturally), and she develops a clever strategy which will enable him to be shared by them both. Tallulah's plum lines were, 'I think you're behaving like a cross between a god and a lunatic!' and 'Conscience isn't like a liver – you can get by without it!', both of which enabled her girls to raise the roof.

Tallulah developed a profound admiration of Cathleen Nesbitt, then married to the MP Cecil Ramage and nursing a baby son, who would once a day be brought to the theatre by his nanny so that Cathlee could breast-feed him in her dressing-room. Tallulah asked if she might watch the ritual and she spoiled the child rotten with costly but well-chosen gifts. 'The baby was much more interesting than anything we did or said on the stage,' she cracked. Even more bizarre was her predilection for delving into Cathleen's personal life, particularly when she was told that the actress had been engaged to Rupert Brooke at the time of the poet's death, at 27, from septicaemia.

Brooke fascinated Tallulah, who read his published letters to Cathleen, edited by the poet's mother on account of their ambiguous sexual content, in a single sitting. One line made her cry and she often quoted it in public, 'If you don't know you're the most beautiful thing in the world, either you're an imbecile or something's wrong with your mirror.' She learned too from her Bright Young Things that at Cambridge, Brooke had been wooed by several soon-to-be-famous young men, including Lytton Strachey and the economist John Maynard Keynes, and when she described these individuals to her friends as 'suckers for Rupert', the intent was obvious. One of the great Bankhead philosophies was that any man capable of getting it together with one of his own sex *had* to be admired and set upon a pedestal. Thus, her inter-performance debates with her friends over whom Rupert Brooke had slept with made a boring play just that little more bearable and she was pleased when it closed.

Believing, and rightly so, that she was getting all the wrong roles, Tallulah decided that she would retire from the stage for a while and luxuriate in the company of Olga Lynn. Audrey Carten, her co-star in *The Dancers*, had taken this unusual step at the age of 23 at the height of her popularity, and could not be tempted back to the boards at any price. Tallulah still walked around the house stark naked, or received guests while languishing in her bath and her behaviour in public was not much better. When an eminent Member of Parliament and his wife stared at her continuously in the Savoy, she marched up to his table and announced, 'What's the matter, darling – don't you recognize me with my clothes on?' She soon pulled herself together, though, when she received an unexpected letter from her Aunt Marie. Suffice to say it was addressed TALLULAH

BANKHEAD, ACTRESS, ENGLAND and it informed her that her father and a colleague, Senator Hughes, were on their way to London on very important congressional business.

Eager to impress upon her father that she was doing well, and behaving like a Bankhead lady, Tallulah rapidly set about putting things in order. In June 1924 she accepted a role opposite Nigel Bruce – later famed for playing Doctor Watson opposite Basil Rathbone's Sherlock Holmes – in another Knoblock play, *The Creaking Chair*, not because the script had much merit but because she did not want Will to find her unemployed. 'On the surface all confidence, all swagger and strut, inside I churned with doubt,' she wrote. 'Any minute the clock might strike twelve and I'd be back in a hall-bedroom at the Algonquin – worse yet, in Grandfather's yard in Jasper.' In fact, the first night audience thought the play so bad that when Edward Knoblock walked on to the stage to take a curtain call, he was booed. Will Bankhead never got to see the play but he did accept an invitation to visit Tallulah at Olga Lynn's house, and The Bright Young Things were conspicuous by their absence. A few evenings later he escorted her to a governmental dinner at the Savoy, an establishment which had not made her welcome since the Gladys Cooper incident, and they sat at the same table as Lord Beaverbrook. Tallulah was disappointed that no royalty was present, though the staff were relieved – besides baptizing Gladys Cooper she had once bellowed to one of the waiters, 'I really do get fed up of all those royal lesbians following me around, darling!'

Will Bankhead did witness his daughter's splendid impersonation of the great French actress Sarah Bernhardt, acknowledged by some critics to have been so movingly accurate that even the hardest of men burst into tears on seeing it. A few years later she was photographed in the role by Cecil Beaton and the prints were exhibited in a London gallery. It is an unusual, and indeed emotional study, practically impossible to distinguish from the real Sarah, and is thought to have been inspired by Beaton's trip to Paris where he had seen the great *chanteuse*, Maryse Damia, the very first artiste to appear on stage with the spotlight directed straight at her face, illuminating just this and her hands.

What Will Bankhead did *not* see were the reviews for the play, which were dreadful. Many years later Emlyn Williams remembered her voice in *The Creaking Chair* as having 'a timbre steeped as deep in sex as the human voice can go without drowning'. In 1924 Tallulah had to make do with being written off as 'typically plump and sophisticated', and she threatened the London *Evening Standard* with a writ when the caricaturist, Tom Titt, drew her as a cottage-loaf supported by very spindly legs.

If any good came of the play it was Tallulah's and Nigel Bruce's innovation to turn it into a farce by sending up every line, forcing 235 sell-out performances and allowing Tallulah to save up for her first car, a smart green and cream Talbot Coupé. This came about when the actor-manager C Aubrey Smith, who appeared in the play, retained £10 of her salary each week, finally handing the money over with interest. Though she took driving lessons and fared reasonably well – this had much to do with her instructor being handpicked, and thus possessed of the essential stud qualities – she graduated as a hopeless navigator. During the short journey between Catherine Street and the theatre she became lost so many times that she took to hiring a taxi to 'lead' her towards her destination, but at a snail's pace so that she could follow. After a few weeks of this nonsense, however, and realizing that she was getting nowhere fast, she traded her car in for a string of pearls ...

4

Fallen Angel

During the run of *The Creaking Chair*, Tallulah saw little of her two 'escorts', Naps and Laking, preferring the reserved company of Audrey Carten and virtually becoming surrogate mother to Audrey's 11-year-old brother, Kenneth, who came up from Eton during that summer of 1924. Tallulah bought the boy a copy of Lewis Carroll's *Through the Looking Glass* and became an avid supporter of his enterprising tennis career. A few years later, before swapping his racket for the stage, he became the Under-Sixteens Junior champion and Tallulah attended as many important matches as her hectic schedule would allow – on one occasion, a Wimbledon official escorted her off the court after she had yelled at a crucial point in the game, 'Hit it, you no good son-of-a-bitch!'

In January 1925, after Will Bankhead had returned to America and the all-clear had been sounded, Tallulah moved out of Olga Lynn's house and rented a service-flat in Curzon Street. This coincided with the most exciting offer thus far in her career – the opportunity to play Sadie Thompson in *Rain*, adapted from Somerset Maugham's short story, 'Miss Thompson', about a prostitute who corrupts a clergyman. Tallulah had been invited to play similar roles in two other plays – *Spring Cleaning* and *Tarnish* – but confessed, 'I wanted Sadie to be my first all-out hussy.' For three years, *Rain* had been playing to packed houses all over America, with Jeanne

Eagels as the heroine. Tallulah's chance to interpret the one role she believed she had been created for occurred when the producer Basil Dean succeeded where Cochran had failed and acquired the British rights to the work and when Jeanne Eagels – nearing the end of her life and hopelessly dependent on heroin – refused to come to London. Tallulah was *so* intent on playing Sadie that she told Dean she would accept half of her regular salary for the privilege. The producer was financially insecure, though within a few years he would earn a fortune directing films for Gracie Fields, and he knew that only an actress of Tallulah's standing and reputation would get him out of the red. The last word, however, rested with the author, a man renowned for his reticence. In this respect Tallulah tried to be understanding – she signed a contract stating that she would appear in *Rain* for £40 a week but only if Maugham approved.

Basil Dean cabled Maugham, who was in New York, and when there was no reply he set off to plead personally on Tallulah's behalf. Not content with this, Tallulah herself sailed on the SS *Berengaria*, arriving in New York on 25 February. Her impatience was such that she rang Dean from the customs house and, when told that Maugham still had made no decision one way or another, she told the press that she would sort out 'that fucking old wasp' personally. Nothing is recorded of her conversation with the author once she did catch up with him, more's the pity – suffice it to say that she stormed out of their meeting, then spent a few days with her father while waiting for the dust to settle. Before returning to London she travelled to Pittsburgh, where Jeanne Eagels and her company were touring with the play. Having already learned the script by heart, she attended several performances, memorizing the great star's every gesture.

A few days later, Somerset Maugham and Basil Dean set sail for England on the *Aquitainia*. Tallulah had booked a berth on the same ship but she changed her ticket to avoid another confrontation. All that was available at such short notice was a cabin on a cattle-boat, next to one that contained a corpse. Tallulah spent most of her time rehearsing her part and playing the jazz records, full blast, which would be used in the play.

'This brought half the passengers to my door,' she recalled. 'Many of them were convinced that the tub, not content with a corpse, also boasted a lunatic.'

In London, Dean arranged two readings of the play, with Maugham sitting in a corner of the darkened auditorium. Tallulah always maintained that she gave the performances of her life – and for nothing. Maugham refused to speak to her after the first run-through and left the theatre during the second. She did not get the part: the official reason, from Maugham, was that she lacked personality, a statement that only added to her anger when, the next morning, she received a £100 cheque from Maugham and a note suggesting that she should get away from London for a while – presumably so that she would not discover the name of the actress who *had* been given the part of Sadie.

Tallulah returned the cheque, along with a curt note of her own. Secretly she blamed her failure on her mimicry of the author's stutter, which she had performed several times at the Ritz, and she was probably not far from the truth. The most bitter blow of all, however, came two days later when she read in a newspaper that her most cherished role had gone to the Anglo-Norwegian character actress Olga Lindo.

> The roof fell in and I was buried in the debris … I wanted to drain the hemlock cup. That night I gave one of my phoniest performances. Returning to my flat I put on Sadie's Pago-Pago costume, gulped down twenty aspirin tablets, turned on Sadie's record. Then I stretched out on my bed to await the end – but not before scribbling this note: IT AIN'T GOIN' TO RAIN NO MOH! I went to sleep, dramatizing every detail of my suicide. The curious and muted crowds at my door! The stern calm of the bobbies and the coroner! Maugham stoned in the streets! The cables aquiver with the death of the American beauty who had conquered England!

It would 'rain' a-plenty for Tallulah many lears later when, in her autobiography, she wrote, 'Olga Lindo opened in *Rain*. It was an immediate failure.' Probably afraid of taking on the mighty Bankhead, Olga Lindo instead sued Victor Gollancz,

Tallulah's British publishers, and won the case because the play had *not* been an immediate failure – moreover, the five offending words had to be removed from all future editions of the book.

Tallulah's suicide-bid was of course deliberately contrived to draw attention to herself. It failed splendidly, though there was a strange twist of fate when, the very next morning, she was awakened by an urgent telephone call from Noël Coward, then about to launch *Fallen Angels*, the most controversial play he had penned thus far in his career. Coward was faced with a dilemma. His piece contained just two characters, for which he had contracted Edna Best and Margaret Bannerman. Now, the production was one week off its première at the Globe Theatre and Bannerman had dropped out through nervous exhaustion. Coward asked Tallulah if she would be capable of learning a part comprising over 100 sides in four days and she replied that if need be she would learn it in four hours. Coward then inquired about her salary and she told him £100. When he argued that this was over twice the amount she had been offered for *Rain*, she boomed, 'The difference, darling, is that I wanted to play in *Rain*. I don't give a shit whether I appear in your play or not!'

Coward engaged her.

Although the production team for *Fallen Angels* was willing to extend the rehearsal period for the play, Tallulah insisted that the opening night should be 21 April 1925, as scheduled. This was to show Somerset Maugham that she was not one to let things get her down. She had the last laugh in the end for the Coward play ran longer than Olga Lindo's *Rain*. She also attacked Maugham during her first performance by changing one of Coward's lines. During a scene where she had to look out of the window and say, 'Oh Lord, more rain', she strode up to the footlights and bellowed, 'My Gawd, *rain*!'. Hundreds of Gallery Girls screamed their approval and the next morning Tallulah made the front pages of the newspapers.

Once Tallulah began finding her feet, she risked improvization more and more, and always with great success. 'Sanders, bring in the coffee now,' became, 'Coffee, bring in the Sanders now.' She also played practical jokes on Edna Best – substituting the coloured prop-drinks with real whisky and champagne, or at a dramatic moment in the play by suddenly collapsing with a fit of the giggles, or by turning cartwheels. This is precisely what Somerset Maugham had been afraid of. She would also tell reporters that she 'could not stand the mortal sight' of Edna Best, then turn up for a party linking her arm, intimating with a well-chosen remark that there was considerably more to their friendship than met the eye, which of course there was. Maugham even invited the pair to lunch. Tallulah was polite throughout the engagement, but when she was ready to leave and the author remarked that *Fallen Angels* was the best comedy performance he had ever seen on the British stage, she turned on him and said, 'Mr Maugham, I have only two words left to say to you, and the second one is "off".'

Because the script of *Fallen Angels* was not drivel, people who might not have bothered going to see a play went to see Tallulah, to find out what all the fuss was about. And of course she injected as much of herself into the role as she possibly could simply to shock the prudes and moralists. She told one reporter that she had put on a stone in weight halfway through the run of the play because her part demanded that she be eating all the time while on stage, adding, 'And you know me, darling, I've always been partial to chocolate cake and big bananas.'

Tallulah also spread the rumour that she had recently had an abortion, claiming that it had been by no means her first. The theatre critic James Agate, denouncing her as obscene, wrote in his column that she was 'a joyless creature whose spiritual home is the gutter'. The *Daily Express* ran the headline, DRUNKEN YOUNG MARRIED WOMEN BOTH CON-FESSING TO IMMORAL RELATIONS WITH THE SAME MAN! leading to a campaign aimed at closing the play, headed by the anti-smut campaigner Mrs Charles Hornibrook, who had earlier caused chaotic scenes when attacking the works of Eugene O'Neill. One evening, when Tallulah and Edna Best were camping it up, Mrs Hornibrook rushed up to the front of the stage and shouted, 'This is a protest. This filthy play should not go unchallenged!' There followed a stream of abuse from the galleries, which Tallulah silenced by raising one tiny hand. Turning to the orchestra leader she growled, 'Play "I Want To Be Happy", darling, and get this creature outta here!' The song was from *No! No! Nanette!*, then packing the crowds into the West End. Everyone joined in, including Tallulah, as Mrs Hornibrook was escorted red-faced out of the theatre.

A confession from Winston Churchill, a few weeks later, that he had seen the Coward play five times and that in his opinion there was nothing wrong with it, gave an enormous boost of confidence to the others in the play. Ten years before, the politician had asked the controversial French star Gaby Deslys to leave England because of her 'embarrassing exhibitionism' – this had led to a young lord flinging himself under the front wheels of her car – and few people would have argued that compared with Tallulah, Gaby had been a saint. Through her friend Lord Beaverbrook, Tallulah actually got to know Churchill. She was driven to his house at Westerham, where over dinner he surprised her by confessing that he had had an affair with Ethel Barrymore when she had appeared on the London stage.

Noël Coward's popularity, which had made him one of the mascots of The Bright Young Things, earned Tallulah a whole new group of fans – there were now Gallery Girls of both sexes, so to speak. As such she was probably the first female artiste to acquire a cult, mixed-gay following, a tradition which she shared at that time with Damia in France, and with 'gender-bender' stars, such as Harry Pilcer in America, and which would later be continued worldwide by Dietrich, Garland and Piaf. Tallulah's fans, however, were unique in that they were allowed to queue for tickets to her shows without actually being seen. Most of them hired '48-hour pogs' – stools, too tiny to be sat upon, which were rented out by Woolworths or the theatres themselves for a nominal fee. Each pog came with its personalized name-tag. They were chained to the railings closest to the theatre, and one hour before each performance the 'gallery-ites' who did queue were served hot tea and muffins by their sisters. The leader of the Gallery Girls was called Fat Sophie, a butch lesbian who invariably wore male attire and carried a large black umbrella which she used when defending her territory and that of her girls from 'intruders' – the young bloods of the East End who, though rarely as violent, were the 'gay-bashers' of their day.

It was Fat Sophie who invented 'Talle-lulah, Hallelujah!' which her followers chanted each time she raised her umbrella in the theatre, and who gave cues to 'scream' or 'swoon', all of course depending on the scene being enacted. And whenever Fat Sophie announced that a particular play was good, which was always the case with Tallulah, her girls would often see the same production as many as six times in one week. Remarkably, though Tallulah was generally indifferent towards most theatre critics, she always found time to listen to Fat Sophie – if a line or gesture did not seem right to her, it was changed.

On 2 September 1925, Tallulah opened at the Adelphi Theatre in Michael Arlen's *The Green Hat*, an obvious step-down from her last play – she branded it as 'an Armenian mish-mash' owing to the fact that the playwright had been born Dikran Kouyoumdjian in Roustchouk, Bulgaria, of Armenian parents. She played the *demi-mondaine* Iris March who, having been ostracized by the society she had gathered about her, ends her life by driving her fancy yellow car into an oak tree at 70 miles an hour. Tallulah had three specific reasons for accepting the part. Firstly, some critics were comparing her to Katherine Cornell, who was playing Iris to rave reviews on Broadway. Secondly, the role had been rejected by Gladys Cooper. Thirdly, it was no mere coincidence that the other major character in *The Green Hat* was named Napier, and that he went with her to a swim-party as the real Naps had once done, making a complete fool of himself. Napier Alington was reminded of this when he attended the première with his lover, Edward Latham. One of Iris's lines in the play went, 'I have never given myself in disdain, in desire, with disgust, with delight ... but I have kept to that silly, childish boast!'

Tallulah was also subjected to a good deal more hype than usual and photographed for the *Sketch* by Dorothy Wilding. One shot, for the puritans, showed her in a dowdy coat and hat.

The other, for the Gallery Girls, showed her bare-headed and sultry-looking, dripping in jewels and furs. Hundreds of fans who had never bought a newspaper in their lives bought the *Sketch* just to cut out the photograph and pin it to their bedroom walls. Nothing, however, could compare with Tallulah in the flesh, which is what she was almost in when, halfway through the first act of *The Green Hat*, she stripped down to her underwear to be told by her lover, 'You are a woman with magic eyes, and a soft white body that beats at my brain like a whip!' The critics dismissed the play as banal and ridiculous but this only served to increase its popularity. David Lloyd George, though he did not see it, was so impressed by the newspaper reviews that he invited her to his Surrey home for tea, took her into his garden, and cut a rose for her to wear in her hair. Tallulah's friend, Hannen Swaffer, under his nickname 'The Pope of Fleet Street', wrote in the *Daily Express*:

> Tallulah Bankhead is almost the most modern actress we have. she belongs to the semi-exclusive set of whom Michael Arlen writes. She has beauty and a shimmering sense of theatre and has moved starwards in great strides during the last year. Her art saved *Fallen Angels* from dreariness; now she has succeeded in a part about which even Gladys Cooper felt nervous.

The Green Hat was a much greater success in New York than in London, mainly because of Katherine Cornell, who in real life was as unlike the play's heroine as Tallulah was almost a carbon copy. Cornell said in an interview, once, 'I had to *work* my way into Iris March. Tallulah was already there.'

Tallulah did not get off lightly with her next play, Sir Patrick Hastings's *Scotch Mist*, which opened in January 1926. It told the sorry tale of a British cabinet minister's sex-hungry wife, and this time Mrs Hornibrook's condemnation had open support from the Bishop of London. Tallulah's friend, Lord Beaverbrook, was so concerned about this adverse reaction that he offered to pay one of his critics to write a glowing review of the play. Tallulah would not hear of this and the piece was a bigger hit than it ordinarily would have been because the bishop was allowed his say. 'There's nothing like a clerical blast to buck up a sagging box office!' Tallulah cracked – then, gave the busybodies something to talk about. Her co-star was Godfrey Tearle, an actor she did not much like, certainly not in the amorous sense. However, when Tearle's intensely jealous actress wife, Mary Malone, began turning up at rehearsals, broadcasting that here was one man who was *not* going to fall into the clutches of the girl from Alabama, Tallulah decided that she would teach her a lesson she would not forget. During one of their love scenes Tallulah flung herself on top of Tearle and almost devoured him. Then, as he was recovering from the shock and his wife could only stare, open-mouthed, Tallulah yelled to Malone in her very best Cockney, 'Good thing I had me drawers on, ain't it?'

Tallulah had now decided to put down roots and, advised by Napier Alington, she signed a 99-year lease on a mews house at 1 Farm Street, just behind Berkeley Square in Mayfair. The house comprised five rooms on two floors, plus another below ground level, a door which opened directly on to the street and a central spiral staircase. She spared no expense having the place fitted out and decorated – spending £3,000 of her own money at the Duke Street shop owned by Somerset Maugham's wife, Syrie, whose speciality was white reproduction Louis XV furniture and made-to-order Marion Dorn rugs. Napier Alington and Francis Laking helped her put the house in order, though Tallulah had started to look upon the latter as a nuisance, and tried to fob him off with a variety of excuses. Her favourite was that she was entertaining Gladys Cooper and Edward Latham, two people he could not stand.

Tallulah also became friendly with the theatrical agent Archie Selwyn, who had made and lost vast fortunes with equal indifference. When Selwyn suggested that some of her hangers-on should be made to donate something to her new home, she asked him to set an example – hardly expecting him to write her a cheque for £300 for a new bed, a tremendous sum in those days. In an interview for an article in *The Sphere* entitled 'The Fun of Open House', she spoke of what it was like to be a society hostess: the secret of success was to hold an open house on certain days of the week, and that all guests should be requested to bring only life's essentials – 'gramophone records, sandwiches, fruit salads, lime juice, soda-water and gin'.

Now that she was earning good money, and was a British resident, Tallulah – who never did anything by halves – decided that she must engage household staff. Her greatest handicap in this respect, she often said, was that as the product of a family whose ancestors had imported slaves she could never regard any other human being as less than her equal. Elizabeth Lock, whom she had hired as her part-time maid and dresser halfway through *The Dancers*, was the first to move into Farm Street. Next came Florence and Arthur Meredith, a Cockney couple who appealed to her because, she said, they looked as though they had stepped out of the pages of a Dickensian novel. The Merediths did not last long. They were unable to tolerate the rave-ups and all-night parties, and would not accept Tallulah's 'new-fangled contraptions'. One of these was a large refrigerator and, when Arthur Meredith threatened to leave unless she got rid of it, Tallulah got rid of him. She then hired a stout Lancashireman named John Underdown to be her butler and his wife Mary to cook and clean. She was delighted when she caught her butler impersonating the lisping, effeminate Francis Laking – Underwood was given a rise in salary, and expected to 'perform' in front of her guests. Her most important acquisition, however, was her secretary–personal assistant, Edie Smith, whom she often referred to as 'my confessor'.

Around her own age, this small, somewhat insignificant woman – Tallulah once said she reminded her of a scrubbed apple – Edie had been a Gallery Girl for two years and was a friend of the highly respected Fat Sophie. One evening, when invited into the dressing-room for a drink and a chat, Edie asked Tallulah if she might have a word in private and was taken back to Farm Street. Edie explained that she had recently seen Tallulah leaving the theatre with Gordon Selfridge Jr, the director of the famous department store. Edie had heard that Selfridge was looking for staff – Tallulah put in a good word, and a few days later Edie was given the job of bakery-assistant at Selfridge's. At around the same time, Elizabeth Lock asked for indefinite leave of absence to look after her elderly mother in Scotland. Unable to cope on her own, Tallulah begged Edie to hand in her notice at Selfridge's and, one week later, she moved into Farm Street, where she very quickly baptized her new boss *die Donner*, German for 'thunder'.

Edie Smith was perhaps the only female friend Tallulah ever had who really understood her almost neurotic mood swings, which one moment saw her highly elated, and the next thrown into the very depths of despair. Edie was on the receiving end of some tantrums which would have put the fear of God into most people, but she also witnessed Tallulah at her brightest and most giving – once, giving the entire contents of her purse to a tramp while they were strolling through Piccadilly. And whenever she accompanied Tallulah on her travels, Edie was always introduced as a friend and never kept in the background.

One of her first duties at Farm Street was to organize a lavish party in honour of Ethel Barrymore, who visited London during the summer of 1926. The actress's entourage had booked her into a hotel, but Tallulah would not allow this, insisting that she should sleep in the guest suite in the basement of the Farm Street house. When the time came for Ethel to leave, Tallulah instructed Edie that her send-off would have to end before midnight so that she would be able to catch her train to Southampton early the next morning. Forty-eight hours later the party was still going strong and, when Ethel was asked why she had missed the sailing for New York by two whole days, she blamed 'the English fog'.

This was also the age of cross-dressing parties, which Ethel Barrymore would have strongly disapproved of, but which Tallulah flung herself into wholeheartedly. One of these, which had just about every reporter in London running around in a frenzy, was a 'treasure-hunt' at the Brook Street house of Captain Neal MacEachern, as described anonymously in the *Sketch*.

Brian Howard went as the Duchess of Portland. Bobby Howard appeared as Joséphine Baker in feathered skirt and tiara. Oliver

Messel went as Tallulah Bankhead in a bridal dress. He wore a mask with long eyelashes which he could move alluringly by manipulating a string. Tallulah Bankhead took off Borotra in beret and white flannels. Captain MacEachern was Mr Lloyd George for the evening, and the Hon Stephen Tennant turned up as the Queen of Romania.

Still feeling guilty that he had let her down by not standing up for her against Somerset Maugham, Basil Dean proposed Tallulah for the lead in his production of Sidney Howard's Pulitzer Prize-winning play, *They Knew What They Wanted*, which had recently taken Broadway by storm. The London production was scheduled to open in the middle of May 1926, at the St Martin's Theatre. The Theatre Guild, influenced by Mrs Hornibrook's preachings, thought the idea of a somewhat disreputable sex symbol playing the part of an ordinary waitress preposterous and opposed Dean in his choice. The producer stuck to his guns, and Tallulah got the part. She played Amy, the wife of an immigrant vineyard owner (Sam Livesey), who prefers working in a cheap San Francisco 'spaghetti joint'. Of course there had to be a handsome lover and in this case it was Joe, a hunky young drifter played by the playboy actor Glenn Anders, fresh from his Broadway success in the same role. Anders was tall, blond, narcissistic and, as Tallulah very quickly found out, 'hung'. The pair became lovers and Anders escorted her to the celebratory bash at the Embassy Club on the evening of the première, where he was observed blowing kisses at himself each time he and Tallulah danced past a mirror.

Not content with having one beau, Tallulah also fell for the dashing Captain Michael Wardell, an associate of Lord Beaverbrook who worked for the *Daily Express*. Wardell had lost an eye in a hunting accident and Tallulah would point to his black patch and introduce him to friends as her 'Spanish Main Swashbuckler'. Telling everyone that she was still sleeping with Glenn Anders, she announced her engagement to Wardell, to the delight of The Bright Young Things who loved nothing more than a scandal.

Tallulah studied the part of Amy, assisted by Edie Smith and a few Gallery Girls who actually worked as waitresses. The majority of her admirers, however, found it hard to accept their idol playing a 'working-class gal', particularly as the photographs taken by Dorothy Wilding promised something completely different. In the past, reviewers had never failed to report how much money was being doled out on Tallulah's stage costumes – in some instances the equivalent of a man's yearly wage. However, when they learned that her clothes bill for *They Knew What They Wanted* amounted to just over £5, the Gallery Girls felt that the time might come when they would have no one to look up to. This led to a private meeting between Tallulah and Fat Sophie, who was asked to relay the news that though the play was expected to have a long run, Amy was definitely a 'one off'. To a certain extent, the fans were placated.

The critic James Agate confessed that he had been 'genuinely shocked' to find Tallulah's performance so convincing:

> Would this piece be yet another incredible fandango of maidens very far from loath, and epigrammatic noblemen too languid to pursue? One's fears were soon allayed. The actress appeared wearing the cheapest of cotton frocks. At once she set about a piece of sincere emotional acting felt from the heart and controlled by the head ... and one would seize the occasion to say that to deplore the misdirection of talent is a very different thing from denying its existence. It would be ungenerous not to recognize that her performance in this piece is one of quite unusual merit.

The Gallery Girls had their Tallulah back in December 1926 when she opened in Avery Hopwood's *The Gold Diggers*, which concerned itself with the entrapment of sugar-daddies by good-time girls. She danced the Charleston in gold pyjamas, bought especially from Molyneux in Paris, and proved a sensation. She was also thrilled to be working with Jobyna Howland, her old flame from the Algonquin. Yet in spite of its season being extended to 180 performances, the critics never stopped giving it a hard time, and Charles Morgan, the British correspondent for the *New York Times*, hated it – particularly when witnessing the mass hysteria which always erupted the instant Tallulah stepped on to the stage. His report was sent winging across the Atlantic.

When she entered they became deafening, mechanical and persistent. Greeting of stars is, in any case, an objectionable practice that destroys the theatre's illusion. Exaggerated, it becomes oppressive and disgusting.

'Oppressive' and 'disgusting' were minor superlatives compared with what some critics (the ones who actually 'lowered' themselves to review it at all) wrote about *The Garden of Eden*, which opened in May 1927. Like its predecessor, it had been transcribed from the original German by Avery Hopwood. 'It is heavily vulgar, as only the German mind can conceive,' one newspaper read. The 'vulgarity' stemmed from the play's strong lesbian theme, and the heroine's tendency to strip down to her expensive lingerie whenever the mood suited her. Tallulah played Toni Lebrun, a dancer in a decadent café who is sacked for spurning the sexual advances of her female boss. Subsequently, she falls in love with a wealthy European playboy, agrees to marry him, then in a fit of bravado climbs to the top of a staircase and rips off her wedding dress, presenting herself but for a moment before her disapproving new family before storming off into the world beyond. More than anything she had ever done before, this final scene drove her Gallery Girls into such frenzy that the applause after the scene lasted almost as long as the last act. The management of the Lyric Theatre was so terrified of a riot that they arranged for two policemen to stand in the wings as Tallulah played the scene. She also had to be escorted to and from the theatre, a task made doubly difficult because each night she insisted on taking half a dozen of her girls back to Farm Street. Once there, she showered them with gifts and allowed each of them to peek inside her bedroom and maybe dab on a little of her favourite perfume – Coty's *Chypre*. This enabled Fat Sophie to invent her latest 'Tallulahism' – for weeks afterwards, each time Tallulah walked on to the stage the girls would begin chanting 'Sheep! Sheep!'

During the run of *The Garden of Eden*, Tallulah alternated her sleeping arrangements with Napier Alington and Glenn Anders, leaving Michael Wardell feeling somewhat confused. Her swash-buckling hero had missed the first two acts of the première because of an important business arrangement. To make up for this he had sent her a valuable diamond brooch: after the performance she told him – in front of dozens of people – exactly where to stick it. She also told him that if he ever stood her up again, she would break off their engagement. The next evening Wardell was again unavoidably detained and she exacted her revenge. Ten times a day for two weeks, the jilted young man telephoned Farm Street only to be told every time that the mistress of the house was in the tub. The crunch came one afternoon when she found a telephone engineer installing a socket in her bathroom. The engineer was sent packing, and so was Wardell.

At around this time, *The Sphere* magazine asked its readers to elect the ten 'most remarkable' women in Britain. Because the winners included royalty – albeit that Tallulah got more votes than anyone else – the names were published in alphabetical order: Lady Astor, Tallulah Bankhead, Lady Diana Cooper, the Duchess of Hamilton, Lady Londonderry, Olga Lynn, the Queen, Claire Sheridan, Edith Sitwell and Mrs Vermet. On the strength of this Tallulah was introduced to the painter Ambrose McEvoy, who executed a profile of her glancing at her reflection through a mirror. The sitting was only half-hearted from her point of view, but when McEvoy sold it a few weeks later 'for a stack of sterling', Tallulah asked him to paint her again, full-face, on the understanding that she would be able to buy the finished work. Shortly afterwards McEvoy died suddenly, and the picture was sold by his estate to Anthony de Rothschild for £600. Though Tallulah offered to buy the painting from him, de Rothschild would have nothing to do with her – Ambrose McEvoy was his favourite painter, and he had a large collection. Tallulah swore that she would one day get even with the man who had 'duped' her but she never did.

When *The Garden of Eden* closed after a record-breaking 232 performances, Tallulah signed to make her first and last exclusively British film for an estimated salary of £5,000. The screen adaptation of Sir Arthur Wing Pinero's *His House in Order* was yet another Gladys Cooper reject – the actress is said to have been horrified to watch her own screen-test. Some time before, Gerald du Maurier had been signed to play the male lead but, when he learned that Gladys Cooper had dropped out, so did he. When filming began at the Teddington studios on 19 October 1927, Tallulah's co-star was Ian Hunter. She disliked the man and the film, which was only a minor success. Seeing her on the screen, the Gallery Girls declared via Fat Sophie, was third rate to seeing her in the flesh because she could not feed them their repartee.

Michael Wardell was replaced in Tallulah's affections by Tony Wilson, the grandson of the Earl of Ribblesdale. Six feet four inches tall, blond and muscular, Tony told her that he had just celebrated his twenty-fifth birthday. In fact, he was only nineteen. Like almost every relationship Tallulah entered into, it would have more than its share of ups and downs.

Tallulah's sister was living in Paris after her second divorce from Morton Hoyt, and tried to follow Tallulah's example by joining in with the in crowd – in her instance the clique that gathered nightly at the Jockey Club. She was often seen in the company of the opera singer Fyodor Chaliapin, then the lover of Maryse Damia, and the singer Kiki de Montparnasse – one of the few entertainers who could out-vulgar Tallulah. Eugenia, whose stage name was Sally Holt, had made a film which had flopped miserably, and on the last day of shooting had been temporarily blinded by an exploding arc light. In the spring of 1928, her sight almost restored, she was approached by Albert de Couville, a London theatrical agent, and offered a part in *The Barker*, for which Claudette Colbert had been contracted following her success with the play in New York.

It was only too obvious that de Couville was hoping to make a killing with a second Bankhead on the London stage, and an article in the *People* tried (and failed) to convince readers that Eugenia was a carbon copy of Tallulah. Tallulah did her best to

support her, attending the première of *The Barker* in
Manchester – disguised in a dark wig and glasses and
accompanied by Alan Parsons, theatre critic of the *Daily Mail*,
whom she hoped would supply Eugenia with an acceptable
review. This ruse also failed. All Parsons wrote about was
Tallulah going to the theatre, full stop. And one or two
unimportant critics merely referred to the fact that 'Miss Hoyt
had executed an acceptable French can-can', no more.

Much more serious was the problem that occurred when
Eugenia was introduced to the irascible Tony Wilson. It was
love at first sight, and the couple shared a number of secret
trysts at the London home of Francis Laking. When Tallulah
found out – from Laking, of course – she threatened to castrate
her former lover and the threat must have been taken seriously.
That same night, after her can-can, Eugenia and Wilson rushed
off to catch the boat-train to Paris. Tallulah would not speak to
her sister for many years, once saying scathingly to a reporter,
'Eugenia's put on some spectacular performances over the
years, darling, but none of them have ever been on the
goddamn stage!' She then tried to camouflage her disappointment over losing Tony Wilson by having another fling with
Napier Alington.

This revival of affections was *very* brief, in effect little more
than a succession of one-night stands, which Naps fitted in
between 'farewell performances' with his legion of male lovers,
now that he was engaged to be married to Lady Mary
Ashley-Cooper, the eldest daughter of the 9th Earl of
Shaftesbury. The marriage, which may have started out as one
of convenience, proved a happy one. Tallulah may have been
pleased about this, though she would never find another man to
take Naps's place, and many times in the future she would
console herself by repeating her favourite Alington anecdote.
Tallulah had stumbled upon Naps when shopping in Paris and
after a wild night on the town, he had missed the train back to
Geneva, where he had been receiving treatment for his
tuberculosis. Seven nights in succession, Tallulah had walked
him to the Gare de Lyon – seven times he had missed the train
and taken her back to his room at the George V. Tallulah had

then been compelled to return to London for a theatre engagement and, at the last moment, Naps had decided to travel to Venice – hiring a taxi for the three-day trip.

In the spring of 1928, Tallulah played Polly Andrews in the political drama, *Mud and Treacle*, where one line – 'The only place where men and women can usually meet is in *bed*!' – had the critics up in arms and the Gallery Girls screaming the place down. After receiving several complaints from Mrs Hornibrook and her supporters, Tallulah received a letter from the prime minister, Ramsay Macdonald. The contents of this have never been revealed, though suffice it to say that once Tallulah had spoken to him on the telephone she was invited to lunch at the House of Commons, and a few evenings later he was seen watching her performance from the front row of the gallery. Not only this, after the show the pair shared a bottle of champagne in Tallulah's dressing-room ... before stepping outside to sign programmes for fans. Tallulah told the press, proudly, 'I got such a great kick the other day, tooling down Piccadilly with the prime minister. It isn't too often, darlings, that you can bag Tallulah and a British PM in one swoop. Isn't it exciting?'

5

My God!
I'm Beautiful!

In August 1928, Tallulah opened at the Lyric Theatre opposite that most English of actors, Leslie Howard, in *Her Cardboard Lover*, a comedy by Jacques Deval and P G Wodehouse. The storyline was trite but the critics and the Gallery Girls agreed unanimously that it was her best play since *They Got What They Wanted*. Shortly before the première she was interviewed by Hannen Swaffer, who asked her if she might care to throw some light on the 'gallery enigma'. Her response was swift and truthful: 'I guess they just *love* to see me in my underclothes, darling!' When, however, Swaffer repeated this in his column, she met him outside the *Daily Express* offices and slapped him across the face – a prearranged publicity gimmick which that evening caused 1,500 hysterical young women to run amok in the street outside the theatre as they waited for Tallulah to arrive, requiring 40 policemen to restore order. There were 12 arrests, several faintings and a heart attack, and further eruptions occurred during the performance itself. When Leslie Howard attempted to take a curtain call Fat Sophie opened her umbrella and he was jeered before the Gallery Girls began chanting, 'Tallulah, Hallelujah!' Afterwards, at a hastily gathered press conference, Tallulah was asked if she might make an urgent appeal to future audiences to show decorum.

She refused, saying, 'I'd be a hypocrite if I said I *didn't* enjoy these demonstrations. And if I *do* take off my clothes, it's only because the *play* demands it, not myself!'

Tallulah was right. She *was* only following the producer's instructions, though what she did not enlarge upon was that, by and large, most of her characters were centred around her off-stage persona. 'There is no difference at all between the Tallulah in the street and the one in the footlights,' one anonymous female reporter declared. 'She has the broad, languorous movements of a blue Persian kitten whose claws are never too far concealed.'

During the run of *Her Cardboard Lover*, Tallulah decided to spend one of her weekends off in Brighton. In her own words, she was 'romping around' with her actress friend, Monica Morrice, when, on the spur of the moment, she decided to go looking for 'it' in a famous restaurant noted for gigolos. Here, the pair espied a handsome, shortish young man dining alone and Monica – not Tallulah – insisted that she had to have him. Tallulah summoned the waiter, and a note was dispatched. The young man announced himself as Count Anthony de Bosdari, an Italianate businessman who claimed he was the cousin of the Italian king. He announced that he was only interested in Tallulah, who wrote in her autobiography, 'He took one look at me, then started to act like Nelson at Trafalgar.'

The de Bosdari–Bankhead affair took off like wildfire and, within a week, was the talk of London. Only days after their return from Brighton, he moved into Farm Street and practically took over the running of the household. He did not *ask* Tallulah to marry him, but *told* her to and, instead of the usual engagement ring, he presented her with a heavy diamond necklace worth almost as much as the house, also promising her a bridal settlement of $500,000. From then on, de Bosdari never ceased to amaze Tallulah with fresh revelations about his 'qualifications' and 'pedigree'. He told her he was two years her senior and a graduate of Winchester, one of the oldest and most prestigious schools in England, where he had captained the cricket and rugby teams, directed a drama group, and even won a gold medal for poetry ... when one of the competitors had been Rupert Brooke. Tallulah was enthralled, and swallowed every anecdote. Rich he certainly seemed to be – besides the necklace he gave her an open-topped, two-seater Rolls-Royce because, he reasoned, she was not getting enough fresh air and so that she could pick him up each evening from his office, like the dutiful wife-to-be. The first time Tallulah told him how much she adored Paris, de Bosdari chartered a plane to fly her there – for Sunday lunch.

Tallulah bought her fiancé a diamond-flecked wristwatch and the wedding was arranged for 22 December 1928, during the Christmas break from *Her Cardboard Lover*. The photograph above the announcement in the *Daily Sketch*, was deliberately unflattering: for reasons known only to herself, Tallulah hitched up her dress so that the photographer could see her panties, and the long ladder in her stocking.

Almost at once, cracks started to appear in the relationship. In the past, Tallulah had always had Napier Alington to advise her – not that she had always listened. Now it was left to her proverbial court jester, Francis Laking, to point her towards the truth. This happened a few days after she had made her politicial 'aspirations' known to a newspaper: 'My ambition is to reverse the performance of Lady Astor, an American woman who got elected to the House of Commons. I will shortly become an Englishwoman through my marriage to Count de Bosdari. Then I will try to capture a seat in the American Congress.'

Tallulah began signing herself Countess de Bosdari and, if Francis Laking's investigations were instigated by jealousy, in the end he did Tallulah a tremendous favour by exposing her fiancé as a charlatan. The first postponement of the wedding was agreed upon mutually, when de Bosdari told her that he had bought shares in the U F A, the German film company which two years later would launch Marlene Dietrich in *The Blue Angel*, and that now was the ideal time to launch Tallulah's European career in films. Laking tried hard to convince Tallulah that de Bosdari was taking advantage of her celebrity and name to further a number of shady business deals and that he did not love her at all. But she refused to listen. The crunch came when Laking supplied her with substantiating evidence that Anthony de Bosdari was actually married to the daughter of a rich Chicago industrialist, but offered consolation that the marriage was not recognized in British law. As her fiancé had never mentioned this marriage, Tallulah asked Laking to dig a little deeper, and even more startling facts emerged: de Bosdari had never even *seen* Italy until three years before their engagement, and the valuable necklace and the Rolls-Royce had not been paid for. Even so, it would take until May 1929 for the British newspapers to report that the wedding had been called off – by which time the business deal for which Tallulah had been used as clincher had been finalized. De Bosdari is alleged to have made this 'worth her while', though there was no truth in the rumour that he paid the $500,000 settlement ... and, rather than return his gifts, Tallulah paid for them herself.

Tallulah was still recovering from her ordeal when, at the beginning of October 1928, the Canadian-born, Los Angeles-based evangelist, Aimée Semple McPherson, arrived in London to begin a sell-out tour of revival meetings. One evening – to cheer herself up, she said – Tallulah organized a 'girls' night out' to see the show and determine what all the fuss was about. Aimée was no ordinary Evangelist – she wore jewels, applied only the most expensive make-up, travelled with a personal beautician and hairdresser and ordered her stage gowns from the top Parisian fashion houses. On top of this, her sexual adventures, widely reported by the world's press, were legion.

Accompanying Tallulah were Beatrice Lillie – whom she described as 'the funniest woman who ever stood in shoe leather' – Audrey and Kenneth Carten, the cellist Gwen Farrar and Leslie Howard. Tallulah eventually met the evangelist at the end of the evening and later commented on her 'beautiful eyes, lovely skin, badly dyed hair and peasant's body'. Aimée, having been told of the 24-hour soirées at Farm Street, declined the offer to join Tallulah for a 'jar', though she did invite Tallulah and her party to her non-drinking, non-smoking chambers where they were subjected to what must have been an interminably boring picture show of Aimée's Angelus Temple in Los Angeles, followed by prayers and readings from the Scriptures.

Although a woman of Aimée Semple McPherson's alleged moral standing would not have dreamed of attending a Bankhead play – although in her early years she herself had wished to become an actress – she was tempted to see Beatrice Lillie in the dress rehearsal of *This Year of Grace*, Noël Coward's sparkling revue which had opened at the London Pavilion the previous March with Jessie Matthews and Sonnie Hale, and closed on the day Tallulah should have become the Countess de Bosdari. Beatrice was also contracted for the Broadway production, and Aimée decided that she would have to warn her against the depravities there. She also agreed, under pressure, to attend one of the Gallery Girls' meetings at Farm Street. As Tallulah remembered many years later, 'We attempted to trick her into admitting some peccadillo, and admitted to depravities and excesses, mostly invented, to test her tolerance. She shrugged them off. "I don't mind these things so long as you don't hurt anyone else by doing them," she said.'

A few days later, Beatrice Lillie was due to sail to New York from Southampton, and Aimée Semple McPherson announced that she would like to be there to wish her bon voyage ... and give her a signed copy of her Bible to soothe her on her way. This was a publicity gimmick devised by her sponsors, The Four Square Gospel Churches, who hoped that they might cash in should Beatrice opt to change her faith. Tallulah saw through the charade and arranged to drive the evangelist to her destination, accompanied by Audrey Carten and Leslie Howard. Whatever plans the trio may have had for shocking Aimée were scuppered when Fate intervened. Running into dense fog on the way back from the port, Tallulah's car broke down. As they pushed it two miles to the nearest garage, the party drank a lot – Aimée excluded – and sang bawdy music-hall songs. Worse still, the press were alerted – quite likely by Tallulah herself – and Aimée's sponsors were horrified to read the next day's headlines: MRS McPHERSON'S ALL-NIGHT JOY-RIDE WITH TALLULAH.

Leslie Howard and Audrey Carten were interviewed by

reporters and of course Tallulah's account of the 'shindig', peppered with expletives, differed completely from theirs, resulting in Aimée's sponsors issuing a formal press statement which read, 'We do not understand Sister McPherson's actions. We may only suppose she went after Misses Bankhead and Lillie because she thought they would be good catches.'

It is not too difficult to imagine how Tallulah's Gallery Girls would have interpreted such a declaration, though by and large the general public turned a blind eye to the episode – a great many of them thought that Aimée Semple McPherson should have known what she was letting herself in for. The public also supported Tallulah when the press discovered that she had run into difficulties with the taxman 'on account of her inability to differentiate between pounds and dollars'. She settled a bill for an estimated £2,000 at once, though the fact that she had almost been branded a thief rankled her sufficiently for her to consider a temporary return to New York.

During the winter of 1928–9, Tallulah spent several weekends in Paris, where Kenneth Carten introduced her to several tennis-player friends. She had a lightning affair with William Tilden, who between 1927 and 1933 never lost a championship match. Known to his colleagues as 'Stinky Stumpfinger' – he had had the tip of a finger on his serving hand amputated after an infection, which only seems to have improved his game, and his intense shyness at stripping off in the locker-room after a sweaty session on court had earned him the first adjective – Tilden told Tallulah that until the age of 18, when he had been allowed to go to school for the first time, his mother had always addressed him as June. For Tallulah, of course, ridding the sportsman of his alleged asexuality ranked as a formidable challenge. Tilden had coached many Hollywood stars, including Rudolph Valentino, Clara Bow, Joan Crawford and Ramon Novarro, and claimed to have slept with them all which, according to his biographer, seems to have been little more than wishful thinking – many years later, he would be twice arrested and charged with child molesting.

Tallulah also admitted to having been another of Tilden's conquests, though some friends have said that with her fanaticism for bathing twice daily and Tilden's reluctance to bathe at all, their relationship is unlikely to have been sexual. She *did*, however, have a very passionate affair with Frank Hunter, Tilden's partner with whom he had won the Men's Doubles at Wimbledon in 1928. If this was not enough, halfway through her sojourn in Paris, she and her 'chaperone', Edie Smith, found themselves in a seedy, American-friendly gay club in Pigalle, run by Joséphine Baker's closest friend, Bricktop. Here, Tallulah set about seducing a tall, dashingly handsome Austrian army officer who had turned up in full uniform for an assignation with the priggish actor, Clifton Webb.

As with Anthony de Bosdari, the soldier was sent a note by way of the waiter. Webb was shown this and left the bar in a huff, only to return a few minutes later with a huge bunch of flowers which he had bought from the street-trolley outside. Executing a mincing little dance, which the no-nonsense Parisians had seen many times before, Webb proceeded to pluck the petals from the flowers and shower the pouting young man with their confetti. Tallulah instinctively knew that if she was going to get anywhere, she would have to act fast. Grabbing Edie Smith's purse (she herself hardly ever carried money on her person) she ran out and gave the flowerseller all the cash she had, wheeled the entire trolley of roses and chrysanthemums into the bar – knocking over tables, chairs and drinkers – and tipped them out at the soldier's feet. Needless to say, she strolled off with the jackpot and was not seen for days. Again, the Gallery Girls lapped up the story once Tallulah circulated it on the grapevine ... though even some of those were not too amused when she became involved in what the press referred to as 'the Wilson *affaire*'.

Having crossed the Channel to meet one lover, only to stand him up for another, Tallulah returned to England with a *third* man – Tony Wilson had ended his relationship with Eugenia Hoyt and had decided to return to his family. One Sunday afternoon Tallulah, Tony and his elder brother, Martin, drove out to Eton to collect their younger brother, Peter, and a friend who were both students there and take them punting, and afterwards to a hotel-restaurant on the Thames. What Tallulah probably did not know was that the boys – both 14 – had not asked permission to leave; this aspect was grossly exaggerated by the press, who alleged that they had been subjected to a 'sexual adventure' against their will. Over the next few weeks the story became ridiculous as the boys grew younger, and the nature of what had transpired during the outing became more and more sordid. If any sexual activity *had* taken place during the outing, this did not prevent the boys from wanting to meet Tallulah again, very willingly, when they travelled up to London to see her in *Her Cardboard Lover*, and to spend the weekend being absolutely spoilt at Farm Street. This caused problems with the Eton authorities, who issued the decree, 'Henceforth all students will be forbidden to witness a Tallulah Bankhead play for fear of corruption'. Tallulah went to see her London lawyer and the headmaster at Eton was served with a writ and forced to make a public apology – though not before someone yelled 'Child molester!' during one of her matinées.

The Wilson *affaire* affected Tallulah badly, though she tried not to let it get her down, and in the spring of 1929 she took *Her Cardboard Lover* on a nationwide tour. Some of her more affluent Gallery Girls trailed after her like itinerant camp-followers, and whenever Tallulah appeared in a new town, the 'gospel' had preceded her by several days. However, she was not happy away from London, even in northern England and Scotland where her popularity caused near-riots and, for the first time in her life, she experienced difficulties eating and sleeping. Halfway through the tour she took a two-week break and flew to Paris, where a second liaison with Frank Hunter helped her to alleviate the tension.

In Paris, Tallulah visited Le Boeuf-sur-le-Toit, hailed as 'the cradle of current Parisian society', where she met Jean Cocteau. The star of the show was Yvonne George, a neurotic bisexual *chanteuse* with a penchant for American sailors, cocaine and a nightly bottle of Irish whiskey which was often consumed on stage. Tallulah was fascinated by the fact that Yvonne – in the latter stages of tuberculosis and close to death – had actually placed an obituary notice in a French newspaper to gauge the public's reaction to her demise before staging a farewell concert, after which she really did die, swallowing a fistful of pills after sharing a night of passion with two sailors. Tallulah was also intrigued that Yvonne was a patient at the same clinic in Switzerland that was treating Napier Alington, who contacted her to arrange a two-week holiday at Evian-les-Bains, near Geneva. Tallulah said goodbye to her pretty little *chanteuse*, and rushed off to her rendezvous, only to find that she had been the victim of a cruel hoax – Napier had gone home to his wife.

While in Paris, Tallulah purchased a copy of Radclyffe Hall's *The Well of Loneliness*, described as the first 'undisguised' lesbian novel. The book had been banned in England by the home secretary but it was openly on sale at the news-stand serving the boat-train at the Gare du Nord. It was badly written and attempted to perpetuate 'the Sapphic interpretation' that a lesbian was little more than a man trapped inside a woman's body, which, while it may have been true in the author's case – certainly did not apply to Tallulah, who denounced the book as 'ridiculous crap'. Even so, Radclyffe Hall's book did cause some critics to comment on 'the undoubtable lesbian spell' that Tallulah had cast over her gallery audience. 'I am told that her feeble attempts at immodesty are for the benefit of the feminine element of her audience. Well, girls *will* be boys!' wrote the anonymous critic of *Theatre World*. Tallulah therefore decided that she would try and abandon her flapper image for a while at least, and search for a vehicle which might add a little more to her credibility.

While in Paris, Tallulah had seen several farces and one of these – *He's Mine* – was adapted into English by William Mollison. It opened at the Lyric Theatre at the end of October 1929, and Tallulah played Wanda Myro, a 'fake Serbian princess', opposite the veteran English stage actor Allan Aynesworth for 98 performances.

At around this time, Tallulah sat for her third portrait, this time by Augustus John. She had met John a few weeks before at the Eiffel Tower, a restaurant off London's Tottenham Court Road. A curious-looking man with long hair and a beard, John was wearing jade earrings and multi-coloured clothes, and was sitting at an adjacent table, apparently doodling on a scrap of paper. Eventually he showed Tallulah the sketch he had made of her face, and asked her to sit for him. Tallulah, remembering how she had lost both her McEvoys, made the condition that, on its completion, John would sell her the work for £1,000. She visited the artist's studio in St John's Wood each afternoon for two weeks. The portrait was only half completed when he showed it to his friend, T E Lawrence, aka Lawrence of Arabia, who offered to buy it for an undisclosed fee. John told Lawrence that he would have to discuss the sale personally with Tallulah and he was dispatched to Farm Street. Tallulah refused to let him have the painting – if he really wanted to please her, she said, then he should 'chug off' on his motorcycle and buy her some cigarettes instead. The idea of being Tallulah's factotum fascinated him and several times over the next few months Lawrence ran errands for her, setting yet another precedent for the future, and the painting was never mentioned again.

Stiff competition for the John portrait next came from the Viscount d'Abernon, Britain's ambassador to Germany and one of the country's acknowledged art experts who, along with Gerald du Maurier and Gracie Fields, was sitting for John at the same time as Tallulah. When d'Abernon told John that the work would probably fetch in excess of £20,000 on the open market the artist tried to opt out of his agreement. John's style did not compare with Tallulah's public image as represented by Dorothy Wilding's studies but as a frail, almost consumptive-looking Brontë-esque creature in a flowing gown and long string of pearls.

Tallulah, however, refused to budge, though she did allow John to hang the portrait in an exhibition at the Royal Academy, where one expert wrote that it was 'the greatest portraiture since Gainsborough's very famous *Perdita*'. It was then taken to Farm Street and unveiled in a ceremony attended by friends, selected Gallery Girls and members of the press. Tallulah was heard to say, 'My God, it's beautiful!' The *Daily Express*, however, enlarged upon this and ran the headline:

TALLULAH SAYS 'MY GOD! I'M BEAUTIFUL!' This 'I-love-myself' tag was added to when she posed for a series of magazine photographs, for she gave instructions to the artist, Sasha, to construct a montage which she called *Face, Hands, Eyes*, a five-segment portrait which was truly remarkable.

Tallulah's next play, *The Lady of the Camellias*, opened at the Garrick Theatre in March 1930, with her revelling in the part of Dumas's dying heroine. The role had, of course, passed into legend courtesy of Sarah Bernhardt, who, although she was to die shortly after Tallulah's arrival in London, had been delighted to hear that there really was another actress more 'off the rails' than herself. The Divine Sarah had often slept in a coffin and, after losing a leg towards the end of her life, presented a bizarre vision of an eccentric old lady in an ill-fitting wig and dentures, who placed all the artificial limbs sent to her as manufacturers' samples in a museum, and kept a lion caged up in her house until the neighbours complained about the stench.

Sarah Bernhardt's Camille had proved definitive and would only be equalled by Garbo's film performance a few years later. Tallulah's interpretation was variously described as 'flat' and 'demanding another kind of talent'. Arnold Bennett, so often her champion, wrote, 'This play is not bad, it is mostly dead.' The Gallery Girls only added to the piece's camp value, shrieking when Tallulah made her entrance in a pink and blue crinoline, and quite literally tearing their hair out by the roots when she played the death scene – which on one occasion caused Tallulah to pause and mutter, halfway into a consumptive spasm, 'It's all right, darlings, I'm still here!' Tallulah's girls did settle down by the end of the second week, but this did not prevent Herbert Farjeon from ending his review, 'They preferred her as *The Lady of the Cami-Knickers*.' The classical actress Mrs Patrick Campbell said, 'Tallulah is always skating on thin ice, and everyone wants to be there when it breaks.'

Tallulah had been sorely disappointed when Laurence Olivier had turned down the part of Armand, afraid that she would only succeed in upstaging him. She compensated for her loss by making a play for her ethereal-looking co-star, Glen Byam Shaw. This strapping six-footer was the former lover of Siegfried Sassoon and, although he is reputed to have 'given service' to Tallulah on a number of occasions, Byam Shaw was very much in love with his new wife, the actress Angela Baddeley (who later played the housekeeper Mrs Bridges in the television drama series *Upstairs, Downstairs*). As if to prove a point, by public demand on 11 June, Tallulah recorded two songs for His Master's Voice, 'Don't Tell Him' and 'What Do I Care?'. (In 1956, by which time her voice had dropped an entire octave, she recommited these songs to shellac and the latter song was preceded by a spoken introduction, 'I give you due warning, I'm going to sing. So turn me off now or never. And when you've recovered from the shock, if ever, I propose to warble to you, in my very best Galli-Curci manner, a little song about – well, I'll give you one guess as to what it's all about!') In 1930, however, each of Tallulah's Gallery Girls thought that she was singing 'What Do I Care?' for her alone, and the record sold thousands of copies:

> Maybe you only love me when there's no one else?
> I guess maybe I'm just your now-and-then ...
> Our affair was accidental,
> You were a welcome stranger!
> We were feeling sentimental,
> But such a pleasant danger!
> Even though you're not mine alone,
> Still, what do I care?

While she was 'magnificently expiring' each evening in *The Lady of the Camellias*, Tallulah received a very lucrative offer from Paramount Pictures in New York, offering her a five-year, five-picture contract worth $250,000. The talkie craze had hit the United States hard on the heels of the Wall Street crash, and that year MGM-Loew had netted a record income of $15 million. Leslie Howard had left England after working with Tallulah and had scored a triumph in *Outward Bound*. Her fellow 'sirens', though she had yet to meet any of them, had soared to unbelievably dizzy heights in Hollywood: Greta

Garbo in *Anna Christie*, Jean Harlow in *Hell's Angels*, and Marlene Dietrich in *The Blue Angel* and *Morocco*. Now, the producers announced, it was Tallulah's turn to take the American film industry by storm – or shock.

Before that, however, Tallulah was honour bound to fulfil her contract to appear in Rachel Crothers's *Let Us Be Gay*, which had recently been turned into a successful film with Marie Dressler, Sally Eilers and Rod la Rocque, whom Tallulah had drooled over in Joan Crawford's latest film, *Our Modern Maidens*. La Rocque was in England at the time, and Tallulah was so keen to act opposite the beefy, six-foot three-inch star that she arranged an audition with the producer, Gilbert Miller. For several weeks, she and La Rocque were virtually inseparable. She introduced him to London society as 'Rod Le Cock' – but he was only interested in seeing the sights of London and keeping their relationship platonic. He was, in fact, a promiscuous homosexual who, in years to come when certain words began attracting wholly different connotations, amused Tallulah by reminding her that he had also starred in *The Gay Bandit* and *The Coming of Amos*. 'Big things really *do* come in big packages,' Tallulah cracked, once she had finally bedded him, with disastrous results. 'Poor Roddy was one fuse which simply would *not* ignite,' she declared.

In *Let Us Be Gay*, Tallulah wore inch-long eyelashes, and glossy carmine lipstick – a forerunner of her famous Elizabeth Arden Victory Red. She was also photographed by Cecil Beaton, hatted with pearls, unhatted and bare-shouldered. The pictures were published in *Tatler*, whose entire print run was sold in less than two hours. The play had its try-outs in Birmingham in August 1930 and it was when she was here that Tallulah was told that her *ami-démon*, Francis Laking, had been taken ill with a rare, incurable form of diabetes and a glandular dysfunction. Within the week, he was dead, aged just 26.

The post-mortem report was made public with obvious delight by Hannen Swaffer – Tallulah's friend and therefore Laking's foe had once witnessed a 'catfight' between Laking and Tony Wilson, when the much bigger Wilson had beaten him senseless over some trifle. The report stated that Laking's condition had been caused by non-development of the brain and that, at the time of his death, he had possessed a mental age of 14. Tallulah mourned him privately, it has been suggested out of a deep sense of guilt – though she had no need to feel in any way responsible – but not for long. In death, Laking had played one last practical joke on her, adding a codicil to his will, 'And to my friend Tallulah Bankhead, I bequeath all my motor-cars.'

There *were* no cars …

At the last moment, advised by Edie Smith that it would only cause a scandal, Tallulah decided not to attend Francis Laking's funeral. She was represented by her friend, Gwen Farrar.

Let Us Be Gay did well at the box office, notching up 128 performances, but this had a lot to do with the Gallery Girls being forewarned that if she accepted the Paramount contract, they would not be seeing their Tallulah for some time. Even though Tallulah objected to two lines in the script – because of her respect for the British royal family, she told Rachel Crothers that she would not deliver, 'Kings and queens are really a kind of joke. The most interesting person I met was a prostitute' – her severest critics and 'moralist' enemies were hoping that she would not be coming back to London for a while, if indeed at all.

The move was swift but not unemotional. Tallulah sold her house on Farm Street, crated up her furniture and her Augustus John, and threw one last all-night party to which she invited as many of The Bright Young Things as she could muster at such short notice: Fat Sophie and several selected Gallery Girls, Hannen Swaffer and those journalists who had pleased her the most during her stay in London, and the Cartens. She posed for scores of photographs – including one with the sculptor Frank Dobson, who had recently completed a 'studious bust' of her, and others with the recently pardoned Anthony de Bosdari, who turned up dressed as a woman impersonating a man. Looking back on these fruitful years, Tallulah wrote:

> I had feasted on fame, revelled in Page One role. Professionally I had advanced from comparative obscurity to international

recognition. I left a lot of debts behind me, a few income tax arrears, but I left a lot of friends behind also. My years in London were the happiest and most exciting of my life.

Hundreds of Tallulah's girls turned up at Southampton, in spite of the freezing cold, to give her the kind of roisterous send-off reserved only for royalty. Tallulah drove herself there, with Audrey and Kenneth Carten, Elizabeth Lock and a young Canadian fan named Dola Cavendish. She told everyone that she would never forget England, and that she would be back. Not one of those witnessing the event disbelieved her, for she suddenly burst into tears – but she did issue a stern warning to any would-be playwright, 'You'd better start finding me better goddamned parts, or else!' Then, as she was about to step on to the gangway – though the move must have been planned in advance – she announced that in the absence of Edie Smith, who had vowed to follow on later, Dola Cavendish was the Gallery Girl she had chosen to sail with her to America.

6

Make My Bed and Light the Light

On 13 January 1931, Tallulah arrived back in New York, where she was greeted by Will Bankhead, now in his mid-fifties, and her stepmother, Florence. The two women were surprised at how well they got on – much of it had to do with Will's well-being, and the fact that Florence had proved a good, faithful wife and not just another gold-digger. Tallulah's parents were somewhat taken aback not to see Dola Cavendish, particularly as they had heard so much about her. The new companion had been detained in Cherbourg because her passport had been invalid.

Tallulah had begun her British career in style by booking into the Ritz. Similarly, her second American phase started off with her renting a suite on the twelfth floor of the plush Hotel Elysée, just off Park Avenue – this had recently been vacated by Ethel Barrymore, in Tallulah's favour, repaying her hospitality for putting her up in London. Here, Tallulah handed out $10 tips to maids, porters and errand boys as though they were going out of fashion, and set up a counselling service for anyone hoping to travel to England in the near future. By and large, most New Yorkers had forgotten her actual plays there, though her reputation still lingered in the memory, passed on by 'the gospel according to St Algonquin'. Many people were shocked to hear her talking openly about Fat Sophie and the Gallery Girls, and London actors who were 'hung like buffaloes'. For those who were not so easily shocked, she at once set up a new fashion for brazen, steely parlance – and made it perfectly clear, from day one, that she would *not* be intimidated by moralists, Bible-bashers, anti-smut campaigners and prudish maiden aunts. The maxim was, 'I am as I am, and so is a stone – them as don't like me can leave me alone!' And as if to hammer home this point, 24 hours after moving into the Elysée, she began parading around her $750-a-month suite stark naked.

At the Elysée she met the entrepreneur Al Woods, famed for his naughty-but-nice bedroom farces. It was revealed that in 1924, when lunching at the Savoy in London, Tallulah had let something slip about her dire financial status and that the next morning £500 had arrived in her mail. Woods' many business interests had since been virtually annihilated by the Wall Street crash of 1929. Upon receiving Tallulah's cheque for the money she owed him – he had completely forgotten about the loan – this hard man collapsed in tears.

Tallulah had less than a week to settle into her new, changed environment before starting work on *Tarnished Lady*, the first of the five films she had contracted to make for Paramount. During this interim period she spent the weekend at the Sands Point home of the torch-singer Libby Holman, who was to teach Tallulah the rudiments of her trade for her part in the film. Though she would later meet and marry a man named Zachary Smith Reynolds and eventually be accused of murdering him, Holman was a lascivious bisexual with a penchant for black women. Olive-skinned and smoulderingly attractive, Holman was described by the critic Brooks Atkinson as 'a dark purple flame'. She liked nothing more than cruising the restaurants and bars of Broadway wearing a man's dress suit and bowler hat, and her scores of lovers included Tallulah, Jeanne Eagels, Montgomery Clift and Joséphine Baker. *Chez* Holman, Tallulah also became acquainted with the aviatrix Louisa Carpenter, a mannish 24-year-old relative of the man who had loaned Tallulah her fare to get to England in 1923. A close friendship developed between the two when Tallulah mistook Louisa for the maid and asked her to run a bath – Louisa's tart response was, 'Run it yerself, lady!' The pair spent most of the weekend walking through the countryside, trailed by Tallulah's Rolls-Royce, in the back of which she had installed a gramophone which constantly played records of Bing Crosby and Russ Columbo.

Tarnished Lady began shooting at Paramount East, on Long Island. Tallulah hated every minute of it – the lack of spontaneity, the fact that scenes were not filmed chronologically and, worst of all, the lack of immediate public response. Her co-stars were Clive Brooke and Phoebe Foster. The former, a snobbish man who she said possessed the acting qualities of a lump of wood, later starred opposite Marlene Dietrich in *Shanghai Express*, while Foster appeared in *Anna Karenina* with Garbo. The script also did not match up to Tallulah's expectations. It told of a young city woman who marries for money in order to save her mother from poverty – a far cry from the vamp roles being offered to Garbo and Dietrich. The film was directed by George Cukor, his first solo effort, and there were tremendous clashes of personality.

Secrecy being unknown to The Bright Young Things, Tallulah was swift as lightning in exposing the director as a closet homosexual. The fact that Cukor publicly ridiculed gay actors to deflect attention from himself rankled with her more than his incessant search for rough trade and, though they eventually became good friends, initially they disliked each other. The fact that Tallulah had always been extremely open about her own sexuality and unabashed at 'outing' anyone else also gave Cukor good cause to fear her in an age where careers could be utterly destroyed with a few words out of place. She was particularly fond of repeating the story of Cukor's run-in with Clark Gable during the shooting of *Gone With the Wind*. When Gable had yelled, 'I won't be directed by a fairy!' Cukor, knowing a great deal of Gable's racy, secret past had responded, 'I prefer working with real men too, dear!'

All the same, Cukor did support Tallulah when, dissatisfied with the Libby Holman school of torch-singing, she decided to get to know how the real blues should be interpreted by renewing some of her old acquaintances in Harlem. She was respected among the black community and often frequented a jazz club called The Hotcha, where for a joint or a few sniffs of

cocaine she would entertain the clientele with a few
'torch-songs' of her own, accompanied by the blind pianist,
Eddie Steele. Noël Coward, in New York during the shooting
of *Tarnished Lady*, usually went along with her.

Tallulah's father strongly disapproved of her forays into
Harlem and is alleged to have 'gone spare' after seeing a
newspaper photograph of her dancing cheek-to-cheek with a
black man. Had he known half the things she had got up to in
London, Will might never have spoken to her again. Now he
complained bitterly to George Cukor, whose only reaction was
to tell Will to mind his own business. Tallulah's friend, the
producer Walter Wanger, then joined in the affray and wrote a
stern letter to Will, reminding him how *he* had been at his
daughter's age. Tallulah felt deeply ashamed of hurting her
father but she did eventually remind him that she would dance
where she liked and with whom she liked, and the matter was
very quickly forgotten once she had finished making the film.

None of the Paramount moguls knew quite how to market
their latest discovery. She was not mysterious enough to be
played off against Garbo and, quite frankly, nowhere near as
good. She could not be looked upon as a new Pola Negri or
Vilma Banky because, they claimed, she did not smoulder.
Ultimately, when they decided that her 'bastardized' speaking,
acting, and life-style were decidedly European, they targeted
her as a new Marlene Dietrich. Many years later, John Kobal
wrote of these 'browless, languid, chain-smoking creatures' in
his biography of Marlene, adding, 'If they weren't born with a
foreign accent, they quickly acquired one.'

Tallulah had thus far refused to even think of being
manipulated by some Svengali as Dietrich had been by Josef
von Sternberg. Garbo was getting most of her own way, she
claimed, because if she did not she always threatened to be on
the next boat to Sweden. Tallulah likewise knew that, contract
or no contract, she would always be assured of success if she
returned to England. She did, however, bathe in the blaze of
publicity for the première of *Tarnished Lady* by posing for a
poster not unlike those commandeered by Joseph von Sternberg
for his films with Marlene Dietrich – brooding beautifully

through a pall of smoke, eyes raised skyward as though beseeching divine intervention. Part of the spiel underneath read: THE PRODUCERS WHO BROUGHT YOU DIETRICH BRING YOU ANOTHER WOMAN-THRILL! TALLULAH BANKHEAD! SHE ENTHRALLED A NATION! ENGLAND'S ADORED BEAUTY ON THE SCREEN! GET WITHIN RANGE OF HER RADIANCE! FEEL THE RAPTUROUS THRILL OF HER VOICE, HER PERSON!

On another poster was printed Tallulah's self-indulgent, self-penned personal credo, one which is said to have made her rivals cringe with embarrassment: MEN ARE AS PLEASANT AND EXCITING TO ME AS THE LAVISH GOWNS I ADORE! I DRINK THE SPARKLING CUP OF LOVE, FOR I KNOW MY HEART WILL NEVER BETRAY ME! I AM TALLULAH THE MODERN!

The Paramount executives then came up with a novel idea of letting the picture-going public realize what a dynamic player their new star had been on the London stage. For the first night at the Rivoli Theatre in New York, the lobby displays containing her photographs were rigged with 'personality sashes' – lengths of braid which, when pulled by the adventurous and curious, effected a small electrical shock. Underneath each gadget was Adolph Zukor's inscription: THIS GIRL WILL SHOCK YOU! HER PERSONALITY REGIS-TERS LIKE A THIRD-RAIL! The gimmick, however, failed to convince audiences that Tallulah's début American film was better than mediocre. It was flattened by the critics, though almost every one of them blamed George Cukor for putting her into the wrong role in the first place. One of America's leading film critics, Richard Watts, wrote, 'Her part in this film has been devised by Tallulah's worst enemy in a particularly cruel moment.' John Mosher commented in the *New Yorker*, 'She proves to be an ordinary young actress, suggesting mostly a feeble resemblance to the more beautiful and able ones, especially to Miss Dietrich. She fails in the end to establish any sort of identity of her own.' Tallulah out-criticized both of them by launching an attack on the people in the cutting-room: 'The picture was made by trial and error. What appeared on the screen showed it. Patched, scissored and victimized by all sorts of hocus-pocus, it wound up a mess.'

A few weeks after the release of her film, Tallulah was asked to attend what some critics predicted would be the première of the year – Archie Selwyn's production of *This Year of Grace*, starring Noël Coward and Beatrice Lillie. The arrangements were made by Walter Wanger and Tallulah's ticket invited her to bring a companion. Wanger suspected that if she was allowed to choose whom to bring, there might be embarrassment all around – either she would bring a female flapper friend, or worse still, she would pluck some muscular young hopeful from a convenient street corner just for the hell of it. Anything was possible with Tallulah. Wanger therefore decided to surprise her and she was told that her escort would turn up with the limousine.

The escort turned out to be Gary Cooper, whom she had only dreamed of meeting since returning to America. In effect, it was an answer to both their prayers. In her own words, Tallulah had not 'experienced a goddamned good penetration' since leaving England – and, for her, three months was an eternity. Cooper had barely recovered from two exhausting love affairs with arguably the fieriest man-eaters in Hollywood – 'Mexican Spitfire' Lupe Velez, of whom he had said, 'She pegged me out and practically drove me nuts!' and the wealthy but horrendous social climber, Countess Dorothy de Frasco. Therefore, to be set up on a blind date with a woman of Tallulah's reputation must have been quite unnerving. She later said that the actor had not uttered one word all evening, not that this prevented them from meeting again the next evening and beginning an affair which, if brief, was considerably less troublesome than Cooper's other two. And, of course, with her apparent sixth sense for singling out men who 'mattered', she was soon telling friends about 'Coop's two-hander trouser-snake', much to the actor's acute embarrassment.

Tallulah also made the point of telling a reporter that she and Cooper were engaged, and this appeared in the newspapers. When she received a wire from Reuter's in London asking her to confirm the details – her response was that she was engaged to *Jackie* Cooper, the child star. The reporter then ran the headline that the prospective bridegroom was *John* Cooper, the ex-golfer, and promptly published a photograph.

My Sin and *The Cheat*, both directed by George Abbott, were Tallulah's next films for Paramount and, according to her, they 'flopped like bad perfume'. She was severely criticized for one sado-masochistic scene in the second film, 'whilst exposing acres of naked flesh' – in reality, scarcely more than her shoulders and back – she was branded by Irving Pichel. Even so, her film career was salvaged by Adolph Zukor and Walter Wanger, when they were finally convinced that the critics had been right all along – she would never be accepted as a second-rate Dietrich. Dissatisfied, Tallulah informed Zukor that she would make no more films in America ... after all, all she had to do was return to London and pick up where she had left off. Zukor tried to get her to change her mind by promising to raise her salary to $6,000 a week, then gave his word of honour that her next film would be shot in Hollywood. Still she refused to compromise and she only gave way when the Cartens arrived from England and agreed to keep her company during the five-day train journey across America. There was a hitch when Tallulah found out that her Aunt Marie had been writing letters to Zukor, asking him to engage her as Tallulah's secretary. Needless to say, Tallulah was not willing for her father to be made aware of her every move and affair by her aunt – she was still extremely wary of hurting or offending him, even though she was almost 30. In the spring of 1932, once she had been convinced that Aunt Marie had been given her marching orders, Tallulah headed west.

According to contemporary reports, Tallulah and the Cartens spent much of the long journey 'giggling, playing cards, doing crosswords and reading Proust'. Tallulah was thrilled to learn that the recently married Douglas Fairbanks Jr and Joan Crawford were travelling on the same train and of course she ensured that her presence was made known. Fairbanks gave her a decidedly cool reception, probably aware that she was out to shock, but Crawford, finding Tallulah a girl after her own heart, invited her and the Cartens to dinner, insisting that this would be a strictly informal occasion. Tallulah later said, 'I turned up in slacks, only to find Joan rigged out as if she was going to the opera.' Crawford admitted, 'Tallulah was very sweet, but she frightened the bejesus out of me!' Fairbanks maintained that she stuck her head around the compartment door and told Crawford, 'I've already fucked with your husband, darling. Soon it'll be your turn!'

Though Tallulah and Joan Crawford never became very close friends, they nurtured a tremendous admiration for one another, and had more than a little in common in their ability to live life to the full. When Joan remarked that the film star William Haines was looking for a long-term tenant for his self-designed mansion on North Stanley Avenue, Tallulah insisted that she should be the one. Haines, one of the biggest stars in Hollywood during the silent era – and nicknamed 'Lavender Lips' for his other talents – had failed his voice test when Louis B Mayer had called him 'lip-lazy', to which he had retorted, causing an uproar, '*I've* never had any complaints.' Naturally, Tallulah unearthed all the juicy details about Haines's past life and loves and she told the real-estate agent, 'Darling, I simply *have* to sleep in the room where Bill Haines got it together with that *divine* Clark Gable!' ... little realizing that the statement would cause an almighty hubbub a few years later, during the shooting of *Gone With the Wind*.

She moved into the mansion at once and proved an important point – creating a furore along the way – by hiring three black servants whom she treated as her equals, much to the horror of some of her openly racist guests. Because she thought her Augustus John looked lonely on her living-room wall, she sent off to England for another – his exquisite portrait of Gerald du Maurier, which the actor had despised – and she purchased a companion Rolls-Royce for the one lent to her by Paramount. 'Cars are like men,' she said. 'It's much better to have a couple on standby in case one breaks down.' She and Edie Smith then spent an entire week shopping around Hollywood for clothes – spending several weeks' advance salary on gowns she would hardly ever wear. Like Marlene Dietrich, she found slacks practical, even if the wearing of them *was* frowned upon by some sections of so-called well-bred society. She took some sensible advice from Walter Wanger on money matters, allowing him to deduct a hefty percentage of her earnings and invest it in a trust fund. Incredibly, though she spent money like water on frivolities and over the next few years persistently claimed she was broke, she never once touched her investment.

Tallulah's first Hollywood film was *Thunder Below*, directed by Richard Wallace and co-starring Charles Bickford and Paul Lukas. It was premièred at the Paramount Theater, Times Square on 17 June 1932 with the 'thunderous' slogan: ONE WOMAN DESIRED, DESIRING – IN A VILLAGE OF LONELY MEN BELOW THE EQUATOR, WHERE CIVILIZATION'S BARRIERS SWIFTLY BURN AWAY! It was lampooned by the critics, and even Tallulah dismissed it as 'a double-jointed dud, maudlin and messy'. A few weeks later she appeared in William Beaudine's *Make Me a Star*, which featured so many movie legends – Ben Turpin, Joan Blondell, Zasu Pitts included – that the producer did not even bother adding her name to the list of credits. Curiously, Tallulah did not lose her temper with Richard Wallace, though when he saw her looking so glum he made up his mind that he would cheer her up in his own inimitable way. Before taking up his Hollywood baton, Wallace had been employed as an undertaker's assistant, so when he asked Tallulah to join him for dinner, their 'evening out' comprised sharing sandwiches and a bottle of champagne in the local mortuary and cracking jokes among the corpses. Tallulah loved every minute of it and decided that she would play a prank of her own on 'that living corpse', Louis B Mayer, whom she accused of deliberately sabotaging her Hollywood career by feeding invented stories to the press – the only way, apparently, that he thought he would ever get rid of her and stop her from slagging off half of Tinsel Town.

A sumptuous banquet had been arranged by Walter Wanger, in honour of Mayer, attended by every film executive in Hollywood and dozens of their most famous stars. Tallulah was invited on condition that she behaved herself. She promised that there would be no problems so long as she was left alone. A reporter asked her if she was having an affair with Gary Cooper and she refused to comment until the young man demanded to know why the actor had sat stony-faced throughout the Noël Coward–Beatrice Lillie première. 'We were playing pocket billiards,' came the reply. From then on her behaviour grew progressively worse as she began making eyes at a waiter who kept plying her with bourbon. When someone asked her to sing her favourite song – anticipating 'What Do I Care?' – she put on a display that few of the guests would ever forget. Smiling sweetly at the guest of honour, she announced, 'And now, here's a number for the Messiah. He tells me that *his* favourite number is "Bye Bye Blackbird".' Mayer had already turned crimson but there was more to come as Tallulah crooned the song ... with one gratuitous adjustment:

> Make me bed, and light the light,
> I'll be home late, tonight ...
> Jew-Bird, Bye-Bye!

The year 1932 was proving a disaster for the entire American motion picture industry, as the country headed swiftly towards the Depression. In spite of the massive pulling-power of Garbo, Grant, Crawford and Harlow – hailed by Tallulah as 'Hollywood's most desirable gals' – MGM-Loew showed a loss of $8 million. Fox and Warner Brothers announced that they were in similar strife and Paramount, reluctantly declaring losses of $16 million, went into receivership. Amid these crises, Tallulah met Marlene Dietrich for the first time ... and almost ended up fighting with her on the set of *Blonde Venus*.

Josef von Sternberg's film told the 'sinfully moral' story of a woman who prostitutes herself so that she may pay for her sick husband's treatment against radium poisoning. Marlene had been contracted to play the lead, opposite Herbert Marshall and a very young Cary Grant, but one of the more controversial scenes in the film – where the mother hides her young son under a restaurant table while soliciting for sex – caused the head of Paramount, B P Schulberg to exclaim angrily, 'This is the godamnest piece of shit I've ever seen in my life!' This led to von

Sternberg walking off the set, taking Marlene with him, and Schulberg immediately brought in Tallulah's friend Richard Wallace to direct the film. Wallace suggested that Tallulah should be offered the Marlene part. Schulberg agreed – to which Tallulah quipped, 'Well, darling, I always *did* want to get into Marlene's pants!' (She also told a journalist, who informed her that Marlene allegedly sprinkled gold-dust in her hair to make it sparkle, 'So what? Now I'll have to start sprinkling gold-dust in my pubic hair.') Tallulah, however, gave up her part in *Blonde Venus* when the offending scene was removed and Schulberg and von Sternberg settled their differences. However she and Marlene crossed swords again a few weeks later at the Ruban Bleue Club. One evening, when both actresses turned up with their respective beaux – Tallulah was with Gary Cooper and Marlene with Maurice Chevalier – Tallulah sent a message to Marlene's table demanding to know why she was wearing gloves. Marlene's response was to send the gloves across to her on a plate and Tallulah returned the message, 'I'd send you my drawers, darling, but I'm not wearing any right now.'

Now more than ever, Tallulah had a burning desire to return to the stage, in spite of the obvious risks involved. Ostensibly, she was prevented from doing so by a writ summoning her for $15,000 in back taxes and at the last moment she signed up for what would be her final Paramount film, and certainly her best one so far, *The Devil and the Deep*.

Charles Laughton had stunned American audiences into taking him to their hearts. Unlike Leslie Howard and Laurence Olivier, he did not typify the regular matinée idol heart-throb and some critics even compared him, unfairly, to the German star Emil Jannings who had appeared in *The Blue Angel* opposite Marlene Dietrich. In fact, had he been handsome and strapping as opposed to corpulent and self-confessedly ugly, he would not have attracted the wealth of character roles that enabled him to become the institution he was. His portrayal of the crazed submarine captain in *The Devil and the Deep* was supreme and resulted in his stealing the film from his co-stars – Tallulah, Cary Grant and Gary

Cooper who played her lover whose devotion is torn between duty to his submarine and his affection for the captain's frivolous young wife. The final scene, of course, cleverly combined kitsch with Shakespearean drama – Laughton going completely insane, trying to drown his adulterous wife, her lover *and* himself by flinging open the hatches, and their eventual evasion of a watery grave by shimmying up a rope, mindless of 'the bends', to safety. The fact that Tallulah was in sequins and stiletto heels only added to the hilarity, as did the film's closing lines:

TALLULAH: I want never to have been born ...
COOPER: There's magic out there. Do you want to kill it?

If Tallulah's early American films had tried to present her as the 'Second Dietrich', some of the shots in *The Devil and the Deep* saw her looking remarkably like Garbo, which was of course unintentional. Because of the film's success, she asked B P Schulberg for a rise, ignoring the fact that as many actors were out of work as in. Her request was turned down, resulting in a tantrum in which Tallulah threatened to leave Hollywood yet again. This time she seems to have meant business, for her tax bill had been settled, and she announced that she was going to help out her family in Alabama, some of whom claimed they were facing financial ruin on account of the economic slump. She had certainly been giving money to her friends the Cartens: in order to support himself and his sister, Kenneth Carten had accepted walk-ons and bit-parts for Paramount, and his small but none the less essential salary had, without his knowledge, been deducted from Tallulah's. Now, seeing her short of funds, and not wishing to sponge off her generosity – not that she would have minded in the least – the pair returned to New York to finalize plans to sail to England. Two weeks later the executives at Paramount came up with a compromise – Tallulah was lent out to MGM.

The loan clashed, in effect, with the Hays office Motion Picture Code. Kenneth Anger, in his best-selling book *Hollywood Babylon*, attacked Hays by describing him as 'a prim-faced, bat-eared, mealy-mouthed political chiseler', which is only slightly more polite than what Tallulah actually said to Hays's face, when she was particularly angry after he had outlawed open-lipped kissing and hirsute chests. For her, of course, telling Hays exactly what she thought of him was insufficient, which is why she gave 'The Tallulah Bankhead I Want a Man' interview to Gladys Hall, of *Motion Picture*.

One can only imagine the impact this interview had on Will Hays, who immediately demanded that MGM drop Tallulah without so much as paying her one cent of the money they had promised her for her film. This did not happen, though Louis B Mayer (who had not spoken to her since being so outrageously insulted by her rendition of 'Bye Bye Blackbird'), did offer a warning via Walter Wanger that she could expect trouble unless she agreed to deny everything she had confessed to Gladys Hall. Tallulah did exactly this, and more. In a 'patch-up' interview she said, 'I have followed Mr Hays's advice and have taken up a completely sexless, nun-like, legs-crossed existence.' As for the new man in her life, a bit-player named Alan Vincent who had recently moved into her home, she scoffed, 'Well, darling. He certainly isn't sleeping in *my* bed!' She then completely ruined this – for her – new whiter-than-white image, when asked about the tall young actor named Anderson Lawlor who had been seen waving to a photographer through her bedroom window: 'Oh, him? He's just the new stud I've engaged until someone better comes along.'

Tallulah's only film for MGM, *Faithless*, was directed by Harry Beaumont and co-starred Robert Montgomery and Louise Closser Hale, a delightful elderly actress who had starred in *Shanghai Express* and who was to die a year later, just as she was making the big time in films. Tallulah was all for having an affair with her good-looking leading man but, a few days into shooting, Montgomery was hospitalized with appendicitis. MGM's immediate reaction was to audition for a replacement but Tallulah would not entertain such 'treason' and shooting was held up until Montgomery was well again.

Faithless was supposed to be a wise-cracking, sophisticated comedy about a rich girl who only becomes a nicer person when she loses her fortune during the Wall Street crash. However there was one line – when Tallulah's character is referring to one of her father's charities, and says, 'I don't believe in delinquent girls' – that had the Hays office champing at the bit. This line, among others, and the film's ending had to be changed. Even so, the critics approved, and Louis B Mayer was told that he had a major star on his hands.

Tallulah again responded to success by demanding a pay rise. The compromise proposed was that MGM would keep her on but at her current salary rate, which meant that she would be faring better than most. Tallulah was having none of this and subsequently she was summoned before Mayer. The resulting 'interview' would have been worthy of any anti-Hays sketch. She was given a specific time for her appointment, turned up five minutes early, and was told by Mayer's secretary that he would see her when he could. Tallulah declared that he would see her on the dot, and he did. Mayer then told her that he was looking for someone to replace Jean Harlow in *Red Dust* – the Blonde Bombshell was about to be fired because of her husband's recent suicide. To do such a thing, however, was against Tallulah's principles:

> To damn the radiant Jean for the misfortune of another would be one of the shabbiest acts of all time. I told Mr Mayer as much. He rose from his throne, became very emotional, and encircled his desk the better to approach me. Purposely I misread his intentions. 'None of that now, Mr Mayer! Stay on your side of the desk!' It gave me considerable satisfaction, deflating this *Nero*!

There was considerably more to Tallulah's meeting with Louis B Mayer than she let on at the time ... for when the mogul began tearing a strip off her because of her sexual adventures, she at once spat out the names of six top MGM actresses with whom, she claimed, she had had lesbian affairs – including Barbara Stanwyck, Jobyna Howland and Joan Crawford – then threatened to expose them to the press. Mayer decided, wisely, not to pursue the matter further. Tallulah threw one last wild Hollywood party, said goodbye to Alan

Vincent – having thanked him for his co-operation in her usual way – then boarded the train for New York, over $250,000 richer than when she had arrived.

7

In Search of That
Scarlett Woman

I *knew* I could play the pants off Scarlett. I looked upon myself
as a symbol of the South, the fine flower of its darkest hours.
Temple bells rang in my head, and I whiffed the scent of the
magnolias.

During the journey to New York, Tallulah read the script of
Forsaking All Others, a spicy comedy penned by E B Roberts
and Frank Cavett, the cameraman from *The Devil and the
Deep*. She had already made up her mind that this would be her
Broadway début, ten years since her last appearance on an
American stage. She rented a modest suite for herself and Edie
Smith at one of the most fashionable hotels in town, the
Gotham, then set about trying to find backers for the play.
None was forthcoming. Any would-be sponsor was terrified of
taking the risk with a woman who, though rapidly on her way
to becoming an institution, was not guaranteed good box
office. This did not deter Tallulah, who had long since drawn
the conclusion that difficulties would only ever stimulate her.
She decided to finance the production herself – buying the
rights to the script – but kept the news from the media so that
she would not undervalue her professional credibility. To cover
her tracks, she brought in her friend, Archie Selwyn, as

producer-titulaire, though legally she was still the play's actress-manager.

Tallulah was benevolent – and reckless – when choosing her team. She read in a newspaper that a well-respected magician named Fred Keating had recently been declared bankrupt with debts of $8,000 and assets of 'a canary worth $1 and a cage worth $8,000'. Tallulah engaged him for what would be his first acting role ... as her leading man! She then decided upon a young hopeful, Ilka Chase, to play her rival – 'a venomous witch full of suspicion and speakeasy brandy' – and gave an important part to Anderson Lawlor who had followed her from Hollywood to take up the position, for the second time in as many years, as stand-in stud. One cannot imagine why Lawlor never became a Bankhead regular, for he possessed all the requirements: tall, blond, blue-eyed, reckless and bisexual – and she admitted to being head over heels in love with him. On top of this, he was Alabama-born and, like her father, had sung with the Glee Club. Finally, she hired Don Oenslanger to design the sets, Hattie Carnegie to design *all* the costumes including the walk-ons, and Harry Wagstaff Gribble as overall director.

Tallulah handled *Forsaking All Others* as she did most other things – impetuously, with too many backstage parties and bust-ups and not enough forward planning. The previews took place in Boston, resulting in some of the most astonishing scenes ever witnessed in an American theatre. The small nucleus of American Gallery Girls who had attended the première of *Tarnished Lady* had grown out of proportion and the chanting of 500 of these near-hysterical women completely drowned out the other actors' lines and the orchestra. If Tallulah uttered a phrase that was remotely funny, they bellowed and stamped their feet until the house lights rattled. When, during the opening scene, Tallulah was jilted by her bridegroom, the hapless Fred Keating was bombarded with hundreds of missiles ranging from coins and orange peel to women's underwear and shoes. In Providence, Ilka Chase had to be escorted to and from the theatre by a police guard ...

In Washington, there was almost a riot when the theatre management announced that, as most of the invited guests were from the political world, none of Tallulah's troublesome girls would be admitted to the performance. Tallulah threw a tantrum, threatened to boycott the production and the manager's decision was overruled. Thirty minutes before curtain up, Will Bankhead entered the auditorium and for the first time realized what his daughter was all about when dozens of pairs of bloomers sailed over his head into the orchestra pit. When they met up after the performance. Tallulah was intrigued that her stepmother was absent from her première and took advantage of the situation by trying to 'get him off' with Jean Dalrymple. It is not known if she succeeded, though with Tallulah anything was possible.

One week before the New York première, Harry Wagstaff Gribble and Jean Dalrymple committed the cardinal sin of criticizing the antics of Tallulah's Gallery Girls to her face – with dire results. Gribble was fired on the spot and replaced the following day by Thomas Mitchell. Dalrymple held on to her job solely on account of her friendship with Will Bankhead. There were further problems when Tallulah accused her agent, Leland Hayward, of cooking the books – Hayward was not even given the opportunity to explain himself. Denounced as a 'parasite', he too was sacked.

New York did not take to *Forsaking All Others* as much as Tallulah hoped it would. She later accused the city of being too middle class, adding that in the past the great music-hall and vaudeville acts had only really played to the galleries – perfectly true, of course. Also, it opened at the Times Square Theatre on 1 March 1933, the day of the bank closures. Attended by Amelia Earheart, Ruth Gordon and the New York equivalents of London's Bright Young Things, the première went well enough. The highlight of the evening was the inevitable cartwheel from Tallulah and the moment when, having been deserted by her fiancé and comforted by the officiating priest, she faced the audience and pronounced in a Southern drawl, 'Now ah *knows* Jesus loves me!' The phrase became the rage of New York but the further the play progressed into its run, the more the box office began to suffer on account of the financial climate. 'This is Miss Bankhead's first appearance in this country since her canonization in England, so let's not be *too* peevish about her play!' opined Brooks Atkinson, in the *New York times*, knowing only too well that the production was dying on its feet. Even so, Tallulah refused to concede defeat and insisted upon it completing its 14-week run, losing $40,000 of her own money in the New York production alone.

Several months later, Tallulah recovered this deficit when she sold the play's rights to MGM. Rescripted by Joseph Mankiewicz and starring Joan Crawford and Clark Gable, the film version was a tremendous success and introduced her to the next man in her life, John Hay Whitney – an unusual liaison in that, while fitting physically into her 'ideal caddy' category, this one was married and neither bisexual nor gay. His father had been Payne Whitney, the famous sportsman who in 1927 had collapsed and died in the middle of a tennis match. Jock, as he was known to friends, was also a sporting fanatic but, upon inheriting what was believed at the time to have been the largest estate in American history, he had changed course to become chairman of Selznick International. Obviously, as an occasional bed-companion, Whitney would also prove useful in other areas, particularly as he was the company's principal stockholder.

Three weeks after closing *Forsaking All Others*, Tallulah read the script of Owen Davis's *Jezebel* and decided that she would use the MGM money to stage this on Broadway. Guthrie McClintic was hired to direct, and the première was pencilled in for September 1933, at the Martin Beck Theater. With a few weeks to spare, Tallulah took a break and rented a bungalow in the former Alla Nazimova complex, the Garden of Allah. Keeping her company were the drama critic Robert Benchley, Tarzan star Johnny Weissmuller, and the composer Vincent Youmans, who played for her at the piano each evening when she sang a selection of his famous show tunes. One, 'Tea For Two', was directed at Benchley, but he was too devoted to his wife to risk having more than the one night of passion with Tallulah. Tallulah therefore set her sights on Weissmuller, asking him in front of everyone if 'it' was as big as the rest of him. When this did not work she made up her mind to seduce him – by diving fully dressed into Nazimova's pool at five in the morning, stripping off under the water and emerging 'naked in Tarzan's arms'. Weissmuller, upon hearing her screaming that she was going to end it all, dived into the pool to rescue her. It is not known exactly what Tarzan did with her afterwards, if anything at all, though Tallulah did later confess that she had been a very satisfied Jane.

During the summer of 1933, Tallulah returned to New York to resume rehearsals for *Jezebel* but in the middle of July she collapsed with crippling abdominal pains. She was examined by Dr Mortimer Rodgers (the brother of Richard) and admitted to The Doctors' Hospital for reports. Her illness was reported in the press in a variety of diagnoses – anything from kidney stones to colic – and was serious enough to keep her hospitalized for another nine weeks, though on good days she still rehearsed her play and created merry hell among the nursing staff and other patients. She also tried to prevent the news of her illness from reaching her father, for no other reason than that she did not wish to worry him unduly. Will had recently suffered his first heart-attack and she was afraid that the journey from Washington might prove too much for him.

Tallulah was discharged from the hospital and ordered by Dr Rogers to take a complete rest. She did – for 24 hours – before returning to the play. She was drinking a bottle of bourbon a day, smoking upwards of 60 cigarettes, addicted to codeine and not eating. She collapsed again and was rushed into the Lennox Hill Hospital with a raging fever and what was at first thought to be an intestinal blockage. In fact, it was much more serious than this. During exploratory surgery her entire abdominal cavity was found to be ravaged with gonorrhoea. Reports at the time claimed that she had contracted the malady from 'that actor from *Morocco*', which of course implicated Gary Cooper. This was unfair, and inaccurate for, taking into account her unusually large number of sexual partners, the 'culprit' could have been almost anyone. Tallulah's condition necessitated a five-hour operation on 4 November 1933, during which a bowel obstruction was removed and a hysterectomy performed. She very nearly died on the operating table and remained critical for another week as her weight dropped alarmingly to 73 pounds. During the first week of December the doctors discharged her but only on condition that she hire a private nurse. Edie Smith, who had never left her side for a moment, saw to this, and the three of them moved back into Tallulah's old suite at the Hotel Elysée. The press had been told nothing about her illness and had merely speculated that with one so promiscuous, it had always been 'just a matter of time'. Though the actual term 'venereal disease' did not appear in newspapers for fear of libel action, some journalists did not shrink away from Tallulah's own admission that she had had 'an inordinate number of abortions', though she had often commented on how nice it would have been to have had children of her own.

For several weeks, Tallulah refused to see anyone but Edie Smith and Anderson Lawlor. Her part of Julie Kendrick in *Jezebel* was given to Miriam Hopkins – it opened in the December and the reviews were dreadful, forcing it to close after four weeks. 'Had I been in it, it might have lasted *five* weeks,' she joked at the time. As for now, she became so depressed that Edie and Lawlor genuinely believed that she would end up in an asylum. However, her 'madness' was the result of her doctor cutting off her supply of codeine and Tallulah's own remedy of large quantities of cocaine and a daily bottle of Old Grandad, which were smuggled into her room, past the eagle-eyed nurse.

By the middle of December, however, Tallulah had put on a little weight and, though still weak and emaciated, she was able to leave New York and spend the Christmas holidays in Jasper – her first visit to Alabama since returning from England. During the first week of January, however, she returned to the Elysée in New York, where she rested for several weeks while planning her next project – her permanent return to London. She also made her radio début on NBC, acting a scene from Arthur Schnitzler's comedy, *The Affairs of Anatol*, in *The Rudy Vallee Show*.

Tallulah cabled Charles Cochran in London early in March 1934, a few days before boarding the *Bremen*, so that the news of her imminent arrival could be 'broadcast to the nation' but what really surprised her was the small, although effective, delegation of Gallery Girls which greeted the ship when it reached Cherbourg. The same thing happened in Southampton but, when she got off the train at Waterloo Station, she was mobbed by 500 near-hysterical young women, armed with placards and banners. When she read the one inscribed: 'WELCOME HOME, TALLU!' she burst into tears. At her press conference she told reporters that she did not expect to do a play in London – she just wanted to rest and catch up with old friends and acquaintances.

Tallulah's first night in London was spent at the plush Hotel Splendide but the next morning she received word from Dola Cavendish, out of the country on business, instructing her that her apartment in Regent's Park was at Tallulah's disposal for as long as she wished. She moved in, but if one journalist described her as 'quieter and more serious than in days gone by', it did not take her long to get back into the swing of things with The Bright Young Things, or what remained of the movement now that many of its founder members had either died or moved on.

She threw a party in Dola Cavendish's apartment to which she invited Ivor Novello – the highlight of the evening was her impersonation of Elisabeth Bergner in *Escape Me Never* and the usual one of Ethel Barrymore. She also gatecrashed a huge social gathering at the Aldwych Theatre, hosted by Charles Cochran who had only desisted from inviting her in the first place because he had been concerned about her fragile health. the guest-of-honour was the Duke of York (later George VI) whom she had been yearning to meet for years. Tallulah had wanted to attend with Douglas Fairbanks Jr as her escort but he refused to go without an official invitation, and at the last moment she turned up on the arm of the outrageously effeminate Stephen Tennant and told a footman, 'Tell Georgie that Tallulah would like to see him, darling.' She was allowed in and when the Duke of York was told that she had recently been very ill, he insisted on meeting her privately so that she would not have to descend the staircase with everyone else.

At another party Tallulah was reunited with her friends the

Cartens. Audrey had written a revue-sketch with her sister Waverley and, for several weeks until the end of April, Tallulah toured the music halls with this and her impersonations – including a new one of the great British actress, Sybil Thorndyke. The sketch was also performed in a benefits concert for the Indian Earthquake Fund. Each of these projects was met with great critical acclaim and, given time, Tallulah might easily have begun a second British career, had it not been for the transatlantic call she received from John Hay Whitney in the May, informing her that he had recently been handed the script for *Dark Victory*, which he was convinced she alone could transform into the hit of the year.

Tallulah returned to New York at once, getting very drunk night after night on board ship, yet still winning a small fortune at the poker table. By the time she moved back into the Gotham Hotel, this near-alcoholism had begun causing her problems. The only person with whom she did not get depressed was Estelle Winwood. During one all-night binge with her friend, Tallulah learned that Sybil Thorndike was staying at the same hotel and announced that she must meet her and execute her famous impersonation in front of Thorndike's face, the way she had with Ethel Barrymore at the Algonquin. Thorndike was currently appearing on Broadway in *The Distaff Side* and getting good reviews. Estelle, however, flatly refused to bring the actress to Tallulah's suite – it was three in the morning – so Tallulah herself asked the switchboard to put her through.

'She walked into the room looking like Joan of Arc,' Tallulah later said, explaining that Sybil's hair had been brushed out over her shoulders and that she was wearing an old-fashioned plaid dressing-gown. Therefore, in reverence to Sybil's sainted image, Tallulah immediately got down on one knee, kissed the hem of her robe and, in a language Shakespeare would have envied, began pouring out every superlative she could muster, ending her speech with, 'Now then, you fucking old miracle, what do you want to drink?' Unblinking, as if she was used to witnessing this sort of behaviour every day, the actress asked politely if she might have a schooner of sherry.

Dark Victory, described by Robert Benchley as 'a Camille

without all the coughing', was not a success, though little of the blame for this was personally apportioned to Tallulah. Many critics simply could not come to terms with the theme – a young flapper who only changed her scandalous life-style when she discovers that she has cancer of the brain. The production was forced to close prematurely because Tallulah suffered a relapse. Toxins present in her body during her recent illness had not been completely eradicated and the effects of trying to squeeze a mere pimple on her upper lip caused a rare infection that laid her low for several months. At one stage she became so ill that her doctors feared it would be necessary to remove her lip to prevent the infection from reaching her brain. The indisposition also cost her what many consider would have been her definitive film role. John Hay Whitney had negotiated for her to appear in the screen version of *Dark Victory*. Like *Jezebel* it was given to Bette Davis, and won her her second Oscar.

Tallulah was next approached by Clemence Randolph and John Colton to appear in their production of *Rain*, the Somerset Maugham play that had caused her so much anguish in London. Sam Harris, the man who had pushed Basil Dean into accepting her for the part then, announced that only Tallulah would be right for the part this time. She herself was not so sure – she would never forget how shabbily she believed that Maugham had treated her and saw no reason why she should be putting money into his pocket. She was also worried that if she did play Sadie Thompson, her American audiences would accuse her of emulating Jeanne Eagels, and she did not want to be confused with the actress who had committed suicide at the peak of her career. Sam Harris finally twisted her arm by offering her the Music Box Theater which boasted the fact that it had never had a single flop. 'Leave it to me,' Tallulah said. 'There's always a first time for everything.'

To a certain extent, she was right. She engaged Sam Forrest to direct, had the sets from Jeanne Eagels's 1923 production copied and even used some of the originals. She then decided to shatter the Eagels image by having her Sadie hail from the heart of Texas ... and when Forrest complained about this, she added a touch of Alabama for good measure.

As usual, *Rain* toured before opening in New York and again proved a massive hit with the Gallery Girls, especially in Philadelphia where Tallulah took dozens of curtain calls every evening. But whereas her fans did not care what she did or how well she did it so long as she was there, the critics, while mostly praising her performances, did suggest that it could be bettered – and, of course, all the newspaper clippings were being forwarded to Somerset Maugham in England. The New York première went down well – Marlene Dietrich hugged her afterwards and told her how she had clapped until her hands were sore. The critics, however, were severe. Even her friend Brooks Atkinson was confused by what he had seen. 'She plunged into the part with the raffish gusto of a gaudy strumpet,' he wrote, adding that one did *not* ad-lib and turn cartwheels in the middle of a play which was supposed to be serious. Therefore, after 47 performances, *Rain* closed.

Tallulah tried briefly to recreate the glories of her London years by accepting the Shubert Brothers' *Something Gay*, opposite Walter Pidgeon. 'Neither singly nor together could Tommy Mitchell and I get blood out of *that* turnip,' Tallulah said of the production which most people agreed was the most dire she had ever appeared in. 'It was a goddamn entombment!'

John Mason Brown of the *New York Evening Post* went to see it, proffering sound advice to Tallulah's would-be producers:

Tallulah Bankhead is so obviously an actress of uncommon possibilities that it is a pity that plays worthy of her talents do not seem to come her way. She has an unquestionable aptitude for the names of comedy as well as sure command of many rapidly shifting moods. What she needs above everything is to find a new play that is in any way equal to what she has to bring to it, and then to discover a director who can control her in her many moments of wasteful restlessness.

To a certain extent, Tallulah put things to rights during the autumn of 1936 when she appeared in *Reflected Glory*, written and directed by George Kelly. The plot, a relatively simple story of an American actress who is compelled to decide between an enterprising career and marriage in the days when the two were rarely compatible, resulted in the play becoming a huge hit when it opened in San Francisco, and Tallulah eventually took it on to the road – an adventure she would not forget. Away from the West Coast, it was savaged by the critics. 'Had it been written by a lesser playwright, they would have loved it,' Tallulah said bitterly, adding that Kelly had been a victim of his own high standards. Along with Thornton Wilder and Tennessee Williams, George Kelly was one of three playwrights who would always be set upon a pedestal.

In June 1936, the speaker of the House of Representatives, J W Byrnes of Tennessee, died suddenly. A few hours later, Will Bankhead was sworn in as his successor, making him the third most powerful man in the United States. One of his first moves as speaker was to introduce the Farm Tenancy Bill which enabled thousands of farmers to acquire affordable loans from the government to help them cope with the almost constant drought. Will actually signed the Relief Deficiency Bill papers in his box at the Washington theatre when waiting for the curtain to rise on the première of *Reflected Glory*. After the show, he presented Tallulah with the 'lucky' rabbit's foot which never left her presence for a moment, and which accompanied her to the grave.

The most important and intensely publicized production in movie history also began in June 1936, setting in motion a confusing and extremely costly machinery of hopes, ambitions, jealousies and emotions in which Tallulah became inextricably embroiled. The battle began when Margaret Mitchell's novel, *Gone With the Wind*, was published and became an instant best-seller, reaching the million-copy mark in less than five months. David O Selznick had read the book in galley-proofs, all 1,037 pages of it, and in July 1936 he bought the screen rights for $50,000. *Gone With the Wind* was to have been the very zenith of his achievements since leaving MGM the previous year to found his own company, but unable to finance the film himself he now approached his father-in-law, Louis B Mayer, for an injection of funds. On top of this, feeling guilty about the 'pittance' he had paid Margaret Mitchell, he offered her another $50,000.

The general consensus of opinion in Hollywood was that no one should play the hero of the film, Rhett Butler, but Clark Gable, and the actor came as part of Mayer's $1¼ million investment, an estimated one-third of the total projected production cost for the film.

Initially, the part of the tempestuous heroine, Scarlett O'Hara, was given to Norma Shearer but one month later she changed her mind, beginning the longest movie 'search' of all time, a process which would drag on for another two years and involve the interviewing and auditioning of 1,400 actresses, ranging from unknown hoofers to Hollywood legends, such as Bette Davis, Katharine Hepburn, Margaret Sullavan, Carole Lombard, Claudette Colbert and Joan Crawford. 'They saw everybody but Maria Ouspenskaya,' Tallulah cracked, referring to the Russian-born star who was unfortunately renowned as 'the ugliest, oldest dwarf in Tinsel Town'. Olivia de Havilland was briefly considered, but then given second lead along with Tallulah's friend Leslie Howard. Tallulah's name was put forward by John Hay Whitney, in his capacity as Selznick's ex-chairman, and Selznick himself was persuaded to see her in *Reflected Glory*. He was so impressed by her beauty and natural vivacity – reputations did not count on this one, or he would not have had so large an audition list – that he immediately wired Louis B Mayer: WE'VE GOT SCARLETT! Louis B Mayer *did* believe in reputations, however, or at least in avoiding them, especially in Tallulah's case and, though he did not reject his son-in-law's proposal straight out, he did advise him to 'look a little further'.

Selznick was utterly convinced that he would never find a better Scarlett … and so was Tallulah.

I felt I had qualifications beyond any of the hundreds of candidates … the looks, the Southern background and breeding, the proper accent. For months I was leading the field in the Scarlett Derby whilst Selznick and his aides kept looking in treetops, under bridges, in the Social Register, and on lists of parolees from reformatories. But my bones told me I wouldn't get the part …

The *Gone With the Wind* production team received literally thousands of letters supporting Tallulah and this the unlikeliest of campaigns was spear-headed by her Aunt Marie Owen, culminating in a petition signed by thousands of women on behalf of the Alabama Public Service Commission and the National League of American Pen Women. Marie made such a nuisance of herself while collecting signatures that Bibb Graves, the governor of Alabama, sent a telegram to David O Selznick which read: WHY DON'T YOU GIVE TALLULAH BANK-HEAD THE PART AND HAVE DONE WITH IT? Finally, on 21 December 1936, Tallulah travelled to Hollywood to make the two Technicolor screen tests – wearing one of Garbo's costumes from *Camille* – which were then 'filed' with the other hopefuls in an amazing archive of 13,000 feet of Technicolor and ten times that amount in black-and-white which, some years later, was edited to form a fascinating documentary about the *Search For Scarlett*.

The director of *Gone With the Wind*, initially, was George Cukor, though he was suddenly and seemingly inexplicably replaced by Victor Fleming and, after Fleming's nervous breakdown three months into shooting, by Sam Wood, the man responsible for the Marx Brothers' *A Night at the Opera*. Tallulah, of course, knew *exactly* why Cukor had been relieved of his command – long before the director confessed all. Cukor, a close friend of Bill 'Lavender Lips' Haines – who since failing to make it into the talkies had ploughed his vast fortune into a hugely successful interior-design business – had hired Haines to work on his new house and it now emerged that some years before, the pair had been lovers. Clark Gable, long before becoming famous, had also had a relationship with Haines and, terrified that Cukor might have been made aware of this, Gable, in one of his 'faggot-hating' phases covered his own tracks by reporting Cukor's 'indiscretions' to David O Selznick. As Kenneth Anger so aptly observes in *Hollywood Babylon II*, 'One of the great directional shifts in film history took place in 1939 because of a few blow-jobs given by Bill Haines, who was certainly not lip-lazy back in 1925.'

Tallulah went to see Selznick, pleading with him to reinstate

Cukor, but the mogul would not listen. She also knew that if she threatened to 'out' Gable to the press, which she wanted to do, she would lose all hope of ever getting the part of Scarlett O'Hara. Henceforth, she loathed Gable with a contempt second to none and blamed him for setting up Bill Haines to be arrested in a downtown Los Angeles YMCA by vice-squad officials who had seen him pick up a young marine. She also suspected him of being behind the unnecessarily nasty and unprovoked attack in the press by the acid-tongued Louella Parsons. Reminding her readers that one of Tallulah's friends was part-financing the film, while another was directing it, Louella concluded,

> ... So, I'm afraid she will get the part. If she does, I personally will go home and weep because she is NOT Scarlett O'Hara in any language, and if David Selznick gives her the part, he will have to answer to every man, woman and child in America.

Tallulah was heartbroken when, in 1938, the most coveted role in movie history went to the British starlet Vivien Leigh. 'I'll go to my grave *convinced* that I could have drawn the cheers of Beauregard and Robert E Lee, had I been permitted to wrestle with Rhett Butler,' she said, blinking back the tears. Meanwhile, as the dust was settling in Hollywood and hundreds of other young actresses were similarly licking their wounds, she decided to take a short holiday in England.

8

As Pure As the
Driven Slush

Will Bankhead had already questioned his daughter's reluctance to marry. Having now had two heart-attacks and been told that he was living on borrowed time, Will's greatest wish was to see Tallulah settled down with children of her own. Obviously, he had been kept in the dark about her hysterectomy. Neither did he have much confidence in Eugenia providing him with a grandchild. She had married Morton Hoyt for the third time in 1929 and divorced him soon afterwards to marry the footballer, Wilfred Lawson Butt. This union, like her first to Hoyt, was annulled and her 1930 marriage to the aviator Howard B Lee lasted just ten days. Her sixth marriage, to a Mr Smith who soon afterwards turned out to be a Mr White, also ended in the divorce court and what would have been a seventh to a Mr McConnell was called off two hours before the ceremony. Since this time, during a trip to Italy, Eugenia fell seriously ill with pneumonia – so ill that a coffin was ordered and carried into her lodgings. Tallulah sent her $100 on her recovery and a copy of Gone With the Wind, 'to help her pass the time between husbands'. Therefore for Will, every hope for the continuance of his direct line depended upon Tallulah.

There had, of course, never been any shortage of suitors – not that Will would have considered any of Tallulah's men either respectable or suitable breeding stock. Jock Whitney and Tony de Bosdari had been approved of – until one had turned out to be married and the other a charlatan. This left only Napier Alington, recently widowed and reverting to his promiscuous ways – still clinging to his small clutch of Bright Young Things even though their brightness had long since begun to dim. Within one day of arriving in London in May 1937, Tallulah was pursuing him with her former reckless abandon. One soirée, chronicled by Cecil Beaton in his *Diaries* and quaintly referred to as 'Tallulah's Walpurgis Night', took place at the home of the wealthy interior designer, Sybil Colefax.

> Tallulah danced frenziedly, throwing herself about in a mad apache-dance with Napier Alington. After he left she wept and bemoaned the fact that he had never married her. Then she threw off all her clothes, performing what she called 'Chinese classical dances'. In the midst of these outrageous situations, one had to reluctantly drag oneself away …

Napier told Tallulah quite categorically that he could never marry outside the aristocracy – and she immediately returned to New York. A few weeks later she rented a house on Long Island Sound, ten miles from Westport in Connecticut. Edie Smith moved in with her, and a new caddy named Stephan Cole – of whom almost nothing is known save that he was a friend of Edie's, in his late twenties and a native of Colorado. Another regular visitor was the beautiful Chinese-American actress Anna-May Wong, who had played Marlene Dietrich's companion in *Shanghai Express* – it was she who suggested that the party should spend the evening at the Westport County Playhouse, where there was a touring production of Dorothy L Sayers's *Busman's Honeymoon*. Tallulah enjoyed the play but not nearly as much as she enjoyed watching and listening to the leading man, John Emery, in the part of the sleuth, Lord Peter Wimsey. The 'drama' during this particular performance became very real, however, when a prop curtain caught fire and Emery put it out with his bare hands. Tallulah waited until the quietest part of the denouement scene, then bawled at the top of her voice, 'My Gawd, the man's *divine!*'

With Tallulah it had always been love at first sight but with Emery, even this adage seems to have been inadequate. She had first met him, finding him 'so-so', in Los Angeles some time before when he had been playing the Earl of Warwick in Shaw's *Saint Joan* and she had admired his portrayal of Captain O'Shea in the film *Parnell*, opposite the hated Clark Gable. Now, she invited him back to her house for the weekend. 'I found him intelligent, amusing and exceptionally good-looking,' she would recall. 'He had good manners and was a good listener. This last marked him a rare bird in the set with which *I* travelled.'

One week later, Emery moved out of his New York apartment and Tallulah took him shopping – his one and only suit which she had dismissed as 'a fuck-awful green monstrosity', had been ritually incinerated and was now replaced by a complete, no-expenses-spared designer wardrobe. Two days later, she announced to the press that they were engaged – this had given her time to consult her 'Sibyl', Estelle Winwood, whose words of wisdom were, 'Everyone should be married at least once, dear!' Edie Smith, on the other hand, quipped, 'I always did want to make that trip down to Reno.' Tallulah later said she must have looked into her crystal ball.

Tallulah was impressed by her fiancé's 'pedigree'. Born in 1904 of English and American parents – his grandfather, Sam Emery, is alleged to have been the first interpreter of Charles Dickens on the British stage, and his mother had played Little Eva in *Uncle Tom's Cabin* – he had attended the LaSalle Military Academy, Long Island, and at the age of 11 had been 'taken in' by John Barrymore and his wife, Katherine Harris. Even so, towards adulthood Emery had practically rejected his guardian because of his uncontrolled drinking. Tallulah had also listened to rumours, and half-believed them, that Emery was Barrymore's illegitimate son – there was a remarkable facial likeness but, in fact, most of Emery's 'Barrymoreisms', such as his eyebrows, moustache and the pseudo-eccentric voice, were little more than Hollywood 'additions'. Critics have also observed that Emery's great failing as an actor – he was at his best in costume dramas, playing characters such as Laertes opposite Gielgud's Hamlet of 1936 – was that he always tried too hard not just to emulate Barrymore but to be him.

Neither the bride nor the groom had much say in the marriage ceremony, which was arranged by Will Bankhead and Tallulah's Aunt Marie Owen. The events leading up to the wedding caused inordinate excitement mixed with disgust over some of the couple's antics. Because of his rapidly failing health, Will wanted as little fuss as possible. He arranged for a quiet Episcopal ceremony to take place at the family home in Jasper and excluded all but his closest relatives.

Towards the end of August, Tallulah, Emery, Stephan Cole (with whom she was still sleeping, occasionally) and Edie flew to Alabama. The flight, and the loan of the handsomest pilot she could find, was an early wedding present from her aviatrix friend Louisa Carpenter. The party's original plan had been to fly to Birmingham, then hire a car which Stephan Cole should have driven to Jasper. During the flight, however, the weather was so abominable that the pilot was compelled to bring his plane down on a number of emergency landings. Suffering from a combination of terror and an over-excess of bourbon, Tallulah's behaviour was worse than the weather could possibly have been and she attempted to make love to her husband-to-be in front of the others. When the pilot complained, she ripped off her red silk Molyneux pyjamas, showed him that she was not wearing panties and, hoisting herself up bodily from the roof-straps, wrapped her legs around his neck and screamed at him to perform cunnilingus. The pilot slapped her, narrowly missed crashing the plane, and the others managed to get Tallulah's pyjamas back on. On the tarmac at Birmingham, as Emery was still trying to come to terms with what must have been the most excruciating 48 hours of his life, Tallulah caught him unawares by pulling his trousers down and shouting to the crowd of onlookers, 'How's about that for a two-hander, darlings?'

The couple stopped off briefly at Birmingham's Tutweiller Hotel where Tallulah changed into a dull-brown Hattie Carnegie suit and poke bonnet and fastened a simple string of pearls around her neck, a wedding present from Emery. Trailed by several cars filled with reporters and photographers hoping to witness more fun and frolics, Stephan Cole drove them to Jasper, where they were met by Tallulah's family. She was of course her daddy's little girl again and only erred the once when, as a matter of course, Will asked Emery if he had the health certificate which was required for marriage in Alabama. Tallulah piped, in her sweetest voice, 'John doesn't need a certificate to prove that he's fit. He was examined on the way down.'

The ceremony itself was almost called off when the Episcopal bishop of Alabama refused to officiate because of the groom's former marriage to the British actress Phyllis Calvert. Will Bankhead called in the local judge and Tallulah had a tantrum, refusing to wait until the next day – after her antics on the plane, she was probably afraid that Emery might back out – and the couple were married in the middle of the night on Tuesday 31 August 1937. Tallulah was given away by her father, Stephan Cole was best man, and Edie Smith, who should have been bridesmaid, had her role changed to that of lady-in-waiting. And just to show her new husband that he had officially become her latest piece of property, Tallulah slipped her grandmother's ring on to his finger. The inscription read: TALLULAH BROCKMAN BANKHEAD.

The only remotely solemn part of the ceremony was when Will read Psalm 103. Thinking of her mother, Tallulah broke down. The newly weds then moved to the floodlit garden and their eagerly awaited press conference. Inside the last 24 hours the number of reporters and photographers in Jasper had doubled, owing to an unprecedented article in *Variety*, in which David O Selznick announced that Tallulah would 'definitely' be playing Scarlett O'Hara, and that Emery had also been promised a part in a new film to be directed by Orson Welles. When asked why she had married, Tallulah responded, 'I married for love, darling. Isn't that so very ridiculous?' And

The young Tallulah. Top right: Tallulah aged 4, with sister, Eugenia (left).
(Alabama Department of Archives and History)

Bottom left: Tallulah aged 9. Bottom right: showing her beautiful hair
(Alabama Department of Archives and History)

Tallulah in *The Creaking Chair*, 1922, London. 'On the surface all confidence, all swagger and strut, inside I churned with doubt,' she wrote. *(Alabama Department of Archives and History)*

With unknown co-star in *When Men Betray*, 1918. She would later denounce the film 'as trifling as it was silent.' *(Alabama Department of Archives and History)*

With Paul Lukas in *Thunder Below*, 1932. Tallulah described the film as 'a double-jointed dud, maudlin and messy!' (*Alabama Department of Archives and History*)

Publicity shot for *Gone With the Wind*. 'I knew I could play the pants off Scarlett.' (*Alabama Department of Archives and History*)

Above left: Poster for *The Little Foxes*.
Above right: Tallulah's favourite photograph.
Below left: Publicity shot for *A Royal Scandal*, 1945.
Below right: Tallulah at Windows.
(Alabama Department of Archives and History)

Top: Tallulah with William Eythe and Anne Baxter in *A Royal Scandal*.
Bottom: Tallulah in *The Eagle Has Two Heads*, 1947, with Helmut Dantine.
(Alabama Department of Archives and History)

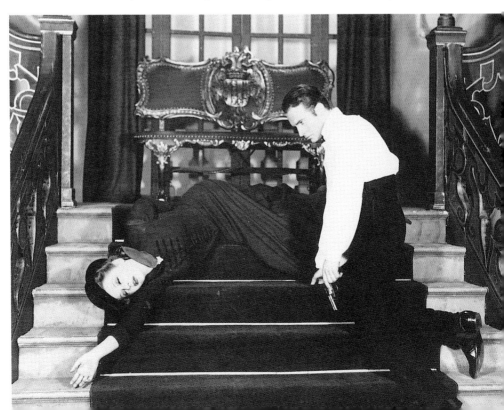

As Amanda Prynne – 'a Riveria doxy of a bigamous turn' – in Noël Coward's
Private Lives. (Al Reuter)

Tallulah with Ethel Mermen and Meredith Willson in 1950 rehearsing for the first *The Big Show*. 'Thank you, Ethel, darling. And may I say you don't look a day over 60!' *(Al Reuter)*

Tallulah with William Roerick, Tom Raynor and Nora Howard in *Dear Charles*, 1954. 'A blithe spirit with a rusty voice is at work here! Hail to her!' one critic wrote. *(Alabama Department of Archives and History)*

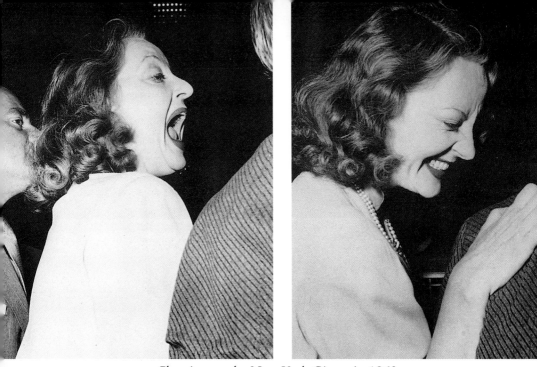

Cheering on the New York Giants in 1963.

'I've stooped not to conquer, and I'm going to do *Batman*!' Tallulah as the villainous Black Widow. *(Alabama Department of Archives and History)*

when asked how she envisaged married life would be, she added, 'Long and hard, darling! Very long, and very hard!' She put in a transatlantic call to London from her bedroom and told H L McNally of the *Daily Mail*, 'We're going to act together, darling, so we'll be partners in business and love. Isn't that absolutely divine?' Michael Mok of the *New York Post* reported:

> You could have knocked the boys over with a pair of passes! They were amazed that the theater's saltiest sophisticate had fallen for a tall, wide-shouldered, narrow-waisted lover like any other mooning matinée-girl ...

The marriage, of course, was doomed from the start. Few people who knew Tallulah expected it to be otherwise. All her life she had been unstoppable and untameable. No man had ever been able to control her and it needed a much stronger husband than John Emery to even try. There was also the added problem of her being the bigger star. Tallulah herself admitted that Emery had not married a mere mortal but an institution and he agreed with her, adding, 'My wife's the only woman I've ever known who can talk, read, listen to the radio, and do her hair at the same time.'

Their honeymoon was spent on Langdon Island but it was by no means a private affair. Reporters who turned up on the spur of the moment for a brief interview ended up staying the week, listening to their hostess describing what had happened during the previous night in the minutest anatomical details – one reporter said that he knew every inch of Emery's body better than Emery himself. Each visitor to the house was expected to file into the bedroom and offer their opinion, while he was sleeping, of her husband's 'equipment'. When he was awake, she humiliated him by telling everyone, 'Well, darling, the weapon may be of admirable proportions, but the shot is indescribably weak.'

During the honeymoon, Tallulah decided that she would like to play Shakespeare. She quipped, 'I've worked with plenty of snakes in my time, I reckon Cleopatra would suit me down to the ground.' With no stage experience whatsoever, Norma

Shearer had recently played Juliet in her husband Irving Thalberg's film version of *Romeo and Juliet* and she had been radiant.
Though she and Leslie Howard had been too old to play the
doomed lovers, the production had worked because the other
players had been 'aged up'. John Barrymore's Mercutio was
definitive and Shearer's limited dramatic abilities had been
enhanced by taking acting lessons from Constance Collier.
Tallulah was actually approached by Collier and offered similar
tutelage. This would have done her some good but she declined
because, she said, she wanted to emulate no one but herself. As a
trial of sorts, she played Viola in the Radio Playhouse production
of *Twelfth Night*, with Orson Welles, Estelle Winwood and Sir
Cedric Hardwicke. This was followed by an appearance with
Henry Fonda on *The Kate Smith Show* where the pair enacted
the whole of *Camille* in 12 minutes. Tallulah then announced
her co-stars for *Antony and Cleopatra*. Conway Tearle came
straight from the Thalberg film to play Mark Antony and she
insisted that no one would portray Caesar but her husband. She
then engaged Rowland Stebbins to produce – he boasted that his
sets 'would put Cecil B de Mille to shame'. Finally, Stephan Cole
completed the team as stage manager and the music was specially
composed by Virgil Thompson.

Broadway had seen nothing to compare with this particular
foray into Shakespeare, even if Tallulah did look more
incredibly beautiful than ever in Egyptian garb. The play
tottered, agonizingly so, for just five performances at the
Mansfield Theatre and the critics who filled the first three rows
of the stalls on the first night solely to lampoon Tallulah's latest
folly certainly were not disappointed. While John Emery
impersonated John Barrymore but at least adhered to the script,
his wife smoked reefers in the wings and stomped on to the
stage stoned, breaking every rule in the book – camping it up to
the nines with *double entendres* and witty, mostly crude, asides.
The reviews have survived better than the memories of what
happened on the actual stage, occasioning Tallulah to remark,
'Shakespeare ought to have left Antony and Cleopatra in
Plutarch, where he found them.' Richard Watts wrote, 'Miss
Bankhead seemed more like a Serpent of the Swanee than the

Nile!' John Mason Brown went one step further, though far from angering Tallulah, his waspish, hilarious comments were incorporated into the sketch she devised for her stage shows of the mid-fifties.

> Tallulah Bankhead barged down the Nile last night – and sank. And with her sank one of the loveliest, most subtle, and most stirring of all Shakespeare's major tragedies. Miss Bankhead can be a brilliant performer, but as the Serpent of the Nile she proves to be no more dangerous than a garter snake.

Antony and Cleopatra did not help the Bankhead–Emery union, though both parties were responsible for it starting to fall apart at the seams before the rice had settled. When asked by a timid woman reporter, halfway through an all-too-polite interview about the joys and sanctity of marriage, to offer her definition of love, Tallulah turned to her hapless victim and quizzed, 'Love? Surely you must mean fucking, darling. That's all love is, isn't it?' Her wit was razor-sharp, too, when she attended the première of Terence Rattigan's *French Without Tears* and announced that she would 'take care' of his very strait-laced mother during the show. Tallulah was all sweetness and light until the end of the evening when she handed the old lady back to the playwright and told him, 'There we are, darling – and I didn't say "fuck" once!' Emery is alleged to have almost slapped her, not that he would have dared do such a thing, in public or otherwise.

All this time, Tallulah was still fretting over whether she would get to play Scarlett O'Hara, now that David O Selznick had issued yet another statement, 'I am looking for a starlet who will not be readily identified with other roles, yet one who has a strength of personality which will not detract from her acting a dramatic role convincingly.' Similarly, Emery was concerned about his own status – his last film had flopped, he did not have a cent to his name and he was living in Tallulah's house, entirely dependent on her generosity, which thus far had been unfaltering. The crunch came on the night *Antony and Cleopatra* closed. When asked by a friend what he was going to do now, instead of replying that he was going home, Emery retorted, 'I'm going back to Tallulah's place.'

Neither did Emery foresee any financial independence from his wife. Because he had entered into a gentlemen's agreement over a film with Orson Welles, he was compelled to turn down several film offers which might have made him a bigger star. But, in the end, Welles's film was cancelled when his sponsors backed out of their contract.

Tallulah also hit a rocky patch. She was offered the starring role in Cole Porter's comedy-musical, *By Candlelight*, which was scheduled to begin an out-of-town tour in February 1938. At the last moment, she was dropped. Retitled *You Never Know*, the show opened in New York with Libby Holman, Clifton Webb and Lupe Velez. There was some recompense in the April when Tallulah and Emery opened at the New York Playhouse in a revival of Somerset Maugham's *The Circle* – 17 years before, Estelle Winwood had triumphed in the original. There were 72 performances, though Tallulah maintained that her only decent review came from Wolcott Gibbs who wrote, 'Tallulah – an intelligent man's guide to worry and adultery – is far too attractive and brilliant to be convincing in *this* play.' The next time she met Gibbs, Tallulah told him, 'If it weren't for getting arrested for bigamy, I'd marry you for those words, darling.' She and Emery also appeared in a radio comedy, Howard Parris's *L Is For Love*.

In August 1938, Tallulah and Emery opened in *I Am Different*, which she put down as 'a Hungarian mishap, decoded for American consumption by Zoë Akins'. But if her husband was hoping for at least a little favouritism, none was forthcoming. Tallulah placed him as far down the cast list as she dared without ostracizing him completely, then engaged her old flame, Glenn Anders, as her leading man. She flirted with Anders backstage, telling him that her sex life with Emery had been virtually non-existent for the last six months and that her only thrills nowadays came from stagehands and whoever happened to be around when she felt the urge. Anders took pity on her and their affair was resurrected.

The critics pounced on *I Am Different* for the mistakes the actors made on stage. In one scene where a shot was fired, Anders was supposed to dash on, stoop over the body and say, 'I heard a shot. It's only a flesh wound.' On the night of the première, he was so busy necking with Tallulah in the wings that he missed his cue and blurted out, 'I heard a flesh wound ... it's only a shot!' Tallulah's ribald laughter drowned everything, including the hoots of derision from the audience, but coming so soon after the high jinks of *Antony and Cleopatra*, this was too much.

The play closed after a brief tour and a dire shortage of funds forced Tallulah to give up her costly house on Long Island Sound and the couple, along with Stephan Cole and Edie Smith, took a suite at New York's Gotham Hotel. Here they languished for just one week, until Tallulah decided that she would be better off in her own apartment. This did not work either – she had become 'addicted' to room service and would not allow Edie to do 'menial' tasks, such as pouring coffee or going out for cigarettes. Therefore the group uprooted for the third time in as many weeks and moved back to the Elysée Hotel, a considerably more costly option. Tallulah coped with the expenditure by selling the sapphire given to her by Jock Whitney, along with some of the trinkets left over from her affair with Anthony de Bosdari.

At the Elysée, there were complaints from the other guests, not just about din made by Tallulah's lovemaking with two men at a time – a permutation of her husband and either Stephan Cole or Glenn Anders – but about her explicit running commentary before, during and after the sexual act. Once, when the management rang her room and asked her politely if she would not mind keeping the noise down, she stormed off into the night and returned to her suite with a couple of street kids, treating them to an evening of entertainment that they would remember for the rest of their lives. The newspapers clamoured to report her scandalous adventures, real or invented, which were frowned upon by her peers and large numbers of fans who thought that, as a married woman, she should have been exercising more control to outgrow her flapper ways. Tallulah did not care when she was told the reason why some people had begun leaving the theatre before the end of her performance, or why sometimes there were fewer autograph hunters outside the stage door than usual. 'For every fan that I lose who's stuffy, two more come along who approve of my life-style,' she declared. 'What I do with my bits and pieces is *my* business. The play's called *I Am Different*, and that's what I am.' The play shuffled along the tour circuit, deteriorating nightly, grinding to a welcome halt in Washington at the end of November 1938.

One particularly nasty incident took place within the Monkey Bar at the Elysée. Rather than attempting to curb Tallulah's drinking, Emery encouraged it, and though she could hold her liquor remarkably well, once she had had a few she was at her sharpest and most insulting. The under-the-thumb husband knew better, however, than to try to calm her down when her storm was in danger of breaking, because this usually had the opposite effect. Therefore when another drunk decided to sling a few sluttish remarks her way, Emery thought he was playing the part of the gallant by knocking the man down. His reward was an almost fatal left hook from Tallulah who, not content with giving him a shiny black eye, had to be dragged out of the bar screaming profanities because Emery had not killed the man ...

Tallulah was rescued from drinking herself into total oblivion by the playwright Lillian Hellman, who approached her with the script for *The Little Foxes*. She instinctively knew that the central role of Regina Giddens – 'a rapacious, soulless, sadistic bitch who would've cut her own mother's throat' – was the best she had ever been offered. All the same, she only accepted the part on condition that besides her generous salary she should receive ten per cent of the box office.

Tallulah also recognized the play's political implications – though she was keeping a watchful eye on the European situation she vowed not to let her anti-Communist views cloud her judgement of what many would soon come to regard as a decidedly Communist work-of-art. The characters in the play, spear-headed by the obnoxious, bitchy Regina, were capitalists who in order to achieve their ruthless, selfish aims deceive, cheat, lie and murder. Many people thought at the time that Tallulah could not really have understood the play's theme, otherwise she would not have acted in it. Others argued that she did understand but, as a highly talented actress who had spent half a lifetime playing all the wrong roles, she was finding it necessary to stay politically impartial now that she had been given something worthwhile. Time would prove both theories wrong.

Tallulah became almost a mother figure to Eugenia Rawls, the teenage actress engaged to understudy Florence Williams, who played Regina's daughter in the play. When Eugenia took over from the actress soon after the première, Tallulah told her, 'You look enough like me to be my own child. I only wish you were.' The photographs taken for the programme do reveal an uncanny resemblance. A few years later, when Eugenia married, Tallulah paid for the reception, and she stayed close to the couple, providing for them in her will. The cast of *The Little Foxes* also included a very young, then unknown Dan Duryea.

Lillian Hellman assigned Herman Shumlin to produce her play – a tough, shrewd but initially caring individual, and one of the few people capable of criticizing Tallulah to her face and getting away with it. Only once did she throw a fit with him. This was when he warned her of the dangers of injecting too much of her own personality into Regina Giddens, a ruse which would not work with *The Little Foxes*. Shumlin instructed her to 'exorcize every last breath of Tallulah Bankhead' from her part and to do this by rehearsing more fervently than ever before. In the past it had always been a question of learning her lines, which she had always been inordinately good at, before letting the flapper take over. Tallulah was putty in Shumlin's hands and she also became very close to the play's Irish publicity agent, Richard Maney – so much so that henceforth he would handle practically everything she did. What made their relationship work better than it normally would have done was the lack of physical attraction and an inveterate love of the bottle. And because she found Maney's company so intellectually stimulating, Tallulah found herself spending more of her spare time with him than with her husband, whom most of her entourage were by now beginning to look upon as an extraneous, costly ornament.

Maney was sufficiently mischievous to occasionally join in with Tallulah's fun and games. On one occasion, when approached by a Bible-thumping reporter for a story about 'the most shameful woman in America', Maney arranged for the young woman to meet Tallulah at the Hotel Elysée ostensibly to prove that she did at least have some heart. The interview went well, with the star making a concerted effort to act 'as virginal as Queen Bess herself'. Smiling radiantly, she did not utter so much as one profanity in over an hour and she even escorted the young woman to the lift, where Maney had organized a delegation of guests and onlookers. Tallulah did not disappoint the curious. 'Thank you for the most *marvellous* interview, darling,' she boomed. 'You're quite the politest lesbian I've ever met!'

The Little Foxes previewed in Baltimore on 30 January 1939 – the eve of Tallulah's thirty-sixth birthday – in a blaze of publicity which for once was not directed at the Gallery Girls. More than at any other time in her career she was terrified of failure – a situation that was made worse three days before the dress rehearsal by an attack of bronchitis. There was also a fierce backstage row with one of her co-stars, Patricia Collinge (who played Birdie Hubbard) when she too developed a cold and asked the management to turn up the heating. The humidity was too much for Tallulah, who refused to do the première until a compromise had been reached – in her favour, of course.

On the night, most of the Bankhead clan were sitting in the front row – Will was next to Lillian Hellman, who had arrived with Dorothy Parker and Dashiell Hammett, the creator of *The Thin Man*. Aunt Marie, who had never seen Tallulah on the stage until *Antony and Cleopatra*, recorded in her journal, 'I've seen Tallulah in *The Little Foxes*, I've seen the World's Fair, and I've seen a fight at the Stork Club. Now I can go home and tell them I've seen everything.'

Tallulah said that her first performance of *The Little Foxes* was disappointing. Probably because she was feeling so wretched, she tried to cheer herself up by over-dramatizing and playing to the gallery. Thankfully there were no cartwheels, though the critic Gilbert Kanour did sum her up when he wrote, 'Tallulah is confusing Regina with Lady Macbeth.' Tempers also flared at the backstage party when, disgusted by the way Dashiell Hammett was treating the waiters 'like skivvies', Tallulah invited a young black usher to sit at her table, and accused Hammett to his face of being racist – an outburst that earned her a round of applause from the entire room.

For some reason, Lillian Hellman did not attend the New York première of her own play, at the 41st Street National Theater on 15 February 1939 – 16 years to the day since the London première of *The Dancers*. Tallulah was still feeling groggy – though more through the Old Grandad and cigarettes 'antidote' than the waning bronchitis – and she later admitted that the first few performances of *The Little Foxes* had been a triumph of mind over matter. Then, quite suddenly, her acting took on a new brilliance. She had told a press conference the day before, 'Regina's a hard-bitten bitch. The audience is going to goddamn hate her, I'll make sure of that!' This she did, in a performance which was so utterly superb that most of the critics went into shock and did not know how to react. The ones who had gone out of their way in the past to revile her could not believe what they were seeing. John Cambridge of the *Daily Worker* wrote, beneath the photograph of Lillian Hellman which had recently been snapped in Russia, thus hinting that the playwright was indeed one of Tallulah's despised Communists:

> Miss Bankhead indulged in a few characteristic mannerisms, which seemed a hangover from the long course of whisky-sodden trollops on which she dissipated her talents for so many years in England. Afterwards, however, she settled down to a fascinating portrait of an evil spirit.

Tallulah's favourite photograph from *The Little Foxes* appeared on the cover of *Life* magazine during the first week of March 1939. In it she was wearing the stunning red gown, designed by Aline Bernstein, in which she made her entrance.

She did not, however, care for the article within. The review she most admired appeared in the *New York Journal*, penned by John Anderson:

> As the vulpine lady, Miss Bankhead is a fox out of hell, sultry, cunning and vicious. Her performance suggests a combination of trade-marked Southern charm, and the spirit of the Borgias to breed a carbolic acid sugarfoot. She is Cindy Lou and Madame Dracula, honeysuckle and deadly nightshade, all done in a magnetic performance that is brilliantly sustained and fascinating.

The Little Foxes was nominated for that year's all-important Drama Critics Circle Award and everyone who saw it would have wagered any amount of money on it running away with the prize. However, at the ceremony on 23 April, the award was not presented because the required '8 out of 11 votes agreement' was not met, the Hellman play receiving only six votes. Tallulah did, however, win the Variety Citation for Best Actress, which for her was a massive official accolade from her theatrical peers.

The second performance of the play was a benefits show for the Abraham Lincoln Brigade, of which Lillian Hellman was one of the sponsors. The money raised was donated to 92 badly wounded survivors from the Spanish Revolution who had recently returned home. Tallulah was willing to waive her fee for the evening the same as everyone else, though for the time being she was more interested in a fight closer to home. When the WPA Federal Theater Project came under threat due to lack of funds, she announced that this would be one fight to the death that she would relish and quickly acquired the title, 'The Joan of Arc of the WPA'.

The problem with the Federal Theater Project came to a head two weeks after the première of *The Little Foxes* when Congressman Martin Dies, in an official statement on why there would be no funds, concluded, 'The Federal Theater Project employs members of the Communist Party and Communist sympathizers.' Tallulah was less interested in some of her fellow actors' political leanings than in the fact that the

Dies Committee threatened to put hundreds of *non*-Communists out of work – and bearing in mind that her play had been branded Communist by Dies's adherents, this meant herself. She therefore headed a campaign to oust the bill from the Senate – travelling to Washington to plead her case, accompanied by a small delegation of actor friends and armed with a huge petition. Her speech to the Senate, in which she extolled all her acting skills and a few strategically placed tears, earned her a standing ovation. Even so, four months later the Federal Theater Project was terminated by an act of Congress.

Tallulah was flung straight back into the mêlée when the House Appropriations Committee blamed its demise solely on Actors' Equity because of its Communist links – a statement that brought forth a torrent of abuse from Tallulah, who had recently failed to gain a minor seat on its governing council. The representative of the HAC who had read out this damning statement, a man named Lambertson, did not accuse Tallulah of having such sympathies – far from it. In the *New York Times* of 9 July he attacked her opponent on the council, the actor Sam Jaffe, as 'an avowed Communist, in preference to that outstanding actress, Tallulah Bankhead'. He then named several of Jaffe's fellow 'reds' from Actors' Equity, including one of Tallulah's friends, Edith Van Cleve, then working as George Abbott's production assistant. Tallulah knew that Edith Van Cleve was not a Communist and she dictated a statement to this effect to a New York journalist, who published it via the Associated Press. She then turned away from politics for a while in order to tackle the most recent plight of her estranged husband.

John Emery had opened in Boston in *Five Kings*, Orson Welles's adaptation of Shakespeare's historical plays. Besides editing the piece, Welles had played Falstaff as remarkably as only he could and Emery had been given the part of Henry Hotspur on the pretext that some theatrical boffins still regarded him as 'the poor man's Barrymore', as opposed to Mr Bankhead. Although the play received excellent reviews, it hit a serious snag when the Theater Guild declined to finance it beyond Philadelphia during a proposed nationwide tour.

Tallulah stepped into the breach. She admitted that she herself was 'up to the chin' in debt, so she telephoned her playwright friend Marc Connelly, who lived in the suite below Tallulah's at the Elysée. He could not afford to bail Welles out, so he brought in Sherman Billingsley, the proprietor of the Stork Club. Still the money was not forthcoming, and soon afterwards *Five Kings* closed. Tallulah then made a further attempt to 'promote' Emery's career when told that he had been contracted by the playwright–producer Randolph Carter to play Heathcliff in his adaptation of *Wuthering Heights*. She rang Carter and asked if she might sit in on the dress rehearsal in order to put Emery through his paces. Permission was granted, and she tore his part to shreds, turning him into such a bag of nerves that he spent the entire night in his dressing-room with the light off, terrified of leaving in case she was waiting outside.

Tallulah's interest in the human condition intensified towards the end of 1939 when Russia made an unprovoked attack on Finland, in what became known as the Winter War, resulting in over 500,000 refugees looking to the rest of the world for aid. The situation was explained to Tallulah at a luncheon hosted at the Algonquin by ex-President Hoover. With Tallulah were Helen Hayes, Gertrude Lawrence, Katharine Hepburn and Lee Shubert, who all promised to raise money for the cause by giving benefit shows of whatever projects they were involved with at the time. Tallulah agreed on behalf of Lillian Hellman and Herman Shumlin that there would be a fund-raising performance of *The Little Foxes*. In fact, neither the playwright nor the producer was interested in the proposal and Hellman even issued a statement to the effect that, in her belief, 'to aid this small, insignificant country would increase America's chances of being sucked into the war, resulting in great loss of life.' Shumlin went one step further by suggesting that the money thus far raised for the Finns should be given to the unemployed actors from the defunct Federal Theater Project.

As such, *The Little Foxes* was one of only three plays on Broadway not to support the cause, though Tallulah did give a substantial donation. She also did a comedy skit in Gertrude Lawrence's new play, *Skylark*, which was touring with both John Emery and Glenn Anders – her co-star was a French midget named André Ratoucheff, who dressed up as Maurice Chevalier and warbled 'Louise'.

By the time the play closed on Broadway, after 408 performances, so that Tallulah could take it on the road, both she and Emery were more than convinced that their marriage was over. He felt that she had publicly humiliated him far too often, though *she* admitted that she had only enjoyed upsetting him because he had always risen to the occasion by letting her see that she was getting to him. What Tallulah truly despised were Emery's racist comments, one of which had been directed at her when he had told a reporter, 'My wife? She's a cross between an Englishwoman and a piccaninny.' For the time being, however, Tallulah was more interested in the inflamed political situation than in her personal problems.

The first week of February 1940 was designated Finland Week, when scores of pretty Scandinavian girls were seen walking up and down Broadway, muffled against the cold and collecting money from passers-by. During this week, *The Little Foxes* began its nationwide tour in Washington, where there were fierce arguments between Tallulah, Hellman and Shumlin which did not go entirely unobserved by the media. Tallulah gave a powerful speech which concluded, 'Mr Shumlin did not hesitate when donating his time, mental activity and money to the Loyalist causes in China and Spain. So why not Finland? Human suffering has nothing to do with creed, race, or goddamn politics.' She did not, however, say what was in her heart – that she had come to despise Shumlin and Hellman because of their Communist beliefs – after all, they had given her the biggest break thus far in her career and she had no desire to join the rapidly lengthening queue of unemployed actors.

The spring tour of *The Little Foxes* was immensely successful. After Washington, it broke box-office records in Philadelphia, Detroit, Boston and Chicago – where she threw a massive party to which she invited her 'three queens': Noël

Coward, Katharine Hepburn and Clifton Webb. In Toronto the partygoers were more on her side of the fence – crowded into her dressing-room were 40 kilted young bloods from the Princess Pat Regiment. She cracked, 'I always did *love* men in frocks!' She was also instrumental in securing American citizenship for a young Viennese production assistant named Otto Preminger, who had arrived in New York in 1935, assuming that it was safe to leave his family in Europe. Preminger had recently attempted to get them relocated to the United States, only to be told that no more Austrians were being allowed into the country. Tallulah appealed to her father on the young man's behalf and as a result of this a new bill was passed by Congress. It was an entirely unselfish act that would bring her much respect from the European film community and personal rewards from Preminger a few years later.

In April 1940, Tallulah and John Emery separated on amicable terms. The news was kept from her now seriously ill father. So far as Will was concerned, Emery was enjoying a successful run in New York with *Skylark* and had to 'suffer' separation from his wife for the sake of his career. He had in fact fallen for the actress-dancer Tamara Geva, whom he had met in suitably bizarre circumstances at the Elysée Hotel. During one of the Emery's more turbulent exchanges of expletives, the noise had risen above that of the party raging in Tamara's suite, immediately above theirs. In order to shut them up – and knowing that to report the matter to the management would only have made matters worse – Tamara invited the couple to the party. Tallulah immediately went into Tamara's bedroom with one of the male guests, leaving her distressed husband to be consoled by the hostess. A few days later, after another fight with Tallulah, a half-drunk, sulking Emery was rescued by Tamara from the Monkey Bar and invited up to her suite for a tête-à-tête, ostensibly beginning a life-long love affair.

Tamara Geva, one of the finest ballerinas of her age, had defected from Soviet Russia during the mid-twenties with her husband, George Balanchine, to join Diaghilev's *Ballet Russe*. In America, she had begun acting and had scored a big success in a play called *Idiot's Delight*, a title which Tallulah often bestowed on her once she had relieved her of her husband. She had first met Tamara some years before at a backstage party given by Clifton Webb and Libby Holman and, if her impression of the ice-cool Russian beauty had not amounted to much then, it slumped beyond redemption when she learned that Tamara had been first choice for *Tarnished Lady*. Tamara's affair with John Emery was the last straw. In Tallulah's book, *she* could dump any man in any fashion but it was woe betide anyone who turned the tables on her. Still thinking of her father, however, Tallulah exercised restraint for the time being and, when interviewed by a suspicious *New York Telegram*, confirmed, 'Of course I'm in love, and what's more I'm *married* to the man I love.'

She was in fact involved with a young English actor named Colin Keith-Johnston. Tall, blond and athletic, he had met her during the auditions for Sir Arthur Wing Pinero's *The Second Mrs Tanqueray*, a turn-of-the century melodrama which Tallulah had decided to 'dust down' for a six-week tour, while the company of *The Little Foxes* was taking a break before the second season of its tour. Tallulah had also patched up her long-standing quarrel with her sister Eugenia (over the Wilson affair in 1928), who had arranged to accompany her on the road.

Before leaving New York, Tallulah called Will, now involved in the Democratic campaign in Maryland. She and millions of others were convinced that provided he lived that long he would make it to the White House, though Franklin D Roosevelt had been elected for a third term. For a while, prior to the last presidential elections, he had been a clear favourite, losing out in the end to Roosevelt's favourite, Henry A Wallace, by 627 votes to 329. Chatting to Tallulah over the telephone, Will did his utmost to convince her that he had never felt better.

The Second Mrs Tanqueray achieved some notoriety on the tour circuit but only because of the backstage squabbles. Since being snubbed by Lillian Hellman and Herman Shumlin, Tallulah trusted no one. Thus the entire touring company – not just the actors, understudies and bit-parts but the carpenters, stagehands, technicians and even the cleaners – were engaged in New York before the tour began, completely disregarding the unofficial theatrical ruling that stated that everyone but the lead parts in a production should be hired in the town being played. When some of the provincial managers complained about this, Tallulah threatened to take her company back to New York without further ado. As usual, she had her own way. Then, because she was so inordinately fond of Stephen Cole and Eugenia Rawls, they too were roped into the production. The play was well received when premièred at the Maplewood Playhouse, New Jersey on 1 July 1940, and when it opened in Berkshire, a critic who modestly signed himself only as KRF wrote, 'Tallulah Bankhead brings a certain majesty that even a playwright could not hope to create with mere words.'

This review was read by an aspiring young playwright named Tennessee Williams, at that time the lover of the novelist Donald Windham, who suggested that Tallulah would be the ideal diva to play Myra Torrance in his new, unread play, *Battle of Angels*. As the pair were constantly hard-up in those days, Williams waited until *The Second Mrs Tanqueray* opened in Dennis, Cape Cod, and even then he had to cycle the 40 miles from his home to see her. Tallulah treated the young man kindly, but refused to have anything to do with his play, which she dismissed as dirty, adding, 'Sex and religion don't mix at all, darling. But you do write well when you're not being filthy!' Stephan Cole then shoved Williams's bicycle into the boot of his car and drove him home. A few months later *Battle of Angels* opened with Miriam Hopkins ... and closed within the week.

During the tour, Tallulah forked out $3,000 for a marmoset, having learned that in France it was all the rage for big stars to have exotic pets. Mistinguett had recently visited New York with a pet ape which had masturbated on cue and Joséphine Baker had been photographed strolling down the Champs-Elysées with a pet pig and a leopard on a diamond-studded leash valued at millions of francs. Tallulah's association with her little monkey ended abruptly when it bit her as she was trying to get it to sleep by crooning 'Bye Bye, Blackbird', so she decided to go one better. During a visit to the circus she purchased a weakling lion cub which she baptized Winston Churchill. This caused even greater problems for everyone when, in true Baker fashion, she insisted on taking Winston everywhere, including the theatre where she fastened him in her dressing-room until it was time for him to share her curtain calls. When asked what she would do once Winston started to become too much of a handful, she replied, 'I'll ask for a bigger dressing-room.'

On 11 September, Will Bankhead was adding the finishing touches to his speech, urging voters to elect Roosevelt for a third term, when he collapsed in his hotel room. He was rushed to a hospital in Baltimore, where doctors diagnosed a ruptured abdominal artery. Tallulah and Eugenia heard the news on the radio and chartered a plane at once. At the hospital they begged the doctors to spare Will from knowing the truth. He was told that he had a bad touch of sciatica and that he would be transferred to a better equipped hospital in Washington within the next few days.

Echoing the insecurities of her childhood, when Eugenia had been Will's favourite, Tallulah asked him, 'Do you still love me, Daddy?' Will reassured her that he had *always* loved her and because there was nothing more she could do and because having her at his bedside would only have made Will realize how serious his condition really was, Tallulah returned to New York, where the company of *The Little Foxes* were preparing to embark on the second leg of their tour.

The tour went ahead as planned. The première, in Princeton, New Jersey, was a sell-out, though Tallulah spoke her lines mechanically. Colin Keith-Johnston and Stephan Cole watched her from the wings, terrified that she would crack under the strain. When she pronounced the line, 'Grief makes some people laugh and some people cry,' then told her on-stage daughter, 'You've had a bad shock today, I know that. And you loved Papa, but you must have expected this to come some day. You know how sick he was,' the audience caught its breath. Two hours before curtain up, a news report had announced Will Bankhead as being close to death.

During the interval, the sisters formulated their plan. Eugenia would take the next train to Washington, Tallulah would follow on after the show. By the time she reached the hospital, however, her father was dead. Eugenia had just managed to get there to say goodbye.

The Speaker's state funeral was held on 16 September 1940, within the House Chamber. The coffin was followed by the three women in Will's life – Florence, Eugenia and Tallulah, all heavily veiled. Behind were his brothers, Henry and John. President Roosevelt sat in the front pew with the family, who had been advised to 'cry like hell' before and after the ceremony but to preserve the dignity of the occasion by not making spectacles of themselves in front of such a distinguished gathering. The next day, the cortège boarded the train for Jasper. The town had declared a day of mourning – more than 65,000 people listened to an emotional Roosevelt delivering the address before Will was interred in the Oak Hill cemetery next to his father, Captain John, whose tomb bore the inscription: HERE LIES THE MAN WHO INAUGURATED FEDERAL AID FOR HIGHWAYS. It is not known if Tallulah actually disapproved of Will's request not to be buried in Huntsville with her mother, though this was not the reason why she declined to accompany his body to its final resting place. 'I need my public,' she said, shortly before going on stage in Princeton. 'Only they can comfort me now. This is what Daddy would have wanted.'

Four months after Will's death, Tallulah visited Oak Hill in strict secrecy to see the gravestone she had commissioned. Her whole heart had gone into the inscription: GOODNIGHT SWEET PRINCE, AND FLIGHTS OF ANGELS SING THEE TO THY REST.

There would be few more trips to Jasper now that Tallulah had lost her anchor and, in any case, she had virtually no reason to see the place, having nothing in common with her relatives there. One cousin, Marion Louise Bankhead Grant, who was very young when Will died, recalled, 'The family saw her a couple of times a year, maybe. She was like a buzzsaw. She was on *all* the time. She *never* got off the stage with anybody.

Really, she wore you out, she never stopped.' Grant's sister, Barbara Bankhead Oliver, spoke of her embarrassment at seeing Tallulah sunbathing in the nude, even in front of her father, yet admitted that she had been unable to prevent herself from eavesdropping when they had been reciting Shakespeare. 'I thought *that* was divine,' she said, in typical Bankhead fashion.

Lane Lambert, writing for the *Huntsville Times* many years after Tallulah's death, offered another personal theory:

The whole town was curious, and Tallulah went ahead doing anything she'd do anywhere else. She was always a distant, if vivid figure, and the fact that she violated virtually every value and sensibility her family held – swearing like a sailor as she did – seems to count for more than the rarity of her visits. People in Jasper, the closest thing she ever had to a hometown, had much the same dual feeling towards her. She offended them, but they *always* tried to get a glimpse of her.

9

Some of My Best Friends
Are Raving Sensations

Only days after Will Bankhead's funeral, Tallulah received devastating news from England that her beloved Napier Alington had been killed in action. Previously renowned as a completely selfish, reckless individual, Naps had put all this behind him by enlisting as a fighter pilot at the beginning of the war, and his plane had been shot down during the Battle of Britain. The fact that he had died so bravely, and in defence of a country she loved as much as her own, touched Tallulah deeply and she is said to have grieved for him for the rest of her life – his death is mentioned in her memoirs but was never brought up in the hundreds of interviews she gave between then and 1968. She did cope with her loss, however, in a patriotic way by becoming one of the principal member-advocates for the CDAAA (Committee to Defend America by Aiding the Allies), attending and organizing rallies across the country, delivering speeches which were as stringent as they were sincere.

When the British began evacuating Dunkirk, Tallulah made a pact – more with herself than with any particular movement – that she would not touch alcohol again until the Allies had given Hitler his comeuppance ... after downing three French 75s, an extremely potent blend of champagne, gin, brandy and lemon juice which, she said, would have flattened a longshore-man.

Though she would more or less stick to her word, Tallulah did 'cheat' occasionally by pretending she had a cold or a stomach upset. Alternatively, she got high by adding a dash of spirits-of-ammonia to her coffee and she never relinquished her essential reefers and cocaine, otherwise she would never have ploughed through her hectic life and work schedule.

The tour of *The Little Foxes* zigzagged back and forth across the American continent. In Cleveland, Ohio, she bumped into Bette Davis, who was harbouring the most terrible secret – that fact that *she* would be playing Regina Giddens in the film version of the Hellman play and not Tallulah. During a brief but well-documented stopover in Jasper, when told that a local journalist, Gretchen Gray, wanted to interview her, Tallulah told the houseman to keep the young woman talking while she made herself respectable then, shedding her clothes she rushed into the garden, where Gray desperately attempted to hide her blushes at the spectacle of the town's most famous star, stark naked and spread-eagled across a sunlounger.

In St Louis, Tallulah 'clashed' with John Emery, who was touring in *Skylark* with Gertrude Lawrence. That she had never forgiven her estranged husband for what she called his 'no-comings rather than his shortcomings' was evident when she told a lady reporter, 'We spent the night in the sack, darlings, just to prove that there were *still* no hard feelings.' In Milwaukee, she was cheered by 200 Gallery Girls and had to break off in the middle of her most dramatic scene to bellow, 'Quiet, darlings. Your Tallulah's about to do something dreadfully evil!' In Tacoma, she was so exhausted – and inebriated – after her performance that she fell asleep in her chair without closing her bedroom window – waking the next morning to find several inches of snow on the carpet. Calling for room service, she requested a glass of neat gin and a shovel. Snow caused further problems in St Paul, where the roads were blocked and only 13 people turned up at the theatre. The show went ahead and Tallulah told the press, 'You must admit, it isn't often that your leading lady invited the whole *audience* back to her room for a tipple.'

In Hollywood there was a surprise party, hosted by a 'mystery' friend who turned out to be Marlene Dietrich, to which had been invited Joan Crawford, Gary Cooper and Cary Grant. John Barrymore gatecrashed and began telling a few Tallulah stories that even she had never heard before but halfway through the evening he became so drunk and uncontrollable that he had to be thrown out into the street. And in San Francisco, Eugenia Rawls announced her engagement to a young law student named Donald Seawell after a whirlwind romance which had caught everyone unawares, most of all Tallulah, who usually liked to know exactly what was going on among her 'team'.

On 5 April 1941, in Philadelphia, the second national tour of *The Little Foxes* ended, after playing in 104 cities covering a total of 30,000 miles. On this very day, Eugenia Rawls and Donald Seawell were married. The company then returned to New York and, during the radio show *Time To Shine* with Eddie Cantor on 23 April, Tallulah was handed a telegram from her friend Anita Loos which read: YOU ARE AN ABSOLUTE RAVING SENSATION. ALL BUT DIED OF CONVULSIONS.

A few days after this broadcast, John Emery, who since Will Bankhead's death had been living openly with Tamara Geva, asked Tallulah for a divorce so that he could remarry. Tallulah agreed wholeheartedly and, as she now had nothing better to do, she left for Reno, where by law she was required to reside for six weeks to make the divorce absolute. She had ended her relationship with Colin Keith-Johnston and was accompanied by the ever-faithful Stephan Cole. On her way to Reno, however, she spent a few days in Hollywood being entertained by George Cukor, who was considering her for a film. This was not forthcoming but she did take Cukor's advice – the fact that to concede to John Emery's demands, thus letting all America know how she had been ditched for another woman (which was true), might prove as disastrous to her career as it would to her dented pride. Therefore the divorce was agreed upon with one condition: Emery was to give his word as a gentleman (which he was) that he would not marry until at least one year after the divorce had been made absolute. Emery decided not to argue – he had cited 'acute mental cruelty' – and on 13 June 1941 the papers were signed. Tallulah told a press conference, 'John could never get used to the fact that he'd married an institution, and the poor fellow had one hell of a lot to put up with. Now, I am free to do exactly as I please, not that being married ever made any difference to that.' John Emery kept his side of the bargain, marrying Tamara Geva exactly one year later. When asked by *Time* magazine what life had been like as Mr Bankhead, he replied, 'Like the rise, decline and fall of the Roman Empire.'

Celebrating her freedom in a very tongue-in-cheek fashion, Tallulah, Stephan Cole and Fred Keating resurrected her old London hit, *Her Cardboard Lover*, and put it into summer stock. It opened in Westport, Connecticut and, after a five-city run, brought them back to Cedarhurst, New York. By this time she had fallen out with one of her co-stars, Harry Ellerbe, and after ringing around several agent friends in the middle of the night spoke to Lyman Brown, who gave his word that a replacement would be found within the hour. Brown was good to his word and brought her Ricardo Montalban, then in his teens. Montalban could not possibly have envisaged his reception. No sooner had he stepped inside Tallulah's hotel suite than he was pounced upon by Winston, now half-grown and with a penchant for devouring shoes while they were still on their owner's feet. After several minutes of sheer terror, the lion was dragged off by Stephan Cole and shut in the bedroom while Montalban desperately tried to pull himself together and learn his lines. Incredibly, by curtain up the next evening he was word perfect, which caught Tallulah on the hop because, as a safety precaution, she had not yet given Harry Ellerbe his marching orders. The torrent of filth, which was exchanged between the actor and Tallulah in the wings only minutes before the performance, was overheard by most of the audience and was followed by an equally vociferous costume exchange between the two actors as the orchestra attacked the overture. Winston, thinking the play was over and that the audience were cheering for a curtain call, bounded on to the stage and had everyone running for cover. When the manager ordered Tallulah to keep her animal under control, or get off the stage, she bellowed, 'Fuck off!' down the megaphone. A few weeks later, the temperamental Winston was packed off to the Bronx Zoo for safekeeping.

On the more serious side, Tallulah continued her campaigning for the CDAAA. She delivered a blistering attack against Lucky Lindbergh and his supporters, who believed that Europe should have been capable of sorting out Hitler and Mussolini without American aid. From the Rainbow Shell at Oriental Beach, on 14 July 1941 – one of several speeches relayed to New York, accompanied by the scattering of thousands of tiny American flags by Navy aircraft – she announced, 'This mortal enemy is threatening us, in spite of what the appeasers are trying to hoodwink you into believing, so let me say this – one flier and his cohorts, in a position to demand respectful attention, are in their blind ignorance more detrimental and destructive to the American way of life than all the subversive elements put together.' Such was the response to this speech that she was invited to the White House to take tea with Mrs Roosevelt. While posing for photographs she said to America's First Lady, 'I knew you'd get around to inviting me to tea one day, Eleanor. You've always been known for you kindness towards delinquent girls like me.'

Around this time saw the beginnings of Tallulah's obsession for baseball, said to have been inspired by Ethel Barrymore, whose knowledge of the game was legendary. She had also been told of the French star Mistinguett's visit to Chicago in the late thirties when, after witnessing a particularly gruelling match, she asked to meet the players in their locker room – where she autographed their jockstraps, while they were wearing them ... Tallulah may not have been quite so adventurous, though she did once say that she had only begun supporting the New York Giants because the team had been 'better-stacked' than any other. Her favourite player was the Number Four, Mel Ott, and she often reckoned that she part-owned him – 'And you don't have to guess which part, darling!' – because a fan had bought her, as a gift, two shares in the team, valued at $20 a year. The Brooklyn Dodgers and the Yankees, on the other hand, she loathed. And of course the sport, with its endless puns on 'bats, balls and jocks' would provide her with enough blue material for anecdotes to last her for the rest of her life.

For Tallulah, in her stance against Hitler and oppression, 17 August 1941 was an important date. After entertaining troops at Camp Langdon, New Haven, she was made an honorary Second Lieutenant in the 22nd Coast Artillery and received a citation from Major William F Nee. She went straight into her next play, *Clash By Night* by Clifford Odets, which after a provincial run opened in New York at the Belasco Theater on 27 December. The producer was Billy Rose, a bellicose little man with whom she did not get on at all. 'He approached the play as if he was staging a rodeo,' Tallulah reflected in an interview, to which came Rose's acid response, 'I once directed an angry herd of buffalo, and I once shot an actor out of a cannon 50 feet into the air into the arms of an adagio dancer, but neither of these events was as tough as saying good morning to Tallulah Bankhead.' Neither did Tallulah approve of her co-star, Lee J Cobb, though she liked the juvenile lead, Robert Ryan. Stephan Cole also appeared in a cameo role, for moral support.

What infuriated Tallulah most of all about Billy Rose was his tendency to address the cast through a megaphone. She complained about this, only to be told that *he* was in charge of the production, not her. To hammer home this point he erected an electric sign above the Belasco Theater which read, BILLY ROSE PRESENT TALLULAH BANKHEAD. For many years, her contracts had stipulated that her name appear first in any publicity material but what angered her now was that, not only had Rose failed to include the name of the play and the other actors, the man could not *spell*. Tallulah stormed into the manager's office and handed him a sheet of paper upon which she had printed, 'If your foul employer insists on BILLY ROSE PRESENT, then you need only add, TALLULAH BANKHEAD ABSENT. Who does he think they're coming to the theatre to see? Fannie Brice's ex-husband or yours truly?' Rose was compelled to remove the first three offending words ... but he promptly erected them on the rooftop of an adjacent building in red neon letters three times the size of the originals. At the press conference on the eve of the première, Tallulah levelled at Rose, 'You're nothing but a goddamn little bully!' The producer shrugged his shoulder and replied, 'How can one bully Niagara Falls?'

The critics who had sung her praises for *The Little Foxes* could not accept her in what most of them considered to be a trashy play. Wolcott Gibbs, who claimed that he admired Tallulah more than any other actress because only she had the guts to appear in some of the lousiest plays ever produced, wrote, 'As the wife of a Polish labourer on Staten island she persistently reminded me of a Southern belle, out slumming.' Gibbs was very enthusiastic about Lee J Cobb, fresh from his success in Spencer Tracy's film, *The Men of Boys' Town*, the title of which alone made Tallulah howl with laughter. Cobb was a fine, stylish actor and, according to many of his contemporaries, knew it. One evening, Tallulah informed Billy Rose, in front of the entire cast, that signing the contract for *Clash By Night* had been the biggest mistake of her life. Rose responded that working with *her* had been the biggest mistake of *his* life. Cobb added that *everybody*'s mistake had been in failing to realize that *he* was stealing the show. Tallulah never spoke to him again, save to mutter obscenities under her breath whenever they were waiting to go on stage. Once, when a group of reporters had been allowed into the auditorium to watch a rehearsal, she screamed at Billy Rose, 'Will you for Christ's sake tell him to stop scratching his ass?'

The tour of *Clash By Night* was a dreadful ordeal for Tallulah, whose tendency to sometimes strut around her dressing-room stark naked brought her down with a chill. She fainted after the first night in Philadelphia, developed a raging fever, and was taken to the local hospital where doctors placed her in an oxygen tent. Selfishly – believing that her illness would affect the advance bookings for the play – Billy Rose booked her in under another name and refused to issue a statement even when she was diagnosed as suffering from pneumonia. She spent three days on the danger list, and two more weeks in the oxygen tent. Upon her discharge she refused to convalesce: she wanted to get the play out of the way. *Clash By Night* opened on Broadway, was disliked by the critics, and struggled through 49 performances.

Tallulah spent most of the year 1942 not on the stage but out raising money for the war effort. She began on 18 January by appearing on *Listen America!* urging people to buy war bonds and created so much interest that she was almost given her own radio series, which one newspaper estimated would have made her the highest-paid radio star in the world. Tallulah actually refused the project because she did not wish to appear mercenary and deflect from public approval at such a critical period in world events. Thus, instead of beginning the series at the beginning of February, she appeared in her first radio mystery play, Dorothy L Sayers's *Suspicion*. On 5 April she appeared with Danny Kaye at New York's La Martinique: for a $10,000 purchase of defense bonds she 'played' Ethel Barrymore's celebrated role of the schoolteacher in *The Corn is Green* and rounded off the evening with a personal donation of $5,000. In the September, Barrymore herself was special guest, along with Charles Laughton, in CBS radio's *Tallulah's Stage-Door Canteen*.

Tallulah's next major play, Thornton Wilder's 'new-age' *The Skin of Our Teeth*, was even more problematic than the one with Billy Rose but she tolerated it because it proved her biggest hit since *The Little Foxes*. Wilder had particularly wanted to have Tallulah in his play, but 37 different producers had rejected it, claiming that they could not understand a single word of the script. The scenario, to begin with, covered a 5,000-year period with Tallulah assigned to four parts: Sabina, an Ice Age family maid who gets to milk a mammoth; Lilith, the alleged first wife of Adam; Lily Fairweather, the hostess from a bingo hall and Miss Somerset, a hyper-active actress. Michael Myerberg, to whom Tallulah took an immediate dislike, finally agreed to take it on, at around the time Wilder, a major with Army Intelligence, announced that he would be working abroad for the duration of the war and that 'supervision' of his work had been left in the hands of his sister, Isabel.

It is not known why Tallulah hated Myerberg so much at this early stage in the production. Until recently he had managed the affairs of another temperamental individual, Leopold Stokowski, who like his new leading lady had always been accustomed to getting his own way, and that Myerberg for once was going to put his foot down and ensure that he was boss and not likely to put up with any of her over-the-top demands. If this was the case, Myerberg lost the first round when Tallulah refused to even speak to him until he had agreed to a suitable salary: $1,500 a week, plus the usual ten per cent of the box office. For a little while, this seemed to appease her ... until she discovered that her co-star, Fredric March, was getting the same amount. Henceforth, the production would rank as a war zone.

In the past, Tallulah had usually had some say in the choice of director for her work and for a long time she had nurtured a soft spot for Orson Welles. She blamed herself, perhaps, for his failure to acquire financial backing for *Five Kings* with John Emery, so she asked Myerberg in one of their rare polite exchanges if Welles might be given a chance, bearing in mind that Wilder's material, like his own, was largely experimental. Myerberg scoffed at the idea and plumped for Elia Kazan, an enterprising young man had who had done great things with the Group Theater. He then delighted in dropping the bombshell – Tallulah had been his and Wilder's third choice for the female lead after Ruth Gordon and Helen Hayes and that she had only been given it now because Hayes, Stephan Cole and Estelle Winwood had begged on her behalf ...

During the rehearsals for *The Skin of Our Teeth*, Tallulah was wilder and more uncontrollable than ever. She would not stay in the same room as Elia Kazan, let alone speak to him. She complained loudly about every line of largely incomprehensible but eloquent-sounding dialogue; she swore at Michael Myerberg; she snarled at Fredric March and did not hide the fact that she positively loathed his wife, Florence Eldridge, whom she had never wanted in the production in the first place. 'She's so goddamn stuck-up and patronizing,' she told the press, who in retrospect were far more interested in the backstage shenanigans than the play itself. Tallulah became such a problem that the management and cast consulted Isabel Wilder, presenting her with a 'Tallulah-Or-Us' petition which even the stagehands had been press-ganged into signing. This had no effect whatsoever, so Florence Eldridge decided to have a girl-to-girl chat, only to be cursed black and blue.

The situation was resolved by Elia Kazan who, unable to get a word in edgeways when he went to see Tallulah at the Elysée Hotel, ordered two stagehands to tie her to a chair and gag her while he read her the riot act. This overt display of machismo, of course, earned him her profound admiration. The pair became friends and allies against Michael Myerberg and a few weeks later Tallulah bought 'Gadge', as Kazan was known to his closest friends, a gold bill-clip decorated with a St Christopher medal which he was still using 12 years later while directing *East of Eden* with James Dean.

On the plus side, *The Skin of Our Teeth* enabled Tallulah to get to know an awesomely handsome but nervous 21-year-old actor from Omaha, Nebraska, who was then desperately trying to hide his homosexuality from family and friends. His name was Montgomery Clift and perhaps, had he taken Tallulah's advice and 'come out' as opposed to being flushed out, his later life might not have become such a tragic catalogue of drink, drugs and self-destruction, which saw him expiring at the age of 45.

Monty was never officially one of Tallulah's caddies, though he did sleep with both her and Stephan Cole several times and supported her against Michael Myerberg who, feeling that his authority had been thwarted once too often, decided to make life as difficult as possible. Whenever there was a cast meeting, he always made sure not to invite the pair along, becoming so nasty to Tallulah that Monty, always the gentlest of men, threatened to 'blow his lights out' unless he treated her with respect. In next to no time, realizing that she was probably not that bad, the cast were on Tallulah's side – all save Florence Eldridge, who would never consider Tallulah anything but 'a tramp'.

The Skin of Our Teeth opened at New York's Plymouth Theater on 18 November, having attracted fabulous reviews for its try-outs, particularly in Washington, where Tallulah was still known as 'the Speaker's daughter'. Wolcott Gibbs described her performance as the most versatile of her career, though she maintained that the notices were good only because the critics had no idea what they were seeing and hearing and did not wish to appear ignorant by admitting this. Her opening scene saw her waving a feather duster, as though exorcizing evil spirits, and announcing to the bemused audience, 'I hate this play and every single word in it! I don't understand a single word of it and the troubles the human race has gone through. The author hasn't made up his mind if we're living back in the caves, or if we're in New Jersey today.' Michael Myerberg seemed to resent the reviews and the applause and, even with record ticket sales, was intent on getting his revenge on Tallulah and Montgomery Clift. He went out of his way to sabotage the first of two benefits performances of the play by giving instructions to the costumes department to deliberately 'misplace' the musicians' uniforms so that they could not march through the auditorium, as planned, before curtain up. Thus the show began late and the audience, who had been kept out in the cold all this time, were understandably unappreciative. Myerberg told the press, smugly, 'Things like that don't happen by themselves. They have to be planned.'

Myerberg's latest indiscretion prompted an appearance by Thornton Wilder himself and the threat of instant dismissal. Tallulah swore that not only would she never speak to this obnoxious man again, she would never allow his name to pass her lips. Throughout the run of the play she and Monty Clift constantly referred to him as 'The Static Slime'.

As for her ongoing feud with Florence Eldridge, this came to a head during the second benefits performance. The actress, experiencing some difficulty remembering her lines, blamed this on Tallulah's on-stage fidgeting – once, when she had not even been on stage. The crunch came during one of the quieter scenes – Eldridge muttered sarcastically under her breath, 'Tallulah, be a good girl,' to which came the basso-profundo response, bouncing off every wall of the vast auditorium, 'I'm sick and tired of being a good girl, and what's more, I'm sick and tired of your fucking moaning!'

Many of the audience, still trying to grasp what the play was about, thought this a part of the script and applauded – even Alexander Woollcott did not know that the expletive was not supposed to be there. He wrote in his column, 'This is a dauntless and heart-rending comedy that stands head and shoulders above anything ever written for the American stage.' Tallulah read this and chortled, 'Alex must have been tanked up on gin when *he* saw the play.'

During the run of *The Skin of Our Teeth*, Tallulah decided that she had had enough of hotels and that, at almost 40, it was time she settled down in a property of her own. She had also received news from her grandfather's house in Jasper that the furniture from Farm Street, stored there these last ten years, was badly in need of renovation. Therefore, accompanied by Edie Smith, Montgomery Clift and Stephan Cole, she set about looking for a house which, she said, would suit her personality. On 1 April 1943 she moved into a five-bedroomed, five-chimney mock-Tudor house in Bedford Village, New York. The house, set in 16 acres of unkempt gardens, was at $25,000 a virtual give-away – the price had been dropped from $65,000 because there was no regular water supply and the entire house required redecorating. Tallulah named her retreat Windows, not because it had 70 of them, but because, she said, 'For the last 20 years, the whole goddamn world and his wife have been looking in on me.'

She dispensed with a small fortune having the place refurbished and was especially proud of her eighteenth-century dining room with its Italian-holly table, crystal and bronze sconces, Waterford glassware and Oriental drapes. She also amassed a sizeable art collection – besides her August Johns there were works by Max Bond, Renoir, Chagall and Toulouse-Lautrec, though she maintained that her favourite Master, aside from the John portrait of herself, was a painting by Beatrice Lillie ...

As she had done with her Farm Street home, Tallulah at once

set about hiring compatible staff. First of all, there had to be a new caddy – Stephan Cole, that most loyal of *chevalier*-servants, stunned her by suddenly joining up with the American Field Service, leaving her out on a limb. A favourite contender for this most hallowed position was Monty Clift, but he was terrified of being in Tallulah's company for too long in case she 'let the cat out of the bag'. Elia Kazan was virulently homophobic and, had he known that Monty was having an affair with another male cast member of *The Skin of Our Teeth* now that Stephan Cole was gone, he almost certainly would have dropped him from the company.

Tallulah's caddies were by tradition if not gay, then certainly bisexual – *never* straight – and they were there exclusively to wait on their mistress hand and foot. Tallulah had never been remotely interested in looking after herself. Because she had a penchant for stripping naked almost anywhere and in front of absolutely anyone, she left clothes scattered everywhere. She became violently frustrated when opening cigarette tins, purchasing make-up, cutting her toe nails, sitting alone on the toilet, bathing, answering the telephone, switching on the radio and television. Even her toothpaste had to be squeezed on to the brush ready for her to use. She could not sleep unless someone was close at hand until she dropped off; often, this would take upwards of four hours, and someone would always have to be there when she woke up. She had an obsession for watching soap-operas and if she ever missed a favourite programme the caddy of the moment had to write everything down and tell her what had happened. She was obsessed with playing cards, insisting that all those closest to her should learn how to play bridge. Tallulah only really did one thing for herself and that was to light her own cigarettes – only her father had been allowed the privilege of steadying her hand while she took her first puff of her 100-plus per day Kents or Craven As. She hated anyone to touch her hands, wrists and arms.

The new caddy was Morton da Costa, a young bit-part player from *The Skin of Our Teeth* who played the broadcasting official but was not actually seen by the audience; standing in the wings, he spoke his lines through a microphone.

There were fireworks when Michael Myerberg threatened to replace the actor, purely for financial reasons, with a recording of Alexander Woollcott's voice – one of his last public acts, for Woollcott died during the run of the play. Tallulah warned Myerberg that unless her lover stayed put, she would boycott the production. She was ignored, of course. Morton da Costa was fired and Tallulah poured a few drops of nail varnish on to the recording so that it stuck and kept repeating the same line. Myerberg had little alternative but to reinstate da Costa, but he did fire him again a few weeks later over some triviality. Tallulah then took the unusual but theatrically 'legal' step of furnishing the management with a doctor's statement. This specified that she had a stomach ulcer, which was a condition that would only become aggravated should she become distressed. When Elia Kazan learned from Tallulah's doctor that Morton da Costa's absence would be the cause of this, he ordered Myerberg to re-hire him.

Tallulah chose Morton da Costa to be her caddy for two reasons. Firstly, though red-headed, she felt that he bore a slight resemblance to Stephan Cole and she learned from a third party that he was good service material – in other words, he would be there, if need be, to keep her bed warm on a night she was between regulars. Secondly, da Costa was an authority on antiques and Tallulah had decided that the furniture at Windows would be at the most tasteful – and costly – that money could buy.

The new caddy excelled himself when it came to sussing out bargains and Tallulah was pleased. He moved into the house with the furniture, passed the obligatory anatomy test with flying colours and that was that. He was introduced to friends and neighbours as 'the most perfect gentleman' she had ever known. The first time she showed him off to the press, she said, 'Morton's so perfect, why, he never so much as bats an eyelid when he hears me break wind.' The young man's perfection was further rewarded when, a few days after moving into Windows, he was allowed to make Madame's bed and wash her stockings.

Estelle Winwood was an early visitor to Windows and one

who ended up staying for two years. After divorcing Arthur Chesney, the brother of the actor Edmund Gwenn, the eccentric, pencil-thin actress had 'erred' by marrying Guthrie McClintic, the ex-husband of Katherine Cornell. Though she would tie the knot twice more, Estelle was not entirely keen on long-term partnerships. Thirty years later she told the American biographer, Boze Hadleigh, 'Somebody once said marriage is an institution – and who wants to live in an institution? And as for wanting to have children, I prefer pets. They never outgrow or outlive you, and they won't contest your will.'

Tallulah had always regretted not having children of her own, though without doubt had she ever become a mother, someone else would have had to do everything for her. Much as these two women cared for each other, however, they antagonized each other a lot. When Estelle fussed over Tallulah's animals – at Windows these were mostly dogs – she would be accused of not feeding them properly. Tallulah once seethed, 'Any idiot knows how to feed dogs!' to which Estelle replied, 'You don't!' This resulted in Tallulah inviting three people to dinner whom Estelle could not stand – Guthrie McClintic, his new boyfriend, and Katharine Hepburn. The actress's two years with her dearest friend may have at times been unbelievably frustrating but they were immensely rewarding. Estelle also told Boze Hadleigh how she was the only person in the world never to have been shocked by Tallulah – which must indeed have been a great testimony to their friendship – and that Tallulah had often regarded Estelle as her only anchor to sanity.

Dola Cavendish also took up residence *chez* Tallulah. Because of the war, her Canadian assets had been frozen and in return for her keep – and a diet that consisted largely of gin – Dola was perfectly willing to become Tallulah's shoulder-to-cry-on. After a while, however, this woman's overt sycophancy became too much for Edie Smith, who moved out for a while. A North Carolina couple, Sylvester and Lillian Oglesby, were taken on to look after the kitchen – a challenging task, for no one, least of all Tallulah herself, quite knew from one day to the next who was residing at Windows. The story was told of how, trying to show her new cook that at least she knew how to make an omelette, Tallulah dropped an egg on the floor and said, never more serious, 'My God, I've killed it!' She also engaged a hunky young black man by the name of Robert Williams to be her chauffeur. She was so taken up by his looks, and the fact that his birthday was 12 April, the same as her father's, that she overlooked the problem that he could not drive. Thus until he passed his test, whenever Robert drove outside the boundary of Bedford Village, Tallulah rang the local police station where she had an arrangement for her Rolls to be escorted by a motorcycle patrol.

Not usually one to try keeping up with the neighbours, the new owner of Windows was a little peeved when, during a rare solitary promenade around her estate she passed the garden of the literary agent, Janet Cohen, and observed a poolside party in full swing. Tallulah decided that she too would like a pool and consulted a surveyor who explained that, on account of the rocks beneath the soil's surface, such a venture would probably cost more than she had paid for the house. Tallulah was having none of this and in order to raise the cash she decided that she would make a film.

In May 1942, her contract for *The Skin of Our Teeth* came up for renewal and there was another bust-up with the troublesome Michael Myerberg when Tallulah insisted on taking the play on tour instead of continuing in New York, where, because of in-house overheads, the money and profits were not as good. For several weeks she dithered over dropping out of the production altogether but, in the end, Myerberg called her bluff and signed the actress Miriam Hopkins as replacement. Thus Tallulah left the show after 229 'agonizing' performances and, though there would be another 130 to go without her, Wilder's masterpiece became just another play – during the subsequent tour, most theatres were reported to be giving away more concessionary tickets than were being sold at the box office. She had the last laugh on Myerberg, too, when she won the Drama Critics Award for Best Actress. The play itself won Thornton Wilder the Pulitzer Prize.

Tallulah had already raised a lot of money for the war effort by doing benefits shows for the USO though, unlike Bob Hope, Danny Thomas and Marlene Dietrich, when asked to work overseas she had declined. With her friend Eleanor Roosevelt she had also helped to found the first stage-door canteen in Washington and it was this charity work that led to her being given a cameo role in the film version of *Stage-Door Canteen*, a light-hearted romp directed by Frank Borzage which enabled her, by way of her friend Guthrie McClintic, to persuade Katherine Cornell to make an extremely rare screen appearance. It was Tallulah too who persuaded Borzage to engage Gracie Fields to sing 'The Machine-Gun Song' and her favourite 'The Lord's Prayer'. The pair, who had not met since 1931 when Tallulah had attended the première of Gracie's film, *Sally in our Alley*, had recently shared the bill on the *All Star Bond Show* in Chicago.

The plot for *Stage-Door Canteen* was publicized as 'The Love Story of a Soldier'. The major characters were played by unknowns – Lon McCallister, the all-American soldier who had never been kissed, and Marjorie Riordan, the girl who has the privilege of helping him to attain his goal. It ran for almost two and a half hours but there were no complaints from the public, most of whom had never even seen Katherine Cornell before – she appeared in a delicatessen scene, reciting 'Romeo and Juliet' to a youth who had played Romeo in a high-school play. The film also starred Merle Oberon, George Raft, Katharine Hepburn, Ethel Merman and dozens of other major stars. 'It is an *embarrassment* of talent!' proclaimed the *Hollywood Reporter*.

Unfortunately for Tallulah, coinciding with the film was the most blistering attack on her private life, penned by a reporter named Bob Rice, which appeared in the political publication, *PM*. Rice, who had never met Tallulah and had no justifiable reason for criticizing her, other than that her views were fiercely anti-Communist, began by referring to her 'capacity for liquor' – one subject of which her public knew little, save that she was fond of having a tipple with friends. Such was her constitution that she could easily polish off an entire bottle of bourbon in an afternoon and still appear sober. Rice made further accusations, claiming that his information had come from 'reliable insiders', about her marriage – under the heading: Poor John – It Was Like Living With a Puma! Worse still, the article said that she and her father had never got on, which was blatantly untrue, and that she had only made *Stage-Door Canteen* for the money, which was perfectly true – so that it could be given to charity.

Tallulah rang the editor of *PM* and told him, 'If I ever meet up with horrible Rice in a dark alley, I swear to God I'll do him to death with my dirk!' Thankfully, she never got hold of Bob Rice, though she would soon have her revenge on *PM*. Meanwhile, she was approached by Alfred Hitchcock and offered $75,000 to play the lead in *Lifeboat*. Thinking of her pool, and the fact that working with Hitchcock would probably be the best move she had ever made, she accepted.

Lifeboat was the very first American film to comprise a single scene, shot in its entirety on a 40-foot boat that had been cast adrift after the ship had been torpedoed by a German U-boat. The cast was small and most of the parts fairly equal in length. Tallulah played the snobbish, sophisticated writer Connie Porter, who is seen alone when the film opens – in mink coat, jewels and perfect make-up, surrounded by the essential props of her trade; camera, jewel case and typewriter, which she loses one by one to the sea. Her antagonist is a brutish, handsome seaman named Kovak (played by John Hodiak, who had made his début that year in *A Stranger in Town*). As the handful of survivors are plucked from the water, each brings a particular problem which, because of the limited location, enables him or her to be 'psychoanalysed' by the others. There is a young Cockney woman with a dead baby, who commits suicide; a dance-mad Brooklynite (William Bendix) who has to have his leg amputated; and a young pickpocket (Canada Lee) who is the only person on board capable of remembering and reciting the 23rd Psalm. Lee, who died tragically young, was Tallulah's personal triumph – it was she who had persuaded Hitchcock to cast him as an *equal* to the other actors at a time when black actors were usually stereotyped into playing servants or criminals.

Most of the action during the film concerns the battle of wits between the rescued German captain (played by Walter Slezak, whom Tallulah referred to constantly between tasks as 'that goddamn Nazi'), and the others, whose capacities for trust rise and fall with the ocean's squall. During the first two-thirds of the film, the Nazi pretends not to understand English, navigating the craft 'towards Bermuda', when they are in fact going in another direction. When, during a storm, his hidden supply of water and food tablets is found, he is unceremoniously beaten to death and thrown overboard.

The dialogue between Tallulah and John Hodiak is all the more interesting because, within a few days of shooting, she had discovered that he was 'hung' and had begun sleeping with him. There were many improvisations that owed more to Bankhead than Steinbeck, upon whose novel the script had been based. When Hodiak strips off his shirt to reveal a wealth of tattoos – the initials of the women he has loved – he says, 'Remind me to show you the rest of them, some time.' When he loses his temper and one of the others tells him to keep his shirt on, he responds, 'I haven't got a shirt … *or* a mink coat,' at which point Tallulah interjects with, 'And *I* thought the common turn was dissolved.' Elsewhere she quips, 'Some of my best friends are women – genus *homo* maketh.' Then, when she and Hodiak kiss at the height of the storm she murmurs, 'We might as well go down together,' after which she adds her initials, in lipstick, to his pectoral gallery. Her mood changes, however, when he is about to succumb to defeat and she snarls, 'Well, Narcissus, shall I put a Q on your chest for Quitter?' Then, in a moment's reckless compassion when forced into a predicament by hunger, she yields her most prized possession, an invaluable Cartier bracelet, as bait to catch a fish which inevitably gets away, with the diamonds, resulting in her having a fit of maniacal laughter. She finally flies into a mad panic when, about to be rescued, she desperately tries to repair her make-up … uttering the most controversial line in the film, 'Some of my best friends are in concentration camps.' And, of course, there was the almost obligatory cameo appearance by Alfred Hitchcock himself – in this instance, a 'before and after' photograph of the director in an advertisement on the back of a newspaper with the caption: REDUCO – OBESITY SLAYER.

Tallulah's part in *Lifeboat* required her to speak a fair amount of German to the Walter Slezak character and, if her command of the language appeared relatively fluent, it was because each phrase was learnt and spoken phonetically, courtesy of her friend and occasional secretary, Paula Miller, who later married the drama teacher, Lee Strasberg. John Hodiak later told the story of how, whenever she ascended the ladder to get into the boat for filming, she teased him by always making sure that he was behind her, so that he would get the worm's-eye view as she hoisted her skirt up to her chin and cocked her leg over the side. 'Tallulah never once had any underwear on,' the actor remembered. The 15-week shooting schedule also made her very ill for, during the storm sequence, the actors were drenched with huge tubs of water and then submerged under billowing clouds of fake fog, while under the studio arc-lights. For the second time in her life, she developed a near-fatal attack of pneumonia.

Tallulah's 'compensation' for suffering came in the guise of the prestigious Screen Critics Award for Actress of the Year – she received 15 of the 18 votes, with two votes won by Ingrid Bergman, and the other by Barbara Stanwyck. She did not get the Oscar, she maintained, because she was not contracted to a major studio. The film was a monumental success, though it did have its critics. Bosley Crowther of the *New York Times* praised it as 'a trenchant and blistering symbolization of the world and its woes today', but drew attention to the fact that the Nazi character, in assuming command of the lifeboat as the others argued among themselves, made everyone else in the story appear foolish by almost outwitting them. The article also added that the film 'sold out democratic ideals and elevated the Nazi superman'. Tallullah dismissed Crowther's theory as 'a lot of balls', and adopted the film's theme for her latest CDAAA campaign – the now unalterable fact that in order to stop Germany from winning, the Allies would have to 'pull out their goddamn fingers and squash Hitler like a bug'.

Lifeboat also caused problems for Walter Slezak. The son of the Czech-born opera singer Leo Slezak, famed for his Wagnerian roles, the actor had already made himself extremely unpopular with the Hitler regime with a film he had made years before the war. *The Story of the Third Sex*, directed by the Dane, Carl Dreyer, in Berlin, had been the first major film to have adopted homosexuality as its central theme. When Hitler attended a private showing of *Lifeboat*, he added Slezak's name to his *Black Book* and, unable to get at the actor personally, exacted his revenge by fining Leo Slezak 100,000 marks for fathering him.

In January 1944, Tallulah halted a press conference at the St Regis Hotel when she saw one of the female reporters wearing a *PM* lapel-tag. She found the publication doubly offensive now because it was Communist and pro-British and what happened next saw Tallulah at her most vicious and perhaps rightly so.

Tapping the young woman on the shoulder, she bawled as the cameras clicked, 'Of all the filthy-rotten Communist rags, this is the most vicious, dangerous and hating paper there has ever been!' She was silenced, momentarily, by a heckler who tried to explain that *PM* had always been a liberal paper, to which she concluded, for once not peppering her statement with expletives, 'Liberal, my eye. It's a stinking paper. Well, not all stinking, I guess. I just love your darling Barnaby. It's the most enchanting comic strip in the world. I always have my maid bring it to me – with tongs.' This brought her a rapturous round of applause but Tallulah had not finished. As the conference was breaking up, she collared the unfortunate reporter again: 'You know, darling, you remind me of a very dear ex-friend of mine ... only she had the fucking sense to commit suicide.'

10

A Royal Scandal
and a Two-Headed Turkey

Within weeks of completing *Lifeboat*, Tallulah signed a contract with one of Hollywood's most distinguished producers, the Berlin-born Ernst Lubitsch, famed for his gently suggestive but refined comedies such as *The Love Parade* and *The Merry Widow*, both of which had starred Maurice Chevalier and Jeanette MacDonald. The new film was *A Royal Scandal*, which recounted an improbably but unavoidably amorous episode in the hectic life of Catherine the Great. The fee was a staggering $125,000 and, if the shooting schedule was beset with problems from day one, few of these were Tallulah's fault. Shortly after negotiating the contract, Ernst Lubitsch suffered a heart-attack and had to be relieved of his command by his assistant, Otto Preminger, the young man Tallulah had helped to become an American citizen four years before. Subsequently she was putty in his hands because, no matter what happened over the next few months, Preminger would always be on her side.

Before shooting commenced, Lubitsch summoned Preminger to his bedside and shared with him the news that had excited him enough to bring on a relapse – Greta Garbo, who had 'retired' from the screen after making *Two-Faced Woman* in 1941, had 'expressed a desire' to play Catherine – a role that had already attained some notoriety by way of Pola Negri (directed by Lubitsch himself), Marlene Dietrich, Elisabeth Bergner and, most recently on the stage, in an outrageously camped-up performance by Mae West.

As Lubitsch would have done absolutely *anything* to woo Garbo back to the screen, he instructed Preminger to buy Tallulah off. This he flatly refused to do, issuing the ultimatum, 'If she goes, so do I!' Lubitsch handed the matter over to Darryl F Zanuck for arbitration, only to receive a shock when he too plumped for Tallulah. Opting to take a leaf out of Michael Myerberg's book, the ebullient little producer decided that he would make life as unpleasant for her as possible.

Firstly, Lubitsch hired Anne Baxter to play Anna, Catherine's spirited lady-in-waiting who is also her rival and, in a series of letters and messages to the set, constantly reminded Tallulah that the actress was 20 years younger than she was, in his opinion prettier and more talented, *and* a Republican. On top of this Anne's grandfather, the famous architect Frank Lloyd Wright, was invited to the studio to watch some of her scenes being filmed. Tallulah refused to act in front of him, though after some deliberation Wright was allowed to sit in on a rehearsal. Tallulah got her revenge on Ernst Lubitsch by deliberately sabotaging the take, which had to be done over 30 times, getting Anne Baxter into a stew and causing her grandfather to leave the set in a huff. There were further tantrums when, in a scene which was supposed to be Anna's moment of glory over Catherine, Tallulah succeeded in acting her into the ground. Lubitsch then attempted to put her in her place by offering a few strong words, only to be out-cursed in such a way that he too left the set, telling Preminger that he would never speak to her again unless she apologized. Tallulah would not do this and, though Preminger did eventually persuade them to shake hands, this was solely for the benefit of the film's publicity agent. *A Royal Scandal* was completed in such an atmosphere of cold disdain that must have made its more hilarious comic moments doubly difficult to enact. Although he sent her a polite letter declaring that her Catherine was the greatest comedy performance he had ever seen,

Tallulah loathed Lubitsch until the day of his death, in 1947. Nor was she the only one to incur his apparent spite. Eva Gabor had been engaged to play the minor role of Countess Demidor but, after an argument with Lubitsch, found every one of her scenes tossed on to the cutting-room floor.

Tallulah's co-star in *A Royal Scandal* was 26-year-old William Eythe, who had recently made a tremendous impact on the film world with *The House on 92nd Street*, a semi-documentary drama about a Nazi spy-ring directed by Henry Hathaway which rivalled anything Hitchcock had ever done. Many critics rated it one of the cleverest thrillers ever made. Six feet tall and ethereally good looking, Eythe became her caddy on and off the screen and Tallulah was soon boasting that he was the 'biggest' man she had fallen for since Gary Cooper. She was utterly devastated by his early death a few years later, just as he was reaching his prime as a fine character actor.

Although Tallulah's Catherine owed much more to the deep South than to Imperialist Russia and, if the dialogue was improbable and at times absurd, the film was a delightful romp through history at a time when the rest of the world was in a mess. Catherine is throwing tantrums and pieces of valuable porcelain at the palace walls when she is told that the unbelievably snide and sycophantic French ambassador (Vincent Price) is waiting without. In fact, she makes up her mind to keep him without as soon as she espies the dashing, unshaven Lieutenant Alexei Chernov (Eythe), who bursts into her chamber and announces, to her delight, that he has ridden for three days and nights to save Russia. From then on, each time Alexei says anything remotely complimentary to Catherine, she promotes him through the ranks: captain, major, lieutenant-colonel, until he becomes commander of the Palace Guard and her lover. The latter is a position which he retains only temporarily before revealing that he is to be married to Anna, an action that results in arrangements being made for her to be sent back to her family and in an inevitable confrontation in which Anna flings a few home truths at her imperial mistress.

Incensed with anger, and sparking off a series of quickfire retorts and *double entendres* which could only have been written by Tallulah herself, Catherine asks her beloved Alexei what they should do with the traitor lurking in their midst. Not knowing that he is condemning himself, he suggests 'prison, torture and death', to which she retorts, 'Let's keep the throne clean!' Then, by way of these arguments, the hapless Alexei is rapidly demoted all the way down the ranks, until he is back to being lieutenant. Several lines also got the pair in trouble with the censor:

> CATHERINE: Oh, Alexei! If I was a little unjust to you, I didn't mean it! Don't think that deep down inside of me I don't appreciate having a knight in shining armor who takes up his spear for me! Is it too much to ask that you get down on your knees?
>
> ALEXEI: On my knees – to beg? I never did that in my life!
>
> CATHERINE: There's always a first time for everything ...

Suffice it to say, Alexei does not beg, and as Anna is sent home to live with her mother, so he is sentenced to face the firing squad. At this moment, fate intervenes. Catherine at long last comes face to face with the simpering French ambassador and is so taken by his over-the-top comments on her greatness and beauty that she tears up Alexei's death warrant, thus enabling all to end well ...

In spite of the inordinate fuss during the shooting of *A Royal Scandal* and a massive publicity budget, the film did not do as well at the box office as *Lifeboat*. But it does remain cult-viewing for all Bankhead devotees, who would have to wait another 20 years before seeing her on the screen again.

On 13 March 1945, one month before *A Royal Scandal* had its première, Tallulah opened at the Martin Beck Theater in Philip Barry's comedy, *Foolish Notion*. The out-of-town try-outs in Baltimore and Washington had not gone at all well and the New York first night did not fare much better so far as the critics were concerned. Her co-stars were Donald Cook, Aubrey Mather and – surprise, surprise – John Emery. After 104 performances in New York, the play toured again, this time a little more successfully but Tallulah lost heart halfway into the run when she received news of Roosevelt's death. She read a moving eulogy on the radio. Many more broadcasts followed, mostly aimed at raising money for the war effort, and a memorable spot on *The Hildegarde Show* when she sang 'Don't Fence Me In'.

Many of Tallulah's friends were surprised when, towards the end of 1946 – a year that had produced only radio shows – she announced that she would like to be given the chance to play the part of Amanda Prynne, should any producer 'worthy of his name' ever decide to revive Noël Coward's *Private Lives*. The Master had written the piece in Bangkok while suffering from influenza. Its plot revolved around the dreadfully snobbish ex-lovers, Amanda and Elyot, who have separated after an 'impossible to live with, impossible to live without' affair, and who meet again in the South of France after each has found someone else. The original production, starring Coward himself and Gertrude Lawrence, had played in New York in 1931 and had only closed because the actors had become bored with it.

Tallulah had already proved with *Rain* that revivals were not always a good idea and when someone did agree to finance and stage it, with her usual percentage conditions, she decided to give Broadway a miss and take it on an extended tour instead. One or two of her closest friends, Estelle Winwood included, actually advised her against doing the play, which some experts had considered grossly outdated even in 1931. Tallulah, however, had a gut feeling that Amanda would give her the greatest role of her career since Regina Giddens, and she was not wrong, though she would often laugh and say, 'I only played her for want of something better to do – to escape the debtor's prison.' There was also a line in the play that convinced her that Coward's heroine could almost have been created for her alone: 'I believe in being as gay as possible, darling!' She also removed some of the character's 'old-fashioned Englishness', imposing a personal stamp which of course only enhanced it. On the negative side, she purposely murdered 'Someday I'll Find You', the play's big hit-song which even Gertrude Lawrence had not sung particularly well. Tallulah's version began half an octave too low and progressed with her struggling *not* to get back into key, much to the delight of her by now largely gay audiences, who loved nothing more than to howl along with her. Only in one respect was she absolutely faithful to the Coward original – this was when she asked Thérèse Quadri, who had played the French maid in the 1931 production, to play her again in the revival. Her co-star was Donald Cook, whose advances she had rejected during *Foolish Notion* on account of his acute alcoholism. Cook now told her that he was cured ... and was believed.

The tour was not without event. Tallulah insisted upon taking the play to Ottawa because Henry Bankhead, her father's younger brother, was stationed there as a diplomat. After the première, Henry escorted her to a buffet, which had been put on at one of the city's most exclusive hotels, where he had arranged for her to meet several Canadian VIPs. Tallulah had earlier held a meeting in her dressing-room, lecturing her entourage on the rights and wrongs of etiquette and instructing everyone to be on their best behaviour. In the event, it was she who let her side down – getting wildly drunk, she ripped off her clothes and ran naked along the hotel corridors, belting out English rugby songs. It was but an isolated incident, and though it made the papers, it did wonders for ticket sales and prompted Tallulah into announcing, 'I *will* do Broadway, and be damned!'

For the time being, however, Broadway was not to be. Tennessee Williams sent her the script for his new play, *A Streetcar Named Desire*, with its superb central role of Blanche Dubois. Though everyone urged her to take up Williams's offer, Tallulah rejected the part at once because one of Blanche's lines contained the word 'nigger' and because the playwright refused to take it out. Williams himself told a different story, that she would have stamped too much of her own personality on

Blanche, though judging by the way she had shaped up to Regina Giddens, this seems unlikely. Instead, she opted for something very different, inadvertently flinging herself into yet another nightmare.

Tallulah had met Jean Cocteau in Paris in the late twenties, when he had introduced her to opium. Willing to try anything once, she had not much cared for the drug, saying, 'For one hour I felt like the bride of Fu Manchu, then I threw up constantly for a week.' She had cared even less for the bizarre playwright, though what had fascinated her was that Cocteau, an unattractive, lizard-like individual, had ensnared as his long-term lover the actor Jean Marais, hailed by his contemporaries as the most beautiful man in France. Therefore, when she learned that the part of the intimidating hero, Stanislas, in his avante-garde melodrama *La Mort Écoute Aux Portes*, had been created for Marais and that there was an excellent English adaptation of the work by Ronald Duncan, Tallulah read both versions, and was impressed.

Duncan had changed the title of the play to *Eagle Rampant*. It told the story of a Bavarian queen who falls in love with the handsome young man who has been sent to assassinate her. It was an extremely demanding role: she had to enact a 30-minute, 20,000-word speech before plunging head first down a huge staircase with a bullet in her heart, while her assassin was drinking a cup of poison. Loving nothing better than a challenge – the tougher the better – Tallulah announced that she would do the play, but with one condition. Working in the sticks, she had seen a young Method actor named Brando and, though she had never cared for 'the Strasberg mumblers', as she called them – she would never forget her difficulties with Lee J Cobb – she was hoping that Brando would prove an exception to the rule. 'A beautiful, dangerous animal – like Monty Clift, without the neurosis,' was how she described him. She was also intrigued that like Monty, Marlon Brando hailed from Omaha, Nebraska – he had been born in 1924, four years after Monty. 'It must be something they put into the water that makes their men so drop-dead gorgeous,' she told John C Wilson, who was to direct *Eagle Rampant*, adding that she would have no one murder her but Brando. The young man was hired.

Tallulah now had more lovers on her hands than she could cope with. Donald Cook was her regular but she was still involved with William Eythe and still sufficiently interested in Colin Keith-Johnston to offer him a small part in the production. In spite of this trio, she nurtured some hope that Brando might return some of the old sparkle to her life, and she took great pains to look like the *grande dame* for their first meeting – buying a new evening gown, hiring a limousine and putting on her best jewels. Brando only shocked her to the core, turning up for their rendezvous in sweat-stained T-shirt, scuffed jeans and old sneakers. 'You'd imagine that he'd show some respect, that he'd put a shirt and tie on to meet me,' she told her friend Kieran Tunney, of whom more later. 'Then, scratching his private parts with one hand, he held out the other and said "Hi". I'm no fusspot, don't stand on dignity but I've worked too long and too hard to put up with that kind of crap.'

Tallulah may have disliked Brando on sight but she *did* recognize his potential and hoped that working with her might cure him of his atrocious manners. The pre-Broadway try-outs opened in Washington in January 1947. As the curtain rose, the audience saw the Bavarian queen, resplendent in real jewels and her Aline Bernstein gown, pacing the stage and recounting how her husband had been assassinated, 15 years before. Tallulah's agent and confidante, Richard Maney – who always referred to Brando as 'the fakir' – described what happened next in his autobiography:

Into her chamber burst Stanislas, a loutish revolutionary intent on doing her in. The conduct of Mr Brando was off-beat. He squirmed. He picked his nose. He adjusted his flies. He leered at the audience. He cased the furniture. He fixed his gaze on an offstage property man instead of his opponent … on cue he plugged the Queen and watched her pitch headlong down the stairway. Then, in defiance of Cocteau, Wilson, and Equity's Board of Governors, he refused to die. Instead he staggered about the stage, seeking a likely spot for his final throe. The audience was in convulsions. Spread-eagled on the stairway, head down, Miss Bankhead was having a few convulsions of her own. Why wouldn't this misbegotten clown cash in his chips? Marlon had been mooning about for a full minute on the apron when suddenly he collapsed as if suddenly spiked by an invisible ray ... If Tallulah could have gotten her hands on a gun, the coroner would have had a customer then and there.

By the time the company reached Boston, Brando's behaviour had become so erratic that Tallulah warned John C Wilson that unless the actor behaved himself, she would leave the production. Brando hung on until New Haven, where Wilson fired him. When Colin Keith-Johnston argued against the decision, he too was sent packing.

Desperately in search of a replacement, Tallulah thought of Monty Clift, whom she heard was still recovering from *his* most recent ordeal – shooting his début film, *Red River*, opposite John Wayne, a man even more homophobic than Elia Kazan, particularly as Monty had been 'caught out' with a male member of the cast. Whatever Tallulah said to Monty over the telephone seems to have worked, in spite of his fear of her, and he arrived in New Haven the next day. Once he had read the script for the play, however, he caught the first train back to New York ... sharing a compartment with Brando. Tallulah then decided that the play's title must have brought her bad luck and asked Ronald Duncan if she might change it, claiming, 'The only thing *rampant* about the goddamn thing was Brando's crabs.' It became *The Eagle Has Two Heads* and as such opened in New York on 19 March 1947 at the Plymouth Theater. She had also worked hard on her opening monologue, reducing it substantially and telling a reporter, 'I've got it down to 17 minutes, darling, but I'm still convinced that everyone will have fallen asleep by the time I have finished.'

Marlon Brando certainly went on to better things. His next role, and his passport to immortality, was in *A Streetcar Named Desire*, which caused Tallulah to utter a huge sigh of relief – had she taken Tennessee Williams up on his offer, she most likely would have starred opposite him. His replacement in the Cocteau play was the equally narcissistic but less tempera-

mental 27-year-old German actor, Helmut Dantine, who five
years earlier had had a small part in *Mrs Miniver*. Tallulah told
friends how she had auditioned Dantine in her bed. 'He was the
answer to any maiden's prayer,' she added, though an alleged
prowess in this department did not pronounce him the
definitive Stanislas. With a $50,000 advance for Tallulah,
superb sets by Donald Oenslanger and a blaze of publicity, *The
Turkey With Two Heads* – the title bestowed on the play not
just by the critics, but by Tallulah herself – closed after 29
performances.

Most of the critics agreed, however, that the play's failure
had little to do with Tallulah, save that her performance had
probably been too stylish – that after her truly magnificent
no-holds-barred monologue, the 'intrusion' of Stanislas –
Brando or Dantine – had been a decidedly poor anti-climax.
Kieran Tunney, a young Irish playwright who had been sent
over to America in the hope of wooing Tallulah back to
London to star in his play, *Aurora* – the mission failed but the
ensuing friendship lasted the rest of her life – believed that the
Cocteau play had all the makings of another *The Little Foxes*
and also blamed Dantine for its failure. In his biographical
tribute, *Tallulah, Darling of the Gods*, he reflected:

> As he burst in on the lonely queen, he looked spectacularly right
> – handsome, butch, bronzed, muscles rippling, hair on chest
> showing. The actor, unfortunately, didn't have the *inner*
> equipment needed. With Dantine's entry, the atmosphere
> achieved by the actress alone on the stage began to evaporate.
> Instead of rising, the temperature fell, as if a vital current had
> failed.

Tunney's book, published four years after Tallulah's death,
was unashamedly and blazingly sycophantic, exactly the way
she would have wanted. Tunney was the lover of Simon
Wardell, the son of her old flame, Michael, and he and Tallulah
had met at her hotel in Buffalo soon after Brando's dismissal.
Two hours later, completely without inhibition, Tunney found
himself perched on the edge of Tallulah's bathtub, sipping
champagne, and that same night he slept in her bed – a purely

platonic act. He was not a particularly successful playwright but she was able to restore his flagging confidence by telling him that it did not matter if he could not make money because his tastes were simple: champagne, smoked salmon and caviar.

After *The Eagle Has Two Heads* closed, Tallulah received an invitation from Orson Welles to play Lady Macbeth in his Utah production of the Shakespeare play. She declined and, while deliberating what to do next, appeared in several radio plays. Her powers of mimicry had not diminished: she had taken to imitating Al Jolson and Gracie Fields with tremendous accuracy, and the first time Gracie heard her version of 'The Biggest Aspidistra in the World', she wept with laughter.

Scarcely pausing to catch her breath, Tallulah flung herself back into *Private Lives*, re-revising the script and conducting rehearsals at Windows with a new director – Stephan Cole, recently returned to the fold, and Tallulah's bed, after his stint with the American Field Service.

Tallulah sat in on the auditions for the secondary male-female leads – in other words, the ex-lovers' current lovers, and it was she who had the last say. When William Eythe unexpectedly walked into her living room, looking every bit as dashing as he had in *A Royal Scandal*, she truly thought that her prayers had been answered. Eythe, however, had merely brought along his new wife, the 24-year-old actress Buff Cobb, the granddaughter of the humorist, Irvin S Cobb. Tallulah pointed at her and told Stephan Cole, 'Well, darling. Seeing as we've both of us ridden the same steed, you'd better engage her.' The part of Amanda's husband was then bestowed upon an actor named Phil Arthur, who had recently toured with Lucille Ball – one good-looking young man who made it perfectly clear from the moment they met that he would not be moving into her bed.

11

In the Wake of the
Human Tornado

Private Lives opened in Westport, Connecticut, on 14 July 1948, in what Tallulah predicted would be at the most a ten-city, six-month run, followed by a month-long break and a spring opening on Broadway. She could not possibly have known then that by the summer of 1950 she would have played Amanda Prynne for a total of 204 weeks, in every American state but Florida, Nevada and Maine and, she joked, 'everywhere but underwater'.

There were problems, naturally: some with Donald Cook, who was often totally inebriated after just one drink – others with Tallulah's Gallery Girls. In Chicago, at the start of a six-week run at the Harris Theater which was extended so many times that the company stayed for seven months, some audiences became so hysterical that the police had to be on standby in case of riots. Buff Cobb said of the première, 'It was just like Benvenuti's first night at Madison Square Garden.' She had camped-up Coward's script with so many asides and *double entendres* that the playwright would not have recognized it. Even so, those critics who had been wildly enthusiastic over the Coward original were unable to find fault with this one.

Tallulah was now grossing $7,000 a week, along with her usual box-office percentage yet, income-wise she was far from being in the top bracket enjoyed by the likes of Hepburn, Davis and Crawford. She also knew from personal experience that one unprecedented success did not guarantee others for the future and, because of this, invested a substantial proportion of her earnings into an annuity fund for her old age. Most of what was left she ploughed into having a good time, with an energy which was quite phenomenal.

Tallulah never wasted time hanging around in the wings waiting for her call, preferring to spend her time chatting non-stop or playing bridge in the wings but she never once missed a cue. She rarely became tired after a performance and would often party until dawn and was extremely tetchy with anyone who could not keep up with her. This was also a brief period in her life when there was no male caddy of sufficient importance to tuck her into bed and stay with her until she had dropped off to sleep. At the plush Ambassador Hotel in Chicago, this job was shared by Dola Cavendish, Buff Cobb – Tallulah was preventing her from sleeping with William Eythe to teach him a lesson for marrying her – and Evelyn Cronin, her elderly dresser-maid. She was also drinking heavily, though with her astonishing capacity for holding liquor, her professionalism was never affected:

> You've heard, I'm sure, about Tallulah the toper! Tallulah the tosspot! Tallulah, the gal who gets as tight as a tick! Let's face it, my dears, I have been tight as a tick! Fried as a mink! Stiff as a goat! But I'm no toper. No tosspot, I. In all my years in the theatre I've never missed a performance because of alcoholic wounds. I have never skidded into the footlights through confused vision. No curtain has been prematurely lowered on a play of mine that the litter-bearers might get an emergency workout.

Tallulah grew increasingly irritable while *Private Lives* was playing in Chicago. She was beginning to find Donald Cook 'an interminable bore'. Though he always behaved admirably on stage, his performances between the sheets were, she declared, 'as flat as yesterday's beer'. She wanted Phil Arthur but he persisted in spurning her every advance and, in spite of

Tallulah's machinations, William Eythe now only had eyes for his pretty young wife. Stephen Cole tried to convince her that her situation would improve and advised her to concentrate on the play, which was making her a fortune. Matters only grew worse when Cole was asked to find an understudy for Buff Cobb, to enable her to spend more time with her husband.

Barbara Baxley had been Method-trained by Sanford Meisner, who had worked with Elia Kazan at the Group Theater, but such a pedigree did not cut any ice with Tallulah. 'Method and in-house actors are pains in the ass,' she told Cole. 'Most if not *all* of them need to see shrinks at least once a week.' Reluctantly, she watched the new understudy in rehearsal but, try as she did, found absolutely nothing wrong with her delivery. At just 19, Barbara was a professional through and through. Tallulah did however have a gut feeling that there was something suspicious about the young woman and what she unearthed shocked her. When an informant at the Harris Theater brought it to her attention that Donald Cook was having an affair with Barbara, Tallulah marched into the understudy's dressing-room to give her a piece of her mind, and there, on top of a pile of magazines, was a copy of the Communist rag, *PM*. Thinking that this could quite easily have been left there by someone else, Tallulah bided her time, instructing the rest of the cast that Barbara would have to be watched carefully. Finally, when the young woman was seen at a Communist rally, Tallulah decided to teach her a lesson. Having now lost all amorous interest in Donald Cook, she had set her sights on a young Canadian actor named William Langford and she had to show him what she was made of – hence her excuse for inviting Barbara Baxley to one of her soirées at the Ambassador Hotel.

The evening went dreadfully wrong. Tallulah 'accidentally' pushed Barbara into a chair, smiled sweetly and murmured, 'I'm *so* sorry, darling!' A little later she tripped her up, and after this she bumped into her several times, always apologetically, until the younger woman could stand no more. Grabbing Tallulah by the shoulder, she sent her careering head first on to the top of the bar, smashing bottles and glasses, before landing face down in the caviar dish. The next evening, Barbara arrived at the theatre, clearly expecting her marching orders. Tallulah breezed past, blew her a kiss and quipped, 'Wasn't it an absolutely *divine* party, darling?' Henceforth, Tallulah's reluctance to punish Barbara Baxley became the punishment – for months, the understudy was quivering under the constant threat of recrimination.

One week later, Tallulah learned that Noël Coward was on his way to Chicago and that he had expressed concern over the way she and her company had 'mangled' his play. This worried her considerably – though Coward had given permission for *Private Lives* to open in New York, she knew that to upset him might result in his changing his mind. Calling an emergency meeting after the show, after a great deal of shouting and swearing she managed to convince everyone that the play would have to be 'put back to normal' while the playwright was in town. Coward arrived in September 1947, was delighted by what he saw and duly gave the go-ahead for Broadway.

At around this time, Tallulah began experiencing severe pain in her right shoulder but she refused to see her doctor. It became so bad, however, that Barbara Baxley – probably worried that she had caused some serious injury – took matters into her own hands when she discovered a very distraught Tallulah standing at the top of a steep flight of steps, unable to move and about to fall. Though she would have suffered any amount of agony sooner than be helped by a love-rival, Tallulah allowed Barbara to guide her down the steps, through the theatre corridors, and into her car where she was driven to a hospital. The doctors there diagnosed neuritis, she was put into traction, and *Private Lives* closed for two weeks until she was fully recovered. From her sickbed she announced, 'If I've got to be a good girl and get myself straightened out, then Donald Cook can go and get himself dried out. Either that, or he leaves the goddamn show.' She was dutifully obeyed.

Tallulah recovered completely – and Cook more or less – and after Chicago the tour progressed with few hitches, zigzagging through Minneapolis, Cincinnati, Cleveland, Pittsburgh, Kansas, St Louis, San Francisco, Los Angeles, with dozens of small towns in between. Tallulah had engaged her most recent lover, William Langford, as Phil Arthur's understudy, and Barbara Baxley took over from Buff Cobb when Buff developed a virus and was advised not to return to the production by William Eythe, who knew just how exacting Tallulah could be. In Los Angeles, where newspapers reported that she was reaping in 25 per cent of the box office, and not ten, there was a big argument with Phil Arthur, which resulted in his being replaced by Langford. This had far-reaching consequences, for Arthur's dismissal resulted in an even bigger showdown with Stephan Cole, who stormed out of Tallulah's life vowing that he would never speak to her again. So far as is known, he never did.

In Philadelphia, on air, Tallulah told a radio reporter who reproved her for 'insulting' Noël Coward by hamming up Amanda Prynne, 'In the play I'm Tallulah, and only Tallulah. Why should I be ashamed of that? Now please fuck off and have a sandwich.'

When the play opened at the Plymouth Theater in New York on 4 October, however, enriched by the presence of Eugenia Rawls, the critics loved it. Brooks Atkinson wrote that she possessed 'a worldly style based on a fine Southern upbringing' and lauded her 'cavernous voice that shivers the galleries'. John Mason Brown, he of the infamous 'Cleopatra' quote, called her, 'The only volcano ever dressed by Mainbocher.' Again, the run had to be greatly extended.

Meanwhile, Tallulah added her very individual support to the Presidential Election Campaign, as an adherent of the underdog, her pal Harry S Truman. Sponsored by David Dubinsky of the International Ladies Government Workers Union, on 21 October 1948 she delivered a fervent speech from her dressing-room during the interval of *Private Lives*. Dubinsky had particularly asked for Tallulah because he had admired her loyalty to her father: he had noted the fact that she had never missed a single one of his speeches. In effect, Truman could not have had a better advocate, for her three-minute address to the American nation, broadcast over the entire ABC network, reaped the largest audience ever to listen to a showbusiness personality. Though it had been edited by her 'political adviser' Richard Maney – solely to eliminate the 'darlings', 'divines' and inevitable epithets directed at Thomas E Dewey, the spivish governor of New York and Truman's rival – the script was all Tallulah's own work, and the radio broadcast presented her at her most sincere:

I would be faithless to Alabama, did I not vote for Harry Truman. Yes, I'm for Harry Truman, the human being. By the same token I'm against Thomas E Dewey, the mechanical man. Mr Dewey is neat, oh so neat! And Mr Dewey is tidy, oh so tidy! Just once I'd like to see him with his hair rumpled, a gravy stain on his vest, that synthetic smile wiped off his face. It seems a great pity to risk exposing Mr Dewey to the smells, noises and ills of humanity. Far better to leave him in his cellophane wrapper, unsoiled by contact with the likes of you and me ...

Mr Dewey is trim and neat and tidy, but is he human? I have my doubts. I have *no* doubts about Harry Truman. He's been through the wringer, by which I mean the 80th Congress. The 80th Congress which ignored his passionate pleas for veterans' housing, for curbs on inflation, for legislation to aid and comfort the great mass of our population ...

What is Mr Dewey for? Again and again he has said that he is for UNITY. Will all the candidates for DISUNITY please stand? Come, come, Mr Dewey. Act like a grown-up. The next thing we know you'll be endorsing matrimony, the metal zipper and the dial telephone. If Mr Dewey has any genius it lies in his ability to avoid expressing an opinion on any controversial subject. Mr Dewey is the great neutral. Harry Truman is the great partisan of our troubled millions. In my lifetime I've enjoyed many thrills. I'm about to enjoy my greatest one. For now I have the distinguished honour to present to you the president of these United States!

Tallulah's script had to be vetted by the White House press secretary before her broadcast. Naturally, there were objections. Ethel Barrymore had already upset Dewey by announcing, also on air, that he was so clean-cut that he could have been mistaken for the bridegroom on a wedding cake. Tallulah was asked therefore to remove her 'cellophane' quote.

'Fine,' she responded. 'So long as you let me put all the "fucks" and "shits" back in.' The reference stayed, though she did cut two more. Describing Dewey's impeccable appearance, she had written, 'Just for once I'd like to see Mr Dewey with his necktie knotted under his ear,' which could have been misconstrued that she had wanted to see him hanged. She also cut the line referring to Dewey's political leaning: 'He ranges far to his right, he ranges far to his left.' This, the censor told her, implied that Truman's chief rival was a Communist.

The next day, Tallulah's speech was printed, verbatim, on the front page of every major newspaper in America and many people believed that the riveting address pushed Truman into the White House. Ten days later, when he gave his inaugural spech at the Madison Square Garden, he invited her to share the presidential platform. She had written a congratulatory speech – shorter than her last one and completely uncensored – which she planned to read after Truman had delivered his. Charles Ross, who had vetted her first speech, tried to dissuade her from approaching the microphone by warning her that she would make herself look a fool if, having listened to Truman, the audience began leaving the stadium. No such thing happened. The president, his wife and a crowd of 20,000 gave her arguably the most important and certainly the most emotional standing ovation of her life.

She was criticized, of course. Wearing no jewellery but her pearls, and keeping her spectacles on throughout, Tallulah's conduct was exemplary – only once did she step out of line, to boo Herman Talmadge, the governor of Georgia. And instead of rewarding Harry Truman with 'one goddamn lipsmacker', as she had promised the press, she had kissed him politely on the back of the hand. Leaving the stadium, however, led to an incident when a burly policeman demanded that she show her credentials. She did as she was asked, then told the man exactly what she thought of him in such strong language that he had to be revived with a whiff of smelling-salts. The incident was reported in the *New York Times* the next day, with a few elaborations. Tallulah was accused of gatecrashing the presidential ceremony without a ticket. Furious, she barged into the office of Edwin L James, the newspaper's managing editor, and demanded a retraction – 'or else'. The apology was printed without delay. She took similar action against the *Daily News* when a photograph of her kissing Truman's hand appeared on its front page with the caption HE'S HER MAN! and with *Time* magazine for implying that she had sat upon his lap during the electoral campaign.

Tallulah won her 'case' with each of these publications – she was not interested in claiming damages but simply in clearing her name. The same applied one day when she switched on the radio and heard the latest jingle for Prell shampoo:

> I'm Tallulah, the tube of Prell,
> And I've got a little something to tell.
> Your hair can be radiant, oh, so easy,
> All you've got to do is take me home and squeeze me!
> I'm Tallulah the tube of Prell,
> And I'll make your hair look so swell!
> It'll shine, it'll glow so radiantly,
> For radiant hair, get a hold of me—
> Tallulah, the tube of Prell shampoo!

This time, Tallulah declared, someone had gone too far. She instructed Donald Seawell, the lawyer husband of Eugenia Rawls, to sue the manufacturers, Procter and Gamble, and the CBS and NBC networks for a staggering $1 million.

'I've yet to endorse a floor wax, a flea powder or wart remover, a cigar or a hookah pipe,' she fumed. 'I'll unjingle Mr Procter *and* Mr Gamble, their aides, their allies and their echoes!' The advertisement was humiliating, she continued, not just because the company had put out the jingle without her permission but because it 'demoted' the image promoted by her name. When the defendants claimed that the surname Bankhead had not been used in their campaign and that the name Tallulah did not necessarily mean that Tallulah, Donald Seawell argued, 'The name Tallulah achieved widespread fame and publicity because of its unique association with Miss Bankhead,' which was of course very true. Tallulah, admitting that she was still washing her locks in dry-cleaning fluid and with no ill effects, told the press, 'My English friend, Max Beaverbrook, once told me that I'm the only person in the world whose first name is instantly recognized as belonging to me. My God, when I was at school, every other goddamn girl was called Virginia.' She was nevertheless willing to settle the matter out of court and did not quibble when only awarded damages of $5,000.

After the Prell episode, Tallulah became restless. She told a reporter from *Variety* that her company had only stayed on at the Plymouth Theater because Lee Shubert had kept them there: part of her contract stipulated that the play would remain on Broadway so long as the box-office receipts did not drop below $14,000 a week. This happened in May 1949, when the show finally closed. By this time, William Langford had moved in with her and the fact that he was almost 20 years her junior did not go unnoticed by the press and neither had the welcoming party for Langford at Windows. At the end of the evening, wearing nothing but her favourite string of pearls and lashings of Victory Red lipstick, Tallulah flung herself backwards over her baby grand and crooned 'Bye Bye Blackbird'. Witnessing this awesome spectacle, Estelle Winwood remarked, 'It's such a shame, you know, when she has so many pretty frocks!'

On 9 February 1949, Tallulah wrote a letter to J Edgar Hoover at the United States Department of Justice. Exactly why she did this seemed unclear at the time and Hoover's speedy response suggested nothing of particular importance, save for one line which read, 'Do not hesitate to call on me at any time.' All was revealed at the end of the month when the singer Billie Holiday, whom she had got to know in Harlem, was arrested and charged with the possession of narcotics. Tallulah knew why Lady Day had to take drugs – a combination of intense racial prejudice, police harassment, and one disastrous love affair after another had rendered her incapable of coping with an immensely successful career. When Hoover pulled a few strings to secure her release, Tallulah secretly put up the bail. It emerged that she had done this sort of thing before and she would come to Billie Holiday's rescue several times more before the singer's death from heart and liver failure in July 1959.

Almost immediately after the Broadway closure, *Private Lives* embarked on a lightning make-or-break Southern tour, fraught with rows and nervous tension, so much so that after the first week the only time the members of the cast actually spoke to one another was on the stage. When the company played a week-long stint in Marblehead, Massachusetts, in the July, Tallulah attempted to alleviate some of the stress by renting a huge, 18-room mansion right next to the sea and inviting the entire company, including the backstage staff, to move in with her. A young reporter who was sent to interview her about the play did not know where to put his face when she answered the door herself. She was stark naked and began talking immediately about breast implants. She then showed him around the house – over her bedroom door was a GENTS sign which she had been given by the landlord of a London pub – and told him that although she was still madly in love with 'a divinely big, big, boy', the real love of her life was Gaylord, her parakeet. She added, scarcely pausing for breath, 'You see, darling, the poor little thing's so dreadfully afraid of the dark that all the lights have to be kept on all of the time and because he's also so very very afraid of bumping into things all the inner doors of the house have to be left wide open no matter who's screwing who!' Tallulah also told the reporter that the house was owned by a Mrs Bloodshot – the name was Blaisdell.

The reporter's visit was followed by an all-night party, after the final performance of *Private Lives*, for the benefit of the local summer-theatre management. This was such a noisy affair that a neighbour called the police and two officers were sent to investigate. Had these been young and good-looking, they would have merely cautioned the rowdies and been asked to join in with the fun when they went off duty. They were not, and when they confronted Tallulah – unclothed again, and smoking a joint – they got considerably more than they bargained for as, in a blind, foul-mouthed fury she fisted one of them in the face and screeched, 'I've seen a better fucking head on a glass of beer!' Ten minutes later she was dragged off, cuffed and kicking, to the local squadroom, where she was locked up for several hours until Donald Seawell bailed her out.

Because none of the local hotels wanted to suffer the 'indignity' of having her on their premises, she was forced to rent a room in a cheap, backstreet boarding house, which she left under cover of darkness to avoid being seen by the team of reporters who were allegedly combing the streets of Marblehead looking for her.

A few weeks after the Marblehead incident, Basil Dean asked Tallulah if she would consider appearing in his forthcoming production of the Mae Cooper–Grace Klein play, *Lily Henry*. It was the beginning of a thankfully brief period of indecision and rejection. Tallulah was certainly interested in working for Dean but she told him that she would have to think about it. She was also approached by Warner Brothers, who informed her that she was in the running for the film version of Tennessee Williams's *The Glass Menagerie*, the stage production of which had been instrumental in relaunching the career of Laurette Taylor, the alcoholic actress whom Tallulah had met many years before at the Algonquin. The director, Irving Rapper, was sure that Tallulah would prove the definitive Amanda Wingfield, the haughty, middle-aged Southern belle and, under normal procedure, Rapper would have been allowed his own way. He had directed many of Bette Davis's films for Warner Brothers, all of them hugely successful, and Jack Warner trusted him implicitly. Davis had in fact turned this part down, saying that she was far too young to play the mother of a grown-up woman – a statement that had not gone down too well with Tallulah, who loathed the actress who had filmed so many of the roles she had created. Jack Warner, who did not like Tallulah and was looking for a legitimate excuse to offer Rapper to ensure that she would not get the part, insisted that she would have to have a screen test. This did not worry her unduly, for she preferred to be employed on merit as opposed to favouritism. She did decide, though, to keep the test a secret from everyone, even her closest friends, and made arrangements to meet Irving Rapper at Windows when only her manservant-chauffeur, Robert Williams, was present.

For several days Tallulah did not drink at all and because Rapper was an unknown quantity she was on her best behaviour, putting a terrible strain on her nerves. She slipped up just the once, when Rapper escorted her to a New York department store to buy her costume for the test. She had never liked hats since the day she had barged into Gerald du Maurier's London office without one and been given the part in *The Dancers* and she told Rapper that she would not be wearing one in *The Glass Menagerie*. He insisted, so she selected several to try on with her other Amanda clothes. Ten minutes later she rushed on to the busy sales floor and announced, 'Well, darling? How do you like my hat?' Unfortunately for Rapper and the dozens of shoppers who had gathered around hoping to get her autograph, she was not wearing anything else.

On 21 August, fearing that she would not be able to keep the secret from her friends, Tallulah moved into her old suite at the Elysée Hotel. Over the next three days she filmed six of the most important scenes from *The Glass Menagerie* and had all but clinched the contract when Irving Rapper caught her on the hop by asking her to put in another day. The young actor, Ralph Meeker, who had just made his film début with Rod Steiger and Pier Angeli in Fred Zinnemann's *Teresa*, had been engaged to play one of the leads and Rapper was eager to see him act with Tallulah. During the morning rehearsal, all went well but, when Rapper and Meeker arrived back at the studio after lunch, they were confronted with a drunken Tallulah who, when advised by Meeker that it might be better to postpone filming 'until she felt a little better', cursed him black and blue and vowed that if need be she would direct the scene herself.

The Warner grapevine was incredibly efficient and within half an hour Jack Warner had received news of the incident at his Hollywood base. Rapper pleaded with him on Tallulah's behalf, to no avail. Warner's official response was, 'I had enough of that sort of thing with Errol Flynn. Drop the Bankhead woman.' A few weeks later, the part of Amanda Wingfield went to Gertrude Lawrence and, in an act of immeasurable spite, Jack Warner gave orders for Tallulah's tests to be incinerated.

Next, and while still waiting for Basil Dean to give her the thumbs-up for *Lily Henry*, Tallulah was approached by an old foe, Leland Hayward, who asked her to appear in Garson Kanin's new play, *The Rat Race*. 'I needed Hayward like I needed a megaphone,' she scoffed, and proceeded to make life for her one-time agent as difficult as possible – demanding 15 per cent of the box office *and* 25 per cent of the profits. She did not get the part and she was also turned down for *Lily Henry*. Feigning indifference but desperate to try something new, on 17 October 1949, Tallulah embarked on another tour of *Private Lives*. The first stop was Boston, where most agreed that the play had been worked to death.

Still mourning Scarlett O'Hara after ten years, Tallulah's favourite phrase from *Gone With the Wind*, was, 'Frankly, my dear, I don't give a damn!' – this was incorporated into the play as the company moved into the deep South, only she changed the 'damn' to something much worse. Most of the cast were still not speaking to each other. William Langford was still sleeping with her but only to keep his job, and her maid Evelyn Cronin was stealing from her.

Tallulah's drinking habits were now starting to match those of Donald Cook – in one scene which required the pair to roll off a couch, they were often so drunk that they could not get back on again, though they never forgot their lines. During one of their character arguments, their off-stage hatred of one another took over and a few choice phrases were uttered which were not from the pen of any reputable writer. To save face, Tallulah invited the press to the sumptuous dinner party which she had put on for the cast at Chez Antoine in New Orleans, on Christmas Eve 1949, but the long faces and snappy dialogue said it all. The reporters drew their swords but what they reported in their respective columns only added tremendous power to the box office. Some theatres actually put up their prices and got away with it.

At the end of April 1950, Tallulah learned that Evelyn Cronin had been 'kiting', or raising the amounts on her cheques, and pocketing the difference. The maid had been caught red-handed by a New York bank-teller who had observed a slight difference in the colour of the ink on a cheque which Tallulah had authorized for $200, but which the maid had kited to $1,300. After informing Tallulah of the alleged crime – she was persuaded by Cronin that the cheque had been a one-off – the bank manager reported the matter to Tallulah's accountant, Benjamin Nadel, who insisted upon a full inquiry. On 23 April, Nadel confronted Cronin in her room at Windows – Tallulah had 'gone out shopping', for in spite of her fiery temperament she had always had a soft spot for her personal staff – with an accusation that between 8 October 1949 and 11 April 1950, in excess of $10,000 had been stolen from her employer's bank account.

Nadel implored Tallulah to prosecute but she refused. Back in Alabama, she explained, 'toting' as it was called had been commonplace among the servants and even accepted, on the assumption that if the lower members of the household were caught and reprimanded, then pardoned, relations between 'upstairs and downstairs' usually proved more amenable. To pacify her accountant, Tallulah dismissed her maid: Evelyn Cronin packed her bags and left Windows within the hour and the matter should have ended there. It did not and the repercussions were severe.

Private Lives closed, finally, on 3 June 1950 and from her dressing-room at the Central Theater, Passaic, in New Jersey, Tallulah announced, 'I've had enough. I'm never going to act in the theatre again, I swear.' She would hold herself to this for another four years. She then returned to New York, where she made the grave mistake of telling the columnist Walter Winchell – a man whom she, with her intense powers of perception, ought to have known not to trust – what had happened with Evelyn Cronin. Winchell promised to keep the information to himself but such a scoop was worthy even of risking the wrath of the woman he had once called 'a human tornado'. Waving his 'Isn't Tallulah a kind and considerate person?' flag, he reported the incident in his newspaper column, hoping that this would placate Tallulah for letting an old woman off the hook – Evelyn Cronin was almost 60 and not in the best of health. This had a catastrophic effect, for the New York District Attorney, Frank Hogan, added to the fray by going to see Tallulah and insisting that she press charges. The trial of Evelyn Cronin was set for the end of the year.

12

The Big Show and
the Cronin Trial

In the autumn of 1950, the National Broadcasting Company made a last-bid attempt to draw away some of the rapidly increasing advertising funds from the television network by launching *The Big Show* – a 90-minute, Sunday-evening radio extravaganza which they promised would dazzle from start to finish with an array of stars, the likes of whom had never before been assembled in one show. The budget for each programme was set at a staggering $50,000, ten per cent of which would be paid to the Master – or in this case Mistress – of Ceremonies. Tallulah was asked to fulfil this role, and obliged. Between introducing the stars, she was more or less given a free rein over what she would do in each show providing her material was not smutty. This was an age when each of the showbusiness 'disciplines' more or less stuck to whatever they were best at and, as Tallulah had so often proved, not everyone appreciated their particular star stepping out of line. The producer, Dee Engelbach, begged her to simply to be herself – nothing more, nothing less. Even so, she developed cold feet a few days before the first broadcast and would have thrown in the towel, had it not been for another telegram from Anita Loos that read: THE DAY YOU GO ON THE RADIO PERMANENTLY SHOULD BE DECLARED A NATIONAL HOLIDAY.

'I walked through the rehearsals like a woman under water,' Tallulah reflected. She coped with this nervousness by dispensing with $5,000 for a series of thrice-weekly injections of Demerol, an opium-based stimulant to which she very quickly became addicted. She took her frustration out on Dee Engelbach by telephoning him at all hours and several times threatened to tear up her contract. The first problem concerned the publicity – spelling out a list of the very cream of American entertainment, it ended, 'All This and Tallulah Too!' Then Ethel Merman turned up for rehearsals at the Center Theater studio and announced that she wanted to perform six songs instead of the customary two or three. This would have the effect of 'squashing' the other guests so close together that Tallulah's participation was more or less reduced solely to introducing them – a job that could have been done by anyone. 'I'd rather starve in a goddamn garret than submit to such shame!' she fumed.

All turned out well, eventually. Merman's set was cut to four songs and Tallulah got her own back by telling her, 'Thank you, Ethel darling. That was wonderful – and may I say, you don't look a day over sixty!' These exclamations of 'ersatz venom', as she called them, were usually meant to be offensive – an antidote to the gross sycophancy with which hosts such as Bing Crosby and Al Jolson had greeted their guests on radio shows in the forties. There was an actual script, supplied by Goodman Ace and Frank Wilson, but many of the jokes were so dreadful – such as, 'Tannhäuser? It used to be known as Fivehäuser, darling, until inflation set in!' – that Tallulah flatly refused to read them out on air. Some of the others were so obscure that she never got the punchline until she was reading them out. Then, millions of listeners would hear her 'pee herself' with raucous laughter.

The first *Big Show* went out on Sunday 4 November 1950: Tallulah's other guests included Frankie Laine, Jimmy Durante, Danny Thomas and Portland Hoffa (the wife of comic Fred Allen), who earned the biggest laugh by addressing Tallulah as 'sir'. The Mistress of Ceremonies then stunned her 30 million-strong audience by attacking 'Give My Regards To

Broadway' in a performance that was so consistently toneless that many critics deemed it a classic interpretation. Jimmy Durante stomped up to the microphone and cracked, 'Tallulah gave her regards to Broadway, and Broadway sent 'em back!' She also crooned the show's theme, 'May the Good Lord Bless and Keep You', composed by Meredith Wilson and played by his 24-piece orchestra and choir. Again, she could only sing it half in tune and half a bar behind the musical director ... while he was humming it in her ear.

The critics loved *The Big Show*. 'They don't come any bigger than this one,' enthused *Variety*. And John Crosby of the *Herald Tribune*, while criticizing Tallulah for using the word 'darling' hundreds (in fact dozens) of times and for having a voice 'with more timbre than Yellowstone National Park', wrote,

> NBC's biggest gamble may have been Tallulah Bankhead, an unpredictable volcano who has been known to sweep away whole villages when she erupts. As Mistress of Ceremonies she was sharp as a knife and succeeded in outshining even the most glittering names on that glittering roster.

The Big Show brought with it several offers – the lead in Edwin J Mayer's comedy, *I'm Laughing*, to be produced by Lee Shubert, and a major part in S N Behman's *Biography*. Tallulah, having now signed an open-ended contract, turned them down, though she did appear in NBC radio's *Screen Director's Playhouse* on 16 November in Howard Wiley's one-off production of *Lifeboat*, guest-directed by Alfred Hitchcock, and with Jeff Chandler taking over the John Hodiak part.

For two more years, *The Big Show* remained the most debated and quite possibly the most popular series on the American radio. There were eight more broadcasts in 1950 – the guests included such stalwarts as Fanny Brice, Lauritz Melchior, Clifton Webb, Douglas Fairbanks Jr and Gloria Swanson, all 'doing their own thing'. The show that went out on the Christmas Eve was perhaps the most memorable of all, with Robert Merrill and Edith Piaf. The Little Sparrow, still mourning the death of her greatest love, the boxing champion Marcel Cerdan (in a plane crash in October 1949), was escorted to the Center Theater by her best friend, Marlene Dietrich. She sang several songs, including 'La Vie En Rose' and 'Hymne à l'Amour.'

The first few months of 1951 were turned over almost entirely to *The Big Show* and by now the content of some of the sketches had become more daring – with friendly slanging matches with guests which, on closer analysis, were often less friendly than they seemed. On 7 January Tallulah's special guest was Marlene Dietrich, who had recently become a grandmother. Many years later, Marlene became my intimate friend and told me that Tallulah had really got up her nose. Part of their sketch, for which I am indebted to my friend, ran thus:

MARLENE: Tallulah, I'd appreciate if it you didn't keep referring to me as a grandmother. You're overdoing it!

TALLULAH: Don't speak to me about overdoing it! Speak to your daughter!

MARLENE: That gown you have on. What colour is it?

TALLULAH: Well, it's a new colour ... battleship grey.

MARLENE: Battleship grey? It's lovely. But isn't it just a little tight around the boiler-room?

TALLULAH: Don't make any more cracks about my gown. I paid a pretty penny for it ...

MARLENE: My goodness, that *was* a clearance sale!

TALLULAH: What are you talking about? You should see the prices they soak you for dresses in Paris. I was soaked at every shop in Paris ...

MARLENE: Yes, I heard you were soaked in Paris!

TALLULAH: Marlene, please let us drop this nonsense. We're too close to go on like this. Now tell me, darling ... whatever happened to that divine chap you used to go out with? Er, Geoffrey?

MARLENE:	Oh, we split up …
TALLULAH:	Really, darling? For good?
MARLENE:	No, only temporarily. He got married. Tallulah, I wouldn't admit this to anyone else but one day last week, I had lunch alone …
TALLULAH:	NO-OH! Well, if you think that's something, as long as you've opened up to me, I'll tell you something. One day, about a month ago, I had breakfast alone …
MARLENE:	It's such a shame. Men seem to be disappearing …
TALLULAH:	They sure do …

In the programme that went out on 28 January, Tallulah was reunited with Gary Cooper. On 11 February she introduced Judy Garland and snarled under her breath at Jerry Lewis. Dee Engelbach and his team had encountered 'certain problems' when negotiating the deal with Lewis and, at the time of their visit to his office, had allegedly been greeted with a display of bad manners. This did not wash with Tallulah, who liked to refer to *The Big Show* production team as 'my boys'. Lewis might have been forgiven had he behaved on the actual day of the broadcast. He was over an hour late for his first rehearsal and, when Tallulah found him in his dressing-room, stripped down to his vest and shaving, she slapped him across the face with the script and levelled, 'That's for being rude to my boys, you no good son-of-a-bitch!'

On 15 February, Tallulah made another appearance in *Screen Director's Playhouse*, playing Judith Traherne in *Dark Victory* and another on 19 April in Fannie Hurst's *Humoresque*, directed by Jean Negulesco. *The Big Show* broadcasts in between included star turns from Beatrice Lillie, Billy Eckstine, Eddie Cantor, Carmen Miranda, and several appearances by the comic presenter, Fred Allen. All over America audiences rocked with laughter when the columnist Earl Wilson, famed for his high-pitched voice, asked Tallulah if on account of her basso-profundo growl she had ever been mistaken for a man on the telephone. Quick as a flash she replied, 'Never, darling. Have you?' The mood was less flippant, however, when along with Eleanor Roosevelt, she was presented with the Honorary Fellowship Award of Merit. The citation read, 'For your contribution to the Theater Arts, Americanism and Human Welfare.'

By the summer of 1951, *The Big Show* had dwindled somewhat in popularity; this was nothing whatsoever to do with Tallulah and her wealth of international guests but more to do with the rapidly increasing interest in television. On 13 June she was again rushed into the Westchester Hospital, suffering this time from an infected gall bladder but the indisposition only gave her the opportunity to relax and think. She decided that she would take *The Big Show* to London – the wheels were set in motion at once, and two days later a deal was clinched between NBC and the BBC. Tallulah was asked to choose a venue for the broadcast and she insisted that it would have to be the very pinnacle of the British entertainment scene, the London Palladium.

Tallulah's British fans expected her visit to be controversial, and it was. On 6 September her plane was just an hour or so from its destination when one of its engines failed and the pilot was forced to make an emergency landing, at Shannon in the Irish Republic. Wearing a three-quarter-length, pink chamois leather suit and a great deal of jewellery, Tallulah tore into the airport lounge and snarled at a reporter who asked her why she had not brought one of her dogs with her. 'You already know the answer to that. It's because of your goddamn quarantine regulations. And what the hell am I doing in this goose town, anyway?' When someone offered her food, she told them, 'Better shove it where the sun don't shine, darling. I'm not hungry.' She did, however, accept a cup of black coffee brought to her by Edie Smith. This, and an entire packet of cigarettes, seemed to calm her down, and before leaving Shannon she announced, 'I'm going to be in London for three weeks, darlings. I'll be seeing dozens of my old friends, some of whom I haven't seen for sixteen years. Now, if you'll excuse me, darlings, I have a plane to catch. God bless you all!'

She was in fine fettle when her plane landed at Heathrow and just managed to catch a glimpse of Princess Elizabeth and her two children leaving for Balmoral. Leaping down from the steps of the airport bus, almost losing her coat over her shoulders, and clenching a long cigarette-holder between her teeth, she yelled at the press, 'Isn't it just shattering, darlings, having an engine steal your thunder? And isn't your princess and her little ones so absolutely adorable?'

Crowded into the airport lounge were a hundred or so of the Gallery Girls who had clamoured to see her in the late twenties, rounder and older, and many of them with Gallery Girls of their own. No less enthusiastic than their mothers had been, they chanted 'Talle-lujah, Hallelujah!' and made a mad dash to get her autograph and shake her hand. Edie Smith turned and muttered to a reporter, 'As you can see, she's still the same old madcap Tallulah!' the young man then asked Tallulah if she was hoping to catch up with any of her 'blue-blooded boyfriends' and she cracked, 'No, darling. This time I'm going to be getting it together with their sons.' She then counteracted the statement by telling someone else, 'No, I don't go to parties any more. I now live in a country house surrounded by acres of beautiful flowers ... and I'm a good girl, now.'

This last utterance was shot to pieces when Tallulah held a press conference at the Ritz on the evening of 8 September, an event which was covered by a reporter from the *Daily Mail* who, as the newspaper was going to press, told the editor he wished to remain anonymous ... for sanity's sake:

With a hoarse cry of 'England, my England!' Miss Tallulah Bankhead stood on a chair in the Ritz ... and took a gulp of champagne from her left shoe ... Waiters averted their eyes as Tallulah boomed at them, 'Darling, bring me a drink!' For two hours this sun-tanned tornado in black silk – 'It's last year's, but it's paid for!' – put on a dazzling cabaret act for 200 guests. Slinking up and down like an amiable jaguar she growled, 'Churchill is my god. I'm just mad about Britain. I love you all like crazy!' ... A middle-aged man who kissed her hand was treated to an impromptu Charleston. The pink-shaded candelabra tinkled as Tallulah, eyes rolling and hips churning, kicked and danced and sang hoarsely. The dance came to an abrupt end when one of Tallulah's stockings broke loose from its moorings. 'I never wear them normally, darling,' she beamed. 'But tonight I had to be polite!' Then she swept out, leaving the room and the guests looking as though a tidal wave had just broken over them.

On 16 September 1951 the Palladium raised its famous big red curtain and Tallulah was greeted with a thunderous applause. Stepping up to the microphone, she boomed, 'Bless you, darlings! Now, let me see. What was I saying when I left England 16 years ago? Oh, yes – make mine a double!' She then introduced her guests, who included Beatrice Lillie, George Sanders, Jack Buchanan, Vera Lynn, Robb Wilton, Laurence Olivier and Vivien Leigh. Though Tallulah's 'ersatz venom' was kept very much under control, she found it hard trying to smile and sound pleasant when introducing the star who had 'robbed' her of Scarlett O'Hara. And there was no stopping her when she told the Palladium audience about her hatred of Bette Davis, which had intensified over the last year since the release of *All About Eve* – not only had her greatest rival 'hijacked' Margo Channing, the role Tallulah had created on the stage, the much-despised Anne Baxter had been assigned to her co-star. Now, Tallulah pronounced vehemently, 'Do you think I don't *know* who's been spreading gossip about me and my temperament out there in Hollywood, darlings, where they made that film, *All About Me*? After all the nice things I've said about that hag, Bette Davis! When I get hold of her, I'll tear every hair out of her moustache!' There were more gibes, less malicious, when Beatrice Lillie asked her if she had seen her début on American television. 'I just loved the close-ups, darling,' Tallulah levelled. 'Your face looked like four yards of corduroy.' She received her comeuppance in her skit with George Sanders. When she told him, 'Darling, I've decided to grow old gracefully,' he retorted, 'And so you have, darling!'

Although Tallulah's British fans adored *The Big Show* and lamented the fact that it was a one-off, the critics were not keen on 'May the Good Lord Bless and Keep You' and they took her to task over her dramatic but sincere rendition of a poem by

Gene Fowler, 'The *Jervis Bay*'. This recounted the fate of the famous freighter which, on 5 November 1940, had been sunk by the Germans after deliberately engaging in battle with their pocket-battleship, the *Admiral Scheer*, so that the rest of its convoy could escape.

One of the problems with the British, from the viewpoint of several of the realist singers who declined to sing in Britain was that, like the Americans and unlike the French, they did not care to be reminded about the darker side of life. Edith Piaf, who had spent part of the previous Christmas with Tallulah, had told her – and over the years would never alter her opinion – that the British had never been into realism and probably never would be. The *News Chronicle* dismissed Tallulah's delivery of the poem as 'a most regrettable breach of taste', and another critic wrote that it was 'as out of place as a boogie-woogie on the organ at Canterbury Cathedral'. Tallulah apologized profusely for her mistake and added, 'I have nothing but praise, love and affection for the British public.' This did not deter Robert Lewis Shayon from writing in the *Saturday Review*:

> Miss Bankhead begins her season ... still billed as 'glamorous and unpredictable'. She is definitely no longer the second. Her vain, rude and temperamental role has worn very thin. She would be well advised to try something fresh.

Tallulah greeted such unnecessary criticism with a few choice but unrepeatable words over the telephone to Mr Shayon and, after saying goodbye to her London friends, she flew to Paris for the French version of *The Big Show*. The performance was broadcast on 23 September from the Empire, one of the city's oldest and best-loved music halls. Tallulah surprised everyone with her fluency in the French language – including Mistinguett, 75 years old and still active in every sense of the word. On meeting Tallulah backstage, La Miss piped for all to hear, 'Mademoiselle Bankhead, you are probably the only woman in the world who has handled more pricks than I have, on *and* off the stage.' The greatest revue star of France should have been on the bill but she had been pipped to the post by her arch-rival, Joséphine Baker, whom she always referred to as 'Banana Tits' but only when she was being kind. Also in the show were Gracie Fields, Georges Guétary, the actress Françoise Rosay and Joan Fontaine. The orchestra was conducted by Paul Durand, one of the stalwarts of the French *chanson*, and the Mistress of Ceremonies howled with laughter when she read the review in *France-Soir*, in which he had described her as 'the great, irresistible one who resembles a Sunday-school teacher'.

On her return to New York, Tallulah announced that she was about to begin writing her autobiography. 'I won't be pulling too many punches,' she said, sending many a shudder through the American and English showbusiness world. With her astonishing flair for honesty, she would be expected to unlock many closets which might have been better left closed, particularly in an age when excessive drinking, drugs, and casual mixed sex – if generally accepted and even promoted in some theatrical circles – was frowned upon by the average man and woman in the street. Tallulah did not care about this. For some time she had been saying to people, 'I don't care what they say about me, so long as they say something!' and this adage spilled over when she was speaking of others. Thus, with time on her hands – *The Big Show* was still raging strong after its summer break but taking up only her weekends – she bought a small tape recorder and began recording her thoughts, memories and opinions.

During this period Tallulah smoked more than ever before – often as many as 150 cigarettes a day – and to take away the foul taste in her mouth she increased her daily intake of bourbon from one to two bottles. Each evening, the tapes were replenished by her secretary and what had been dictated (or ranted) was typed up, ready to be edited into a readable text by Richard Maney. Tallulah was interviewed on 4 December by Don Iddon, one of her favourite British reporters:

The book's to be called *Oh, My Foes! Ah, My Friends!* That's a quote from Edna St Vincent Millay. It will be in the very best taste, darling. Nothing scurrilous. Frank, by all means, but in the best of taste! I've been called a garrulous extrovert, a cello-voiced witch, a honey-haired holocaust, a heretic whose vitality if harnessed to the Sahara might transform that sandy waste into another Eden. Now, my fans are going to know the truth!'

And when Iddon asked her, for his article in the *Daily Mail*, if she intended telling the truth about her age, she growled, 'I was born in 1903, so that makes me 48, darling. And if any cunt contests that, I'll part his hair with a polo mallet.'

Soon after the Don Iddon interview, Tallulah changed her mind about her title of her autobiography, thinking it a little too highbrow to catch on. Even so, she retained a part of the Edna St Vincent Millay poem for the end of the book because, she said, Millay's work ideally expressed her own personal plight and philosophy. The fact that she had been actively bisexual and capable of expressing these feelings in stanzas of great beauty impressed her:

My candle burns at both ends;
It will not last the night;
But oh, my foes and oh, my friends
It gives a lovely light.

Meanwhile, Tallulah was also steeling herself for the Evelyn Cronin trial. Initially, she was so desperate to forgive and forget that she and Donald Seawell engineered to 'bump into' Evelyn in the District Attorney's office. 'Just go dig up the goddamn money, and we'll call it quits,' Tallulah told her. The plea was ignored and the trial opened on 11 December 1950, at the General Sessions Court. It was covered en masse by the world media – as Tallulah later said, afforded more newspaper space than the ceasefire negotiations for the Korean War – and relayed to the British press by Don Iddon. Evelyn Cronin was defended by Senator Fred G Morritt of Brooklyn, of whom Tallulah scathed, 'He picked up all he knows about law from singing baritone in the radio show, *Lucky Strike Hour*, you know.' She had the ever-faithful Donald Seawell on her side and, ironically for her, the judge was Harold Stevens, the first black man to ever sit on a General Sessions Bench.

The first day's proceedings went badly. A long queue formed outside the court house, fighting over the 85 seats like an important première at a small-town theatre. Tallulah arrived on cue, looking nervous, but signing autographs all the same. She was flanked by Donald Seawell and William Langford and had purchased a dull-brown Hattie Carnegie dress especially for the occasion, though on account of the bitter cold she kept it covered most of the time by her mink. She told a reporter, 'Of course I'm nervous, darling – I'm only human!' The defence, however, seemed intent on playing dirty, as was disclosed when Fred Morritt addressed the panel of prospective jurors, 'Certain names, foul language, profanity, perversion and criminality may have to be brought out in court. My defendant will take the stand and tell you what she saw with her own eyes and heard with her own ears.' He then explained why Evelyn Cronin had been compelled to alter her employer's cheques – the fact that they had been made out for 'booze, drugs and sex', all unknown quantities of whose current market value Tallulah had not been aware, and that Cronin had been forced by fear of brutality to add a couple of noughts to her employer's cheques in order to make up her own losses. Tallulah reacted to this revelation like a viper, declaring, 'I didn't have to *buy* sex! I've never had to stoop *that* low!' The jury were sympathetic towards her but, when their spokesman refused to accept that Tallulah's private life could have had anything to do with her maid kiting cheques, he and several other members were discharged and replaced.

On the second day of the trial, Fred Morritt's remarks became more vitriolic. He announced, 'Tallulah Bankhead spent a fortune on cocaine, marijuana, booze, Scotch and champagne ... and sex.' Then, after promising to reveal the names of those with whom Tallulah had smoked pot – including 'a very distinguished radio and television star' – Morritt told the jury that Tallulah had taught Evelyn how to roll 'tea' (marijuana) cigarettes and that she had become so proficient that she had been able to roll 98 in five hours. He concluded, 'Reluctantly, we are going to prove that the lady was never sober, or rarely so. She not only earned more than

$3,000 a week, she hired on that scale. The money was spent on sex! What is more, this woman also physically beat Mrs Cronin at least 50 times!' At this stage, Tallulah began laughing loudly. This developed into a genuine fit of coughing and Morritt begged Judge Stevens to tell her to 'shut her mouth'. The judge reciprocated that he would make that decision, to which Tallulah stormed out of the court house muttering, 'I've got bronchitis, for Christ's sakes. The next thing they'll have me vivisecting my fucking dogs!' Later that afternoon, she breezed into the rehearsal room at the Center Theater. The guests for that week's *The Big Show* included Phil Silvers and Sarah Vaughan, who had listened to fragments of the proceedings on the radio and who were surprised that she was still in one piece. She quipped, 'Well, don't just sit there, darlings. Roll me a reefer!'

On the third day of the trial, probably aware that the whole affair could quite easily turn into a Lupe Velez catfight, Judge Stevens declared that all witnesses should be excluded from the court until required to take the stand. The press could hardly fail to notice that Tallulah was the only witness that day but she made up for being banished to the witness room, the only place in the building where she was allowed to smoke, by answering whatever questions the press flung her way. She said, 'This Cronin woman worked in burlesque before I was born. Her lawyer ought to be in burlesque right now. I'm only here on a matter of principle.' When the news of this particular admission reached Fred Morritt, he demanded a renewed trial on account of Tallulah's 'gratuitous remarks to an irrevocably prejudiced press'. His request was denied.

Tallulah had also been doing her homework – or at least Glenn Anders had, on her behalf. Anders had first encountered Evelyn Cronin in 1913, when she had indeed been working in burlesque, doing *The Dance of the Hours* with the Lovenberg Sisters in Bridgeport, Connecticut. Anders was dispatched to interview the old ladies, and the outcome of this unorthodox detective work – that at the time of the Lovenbergs' first meeting with Evelyn, she had been on a stage wearing nothing but a G-string – delighted Tallulah no end. Though she had agreed not to visit the court house again until summoned to take the stand, she did feed whatever information she could to the press, via Anders, who drove to the court house each morning with Donald Seawell.

There was an outburst next day when Morritt accused Tallulah's lawyer of 'soliciting for public approval' by discussing the trial and pleading her innocence on a television programme and he again demanded that the case be declared a mistrial and Seawell be cited for contempt. Again, he was overruled and Judge Stevens granted Seawell permission to call an accountant from the District Attorney's office to the witness stand. His name was Bernard Dolgin and under oath he stated that when Tallulah had visited his department, sex, or the payment for sex, had not been discussed at all. Furthermore, Dolgin stressed that the accused had 'of her own free will' admitted that the stolen money had been spent on personal expenses, clothing, travel and tips, and some money on liquor, but not a penny on cocaine, marijuana or drugs'. Dolgin's statement was relayed to Tallulah, who quipped, 'And the shit's only started to hit the fan!'

Tallulah took the witness stand on 18 December. She arrived at the court house with Donald Seawell and a photographer was at hand to snap him lifting her over the huge pile of snow that had been swept off the pavement into the gutter – it appeared in a newspaper the next day with the caption: LEGAL AID. Inside the building, huddled into her mink and looking very much the executive actress in her horn-rimmed spectacles, her 25-minute appearance was, certainly for the media, something of a letdown because the words 'sex' and 'drugs' were not used once. The questions were strictly routine, centring around the actual amounts of the original cheques, as opposed to what her former maid had kited them too. Tallulah's 'venomous expression' throughout did not go unobserved by the reporter from *Time* magazine, who wrote, 'Theater-goers who watched fully expected Miss Bankhead to pull a small, pearl-handled revolver from her handbag and shoot both the defendant and her counsel!' the next day, however, Fred Morritt yelled so much at Donald Seawell that

Judge Stevens had him forcibly seated and threatened to bar him from the court unless he modified his behaviour. Evelyn Cronin took the stand and admitted again that Tallulah had regularly hit her and used bad language. After refusing to say aloud some of the things she had heard, she was allowed to write them down, and these scraps of paper were handed to the jury. According to Tallulah's 1972 biographer, Lee Israel, one of these sheets is still in the Cronin-Bankhead files, inscribed with the words, 'I will give you cancer of the breast, you old cunt.'

In her evidence the next day, Evelyn told the court that during the tour of *Private Lives*, Tallulah, along with several friends and members of her entourage, had regularly smoked pot. Fred Morritt even produced Harry Blaisdell, the owner of the seaside house in Marblehead, who dragged up the story of Tallulah's one and only night in jail. According to Blaisdell, Evelyn had herself paid the bail for her employer's release and she had also footed the bill for the backstreet lodging-house, food for the entourage, petrol and a temporary chauffeur for her car because no one had been in any fit state to drive. Morritt then faced the jury and said, 'Mrs Cronin spent this money under authorization from Miss Bankhead. It doesn't matter whether it was spent on booze, marijuana, Coca-Cola or cocaine.' Again, the subject of Tallulah's colourful language was brought up when Blaisdell repeated what she had said to the two police officers who had arrested her.

On the last day of the proceedings before the Christmas break, the question of Evelyn Cronin's so-called morality was brought out into the open. She admitted that in her younger days she had been a stripper but insisted, 'I only went down to my bra and panties, like they do on Broadway today.' She then confessed, under cross-examination, that while working in burlesque she had heard a great deal of bad language, and that four-letter words had never shocked her at all. When questioned about the kited cheques, she explained that Tallulah's rage had been so violent the first time she had 'amended' a cheque that thenceforth she had changed them without her employer's knowledge – solely to reimburse herself for paying William Langford's allowance. The bombshell came when she admitted that legally her name was not Cronin – she was living with a John Cronin, a stagehand who was still married to somebody else. And while the jury were still taking this in, the prosecution announced that the accused had once been questioned by a San Francisco store detective over a brooch she had attempted to steal. Evelyn's reply, that she had picked the brooch up off the floor, caused a ripple of amusement in the court house.

Fred Morritt's summing-up of the case, after the Christmas break, was as pathetic as Tallulah expected it to be. He told the jury, 'This is a dispute between two elderly ladies – one who tries to look young, and one who shows her age rather gracefully. Keats said, "Beauty is truth, truth beauty", and I would like to dedicate this poem to love and justice. I hope that your consciences are clear, and that you will not send an innocent woman to jail. There but for the grace of God goes your mother, sister, or loved one.' Evelyn Cronin was suitably attired for the occasion – she had turned up in a bonnet and shawl.

'Morritt droned on for 72 minutes,' Don Iddon reported. 'Several times, he reminded the court that William Langford was 21 years Tallulah's junior, but that this of course was only her business. On cue, the accused wept.' The prosecution, Jerome Kidder, referring to Evelyn Cronin's futile excuses for stealing from her employer, remonstrated to the jury, 'If in any case of larceny the prosecution has to trace where and how this money was spent, then we might as well shut up shop!' Bernard Dolgin then produced Tallulah's expenditure accounts and the jury saw for themselves that most of her 'incidental' expenses had been paid for by Tallulah's personal cheques and not with Evelyn Cronin's money. This resulted in yet another outburst from Fred Morritt, who now petitioned Judge Stevens to dismiss all charges against his client because of insufficient evidence.

Needless to say, the next day Evelyn Cronin was found guilty on three counts of grand larceny and bailed for $1,000. She and Fred Morritt faced Judge Stevens again on 24 January 1952 –

she to be given a one-to-two-years' prison sentence and he to miss a contempt charge by the skin of his teeth.

The aftermath of the Cronin case was also typically Tallulah. Because *she* pleaded for clemency, petitioning Judge Stevens to take into consideration her former maid's age and infirmity, the prison sentence was suspended and when Evelyn Cronin died in May 1953, aged 61, Tallulah admitted that she felt deep shame for what had happened – not that she should have done, of course. Two months after the case Tallulah filed a suit for an estimated $30,000 against her accountant, Benjamin Nadel, 'for failing to exercise due proper care in examining cheques drawn on my account', and won her case.

13

A Blithe Spirit
With a Rusty Voice

Tallulah received a pleasant surprise between the end of the Cronin trial and Judge Stevens's summing-up when, on 17 January 1952, the New York Philharmonic, under the direction of Guido Cantelli, premièred *A Laurentian Overture*, composed in her honour by the cellist Alan Shulman and dedicated in her name. Shulman had been engaged by Meredith Willson to play in *The Big Show* and Tallulah was so touched that she invited him and his wife to Windows for the weekend. She told the press that the piece had made her cry, adding, 'I guess I'm just an emotional gal, at heart. Until I heard Alan's beautiful music, only old Wagner could ever sweep me away!' When a reporter asked her for her opinion of the Laurentians, however, she was stumped for a reply – she did not know who or what they were, and had to be filled in, to which she responded, 'Well in that case, darling, some of my best friends are Canadians!'

On 20 April 1952, NBC radio finally succumbed to the upsurge in popularity of television and dropped *The Big Show*. For nostalgia's sake, Tallulah's guests on the last show included three who had appeared in the first: Ethel Merman, Portland Hoffa and Fred Allen. She then embarked on a nationwide tour of lecture-engagements for women's clubs, earning $1,500 each evening doing nothing more than telling her life story, with a few songs and more-or-less clean jokes thrown in for good measure. In Dallas she was heckled by the Temperance Brigade, whose spokeswoman demanded to know if she was drinking a real cocktail. Tallulah held up the half-pint glass and said, 'Darlings, I only wish it were!' She was drinking neat gin, coloured with fruit peel.

On 29 September, her much-talked-about autobiography was published – in America by Harper and Brothers and in Britain by Victor Gollancz. She had decided to keep matters simple by calling it *Tallulah*. The finished product was claimed by many who knew her to be not so much about Tallulah but a lengthy catalogue of 'Tallulahisms' edited by Richard Maney. In truth, it had been ghost-written by him but 90 per cent of its content had been dictated into a tape-recorder. As such it was very bold for its day, dealing honestly with sex, booze, drugs and a host of subjects which most publishers considered taboo. It was the best-selling book in America for the 1952–3 season – the first print-run of 100,000 sold out practically as soon as it hit the shelves. It remained on the best-seller list for eight months and was kept in print for seven years. Harry Truman had asked to read the proofs and on 4 August had written to her, 'It is undoubtedly the most interesting book I've had in my hands since becoming president ... the demand on you for more books in the same vein as this one will undoubtedly be your profession from now on.'

Tallulah subjected herself to a marathon publicity shoot with the photographer Richard Avedon, insisting upon every single one of her classic poses: pouting, smoking, laughing, crying, having a screaming session with an imaginary antagonist over the telephone – each of her moods snapped as she was sitting up in bed, surrounded by her dogs and as many copies of her book as could be arranged about her. She was so anxious to get everything right that she missed the ashtray when stubbing out a cigarette ... setting fire to her Maltese terrier ...

Thirty American newspapers serialized *Tallulah*. In Britain, it was serialized by the *Daily Express*. Cecil Wilson, reviewing it in the *Daily Mail*, called it, 'A slick, slangy, self-absorbed outburst of wild life, breathless with passion for the theatre.'

In New York, during a television plug for the book, Tallulah was filmed sitting at a desk in front of a mock-Renaissance backdrop when Adlai Stevenson, the Democratic leader, 'just happened' to be filming at another desk, just yards away on the same set ... Naturally, she had to bellow her very individual support for her friend, by bad-mouthing the opposition, of whom she had recently said, 'The Republican party's an old ship that should be placed in dry dock to have the barnacles scraped off its bottom.' Afterwards, she joined forces with several Democrat stalwarts – Ethel Barrymore, Henry Fonda, Richard Rodgers were but three – in endorsing Stevenson, telling a reporter, 'I was instrumental in getting Truman into the White House, darling. So why not this man?'

A few days before Christmas, she was invited to New York's Pen and Pencil Club to a 'literary' bash which had been organized in her honour, now that she was a bona fide member of the writing fraternity. Harper and Brothers had taken the liberty of inviting most of New York's society, including a large number of celebrities she could not stand. By and large, once she had hunted these people down and insulted them one way or another, Tallulah stuck with her friends. She was photographed in varying stages of inebriation with Zsa Zsa and Eva Gabor, Sid Caesar, Beatrice Lillie and Vivian Blaine, and when the singer Fritzi Scheff performed her famous number, 'Kiss Me Again', Tallulah knelt at the singer's feet, and kissed her hand. Then she offered a recital of her own, which included 'I'll Be Seeing You' and 'Silent Night', after which she blasted into the ambience with a call for the last waltz, announcing, 'It's four in the morning, darlings, and my real fans and myself are about to get down to a real jam-session. So, would the rest of you lovely, divine people please fuck off to your homes.' Most of the 'non-friends' were sensible enough to take her advice and two hours later Tallulah was still on her feet, belting out hymns. The next day, Edie Smith took the call from President Truman who wanted to congra-tulate Tallulah on the sales of her book. She was in the middle of her favourite television soap opera, and asked him to call back after it had finished. He did ...

Between October 1952 and March 1953, Tallulah appeared five times in NBC-TV's *All-Star Revue*, again produced by her friend Dee Engelbach and musically directed by Meredith Willson. Her costumes were by Hattie Carnegie and her television début, on 11 October, saw her in a sketch with Ethel Barrymore and Groucho Marx.

These shows included another close friend, Patsy Kelly. Temporarily down on her luck, the actress from the famous Hal Roach comedies had recently been taken under Tallulah's wing and, at the end of 1952, took up residence at Windows. According to Kenneth Anger, it was a lesbian relationship and Tallulah did not deny it when asked. Shrugging her shoulders, she said, 'Some of my best friends are lesbians! What's new?'

There was also talk of a one-woman show, *A Night With Tallulah*, which Engelbach wanted to stage on Broadway. Tallulah shelved this for the time being – she was having too much fun promoting her book and did not wish to be tied down. She appeared in a couple of radio plays, *All About Eve* and *Magnificent Obsession*, because these kept her in touch with her fans and did not take up too much of her time, and in March 1953 she made a joint appeal with President Eisenhower to raise funds for the Red Cross.

On 20 May 1953, Tallulah began a season of cabaret recitals at the Sands Hotel in Las Vegas for a staggering $20,000 a week: if she had deliberated about the Broadway show, she had not hesitated for one moment before signing the contract for this one. There was just the one regret, the fact that her two most devoted friends, Edie Smith and Glenn Anders, declined to travel with her. Edie had recently suffered a fall. Anders, now in his mid-sixties, had learned his lesson during the Cronin affair when one newspaper had suggested that he had 'pimped' for her on a number of occasions by introducing her to handsome young men. Anders told her to her face that so far as the distinguished Vegas crowd were concerned, she would have to 'mumble through' without him. Tallulah thought about ending their friendship, decided not to, and left for Las Vegas with Patsy Kelly.

Working the Sands Hotel, she declared, was a doddle.

Neither was she expected to be on stage for long – most evenings no more than 40 minutes, after a warm up from a number of regular nightclub acts, including the Clark Brothers, Virginia Hall, and a young ballad singer named Merv Griffin. Accompanied by the Ray Sinatra Orchestra, she strode on, wearing a white, floor-length Hattie Carnegie gown, scanned the equally elegant front row of stage and screen stars – they included Marlene Dietrich, Lucille Ball and Desi Arnaz, Jane Powell and Montgomery Clift – and bellowed, 'AAAAAH, MAH GAWD!' Then, as the orchestra was about to play her into her opening number, she added, 'If anybody tells you, darlings, that this is my first time in a nightclub, don't believe them. I've spent half my life in saloons – only this is the first time I've actually been paid for it!' She followed this up with her baritone drawling of 'What Do I Care' and 'You Go To My Head', the latter song being directed straight at Marlene, who had sung it in one of her films. She chortled, as if reading Marlene's thoughts, 'It's the microphone that's flat, darling, not me!' Then she did several impressions, told a few risqué jokes, danced the black-bottom, recited a part of Dorothy Parker's 'The Waltz', and added, 'Did I ever tell you, darlings, that the divine Miss Parker was into horticulture? She told me only the other day, "You can lead a whore to culture, but you sure as hell can't make her drink!" And did I ever tell you, darlings, about the dreadful dilemma I faced when all the taxis in New York went on strike and I was forced to ride ... on the subway? I'd never been down there in my life, and I said to the darling man on the ticket control, "Darling, be divine and get me a Pullman to Fifth Avenue!" ' Then, whilst the audience were wiping the tears of laughter from their eyes, she launched into 'I'll Be Seeing You' and brought tears of a different kind – and a 15-minute standing ovation.

Tallulah's three-week stint at the Sands Hotel was a fabulous success, though she did spend a hefty portion of her salary at the casino – a problem that was rectified, in a fashion, by the wily Donald Seawell, who arranged with the casino manager to credit every dollar of Tallulah's account for just one cent and pay her winnings pro-rata. Even so, her account ended up in the red.

The Las Vegas season also introduced a new man to her life, for since the Cronin case she had kept her act clean. This was her supporting act, Merv Griffin, whose introduction into her affections was bizarre, but typical. It took place in Griffin's dressing-room, when Tallulah was wearing a low-cut dress, and the singer's gaze mistakenly fell on her cleavage. The newspapers had reported her recent mammoplasty, and of how she had proudly displayed her 'new' breasts to Marlene Dietrich and Otto Preminger in front of hundreds of people at the Stork Club. Exposing one of her breasts now for Griffin to squeeze, she told him, 'See, darling, it's all me. Not plastic!' Later that same evening, Tallulah invited him back to her dressing-room for a drink – she called him into the bathroom, where he found her squatting ingloriously on the toilet with her Hattie Carnegie gown hoisted up to her chin.

Griffin told the story of how she once refused to go anywhere near him when he had laryngitis, saying, 'I only have to listen to Jimmy Durante, and my throat's sore.' She then recounted the earlier episode with Somerset Maugham when, through no fault of her own, she had mimicked his stutter, and added, 'I only have to be told about a car crash, darling, and I feel bruised all day.'

There was a publicized incident at the Sands Hotel casino when, made aware of Donald Seawell's one-cent limit, Tallulah seized all the money she could lay her hands on, won a small fortune at the tables and spent the lot treating those about her to cocktails. She became boisterous and began telling dirty jokes but when a bouncer approached her and told her to behave herself, he was recompensed with such a tirade of filth that he picked her up, tucked her under his arm like a parcel and carried her off the premises. A large crowd had gathered in the foyer and Tallulah had lifted up her head and yelled in her best Southern drawl, 'Well, isn't anybody gonna come up and fuck me tonight?'

Immediately after this episode, Tallulah travelled to Hollywood, where she was contracted to appear in Tay Garnett's *Main Street to Broadway*. She played herself in a sketch with Agnes Moorehead; the cast also included Rex

Harrison, Lilli Palmer, Mary Martin and all three Barrymores – Lionel making his final screen appearance, though he remained on MGM's salary list until his death the following year. The film, premièred on 13 October 1953, was not a great success – and neither was the romance that had blossomed when Tallulah had been making it.

During rehearsals she had observed a handsome, brooding young man sitting in a darkened corner of the studio, chain-smoking and fidgeting constantly. Later, in the canteen, he introduced himself as James Dean and, though nothing is known of their subsequent conversation, Tallulah arranged a date with him which Jimmy, typically, had not kept, though they would be destined to meet again very soon.

A few weeks later, Tallulah was appointed chairwoman of a committee founded to raise $10,000 for the W C Handy Blind Foundation and on the same day she allowed a television production crew to drop in at Windows to film her with her dogs and favourite possessions. She had decided to put her house on the market not because she was short of resources but because, of late, many of her friends had found getting there too much of an ordeal. 'It has become just another home for old actors,' she told the cameraman. 'And you know, darling, I *hate* to be alone. Being alone is worse than having a fatal illness. That's why I have to return to New York, where there's plenty of fresh air.'

Windows was sold very quickly, without profit, and Tallulah at once moved into an imposing, 12-roomed town-house at 230 East Sixty-Second Street. It had a fireplace in each of the six main rooms and a small garden with sycamore trees – enough, she said, to remind her of her last home. She told a reporter from the *New York Times*, 'It is to this house, if I may borrow from Thomas Gray, that I may lie, at evening's close, to sweet repast and calm repose.'

On 5 January, Tallulah appeared in her first television drama, playing the title role in Ibsen's *Hedda Gabler* opposite Luther Adler and Eugenia Rawls. One critic wrote, 'She is a lioness playing Puss in Boots.' As she emerged from the studio, James Dean was hanging about the corridor, Jimmy marched up to her, hoisted up her skirt as she wrapped her legs around his waist and the pair feigned copulation against the wall. The tea-lady, pushing her trolley, could only stare in amazement as Tallulah asked her, 'Well, darling. How was it for *you*?' Jimmy then took his idol out on the date he had promised her months before. 'I got to play with his bongos,' Tallulah later confessed, though for once she was the one who ended up red-faced when he announced, as he was seeing her into her cab, 'You remind me of Edith Piaf. She's another prima-donna bitch whose mouth gives me a hard-on. The next time we meet, I'm going to stick my dick in yours!' So far as is known, Tallulah never encountered Jimmy Dean again and she was heartbroken over his death the following year, saying, 'God has taken away one of His most talented and most beautiful children.'

That same day, 5 January, *Tallulah* was published in paperback, its first print run of 400,000 copies selling within a matter of days. In early August, Tallulah began her second season at the Sands Hotel – this time for a month, supported by Chuck Nelson and the opera star Robert Merrill, who wrote about the occasion in his extraordinary autobiography, *Between Acts: An Irreverent Look At Opera and Other Madness*. Merrill bumped into Tallulah in the bar at the Sands Hotel and, when he informed her that he had been engaged to go on stage after her, she boomed for all to hear, 'You poor, misguided bastard! The only act who could follow *me* is King Kong with a hard-on!' She then filled everyone's ears with a description of her recent breast surgery, exposing one for inspection as she had with Merv Griffin, 'My bazooms are absolutely virginal, darling. Oh, lawdy, have a bite!'

The big event of 1954, however, was Tallulah's return to Broadway on 15 September in *Dear Charles*, adapted from Marc-Gilbert Sauvagon's popular French comedy *Les Enfants d'Edouard* by Fred Jackson. Thinking the central role of the matriarch ideal for Tallulah, now in her early fifties and having assured everyone that she was no longer interested in playing flappers, the producer – the then relatively inexperienced Robert Aldrich – sent a young man named Arthur Penn to 'proposition' her at her town-house. Although Penn had worked on numerous television shows, *Dear Charles* was his first theatre play. He was brash but sensible, talented and, Aldrich believed, capable of taming the tigress. He could not have been more wrong.

Tallulah wined and dined her visitor and chatted away the entire evening without allowing him to get a word in edgeways. Then, at midnight when he was preparing to leave, she began poring laboriously over the script. To begin with, she disliked her character's name and thought that it should be changed. She was discussing this with Penn when Dolores, her Maltese terrier, suddenly jumped into her lap. Penn agreed – *Dolores Darvel* did not sound altogether bad. Tallulah then began working out how she would tackle her role as the mother of three sons and still play an extension of herself. This was when Penn put his foot down, informing her that she would play the character, or forget the whole idea. Tallulah gave way and because he had stood up to her, Arthur Penn was that night granted the honour of putting her to bed and holding her hand until she was asleep.

Henceforth, however, Penn's association with Tallulah was anything but plain sailing. She allowed him to mould her into shape for Dolores Darvel only because she was desperate to get back into a play worthy of her talents and once this was effected she was ready to dominate – so much so that it is a wonder *Dear Charles* survived its pre-Broadway tour. Tallulah hated everyone in the cast with the exception of Fred Keating and a young actor named William Roerick, who played one of her sons but, if she was sexually interested in Roerick, the feeling was in no way mutual. Furthermore, she argued so much with Arthur Penn that he stormed out of the production, allowing her to go back to playing herself for a little while, which of course increased the takings at the box office.

Certain that the Broadway success of *Dear Charles* would rival that of *Private Lives* – a brainwave that came to her one Sunday morning when the company were in Hyannisport – Tallulah had a sudden impulse to call the fashion designer Gene Coffin at his New York home and requisition 'an evening gown, a morning dress, a cocktail dress, and something to cut flowers in'. She also demanded that Coffin fly out to Hyannisport that very afternoon with the designs. The man panicked, but the designs were ready within the hour – sketched on any scraps of paper he could find at such short notice when the shops were closed – and Tallulah drove to the airport herself to pick him up.

Tallulah fell in love with Coffin's designs and, unable to make up her mind which ones to have, ordered every single one. The fittings took place at her home after the tour, when the designer was accompanied by his nervous, easily shocked, middle-aged Italian seamstress. Most of the dresses fitted beautifully but Tallulah declared that the cocktail dress was too heavy. When the seamstress tried to argue, albeit gently, that it was not, Tallulah ripped it off and began running around the room in just her panties, screaming that all Italians were 'shits' and that this one 'had been screwed by Mussolini'. The little seamstress, thinking herself about to be murdered, rushed out into the street and had a fit of hysterics.

Once she had calmed down, of course, Tallulah thought the whole episode hilarious. By way of an apology, she brought the woman back and sent out for the largest bunch of flowers she had probably ever seen – and then tore a strip off Coffin for not forewarning the seamstress about her ferocious temper in the first place.

Dear Charles premièred at New York's Morosco Theater on 15 September 1954 and ran for 155 performances. Most critics liked it but came to the conclusion that it was just an average production that had succeeded only because of Tallulah's reputation and name. Walter Kerr wrote in the *Herald Tribune*:

> We are getting Bankhead in comfortable beige, Bankhead in dazzling red, Bankhead in sequins, Bankhead with flowers, Bankhead enveloped in smoke. I'd say that the play was appalling for this day and age, but that it's difficult to remain honestly appalled while you are rapt with admiration. A blithe spirit with a rusty voice is at work here! Hail to her!

That other 'Tallulah-friendly' journalist, Cecil Wilson, having expressed his surprise and delight that she could play a middle-aged matriarch and still thrill the Gallery Girls and Boys, concluded in a feature that was relayed to the *Daily Mail*,

> Somehow she hammers the play so persuasively into her own shape, and the force of her performance leaves the rest of the cast with so few legs to stand on between them. I used to think of Tallulah Bankhead as largely an illusion: a lope, a croak, a shrug, a toss of the hair, a puff of cigarette smoke. Now, after seeing how she can turn a play inside out to suit her own theatrical ends, I accept her as a true technician.

On the strength of Wilson's piece, a British reporter named Macdonald Daly was sent to New York to get an exclusive on Tallulah for *Illustrated*. Interviewing her at her still-retained suite at the Elysée Hotel, however, resulted in a feature headed 'Pets of the Famous: Tallulah's Terrier Is the Best Yet!' – an in-depth portrait of the only important Dolores in the world, her dog. Tallulah offered a potted history of the Maltese, showed Daly the pile of soggy newspapers in one corner of her bedroom which represented Dolores's toilet and mentioned nothing at all about her love life, probably because she was going through a rare but temporary period where nothing much was happening in this department. There was a new young Canadian secretary, Philip Hall, who admitted that though he and Tallulah had several times shared a bed after all-night drinking sessions, he had never had sex with her. This left only her co-star, William Roerick, whom she made one last attempt to seduce during the closing week of *Dear Charles*. Roerick's rejection, 'I want nothing whatsoever to do with you – you have the most hideous public personality I've ever known,' was met with a curt, 'And fuck you too, darling.'

At the end of 1955, Tallulah went to see her friend Jean Dalrymple, now the director of the City Center, and begged her to find her a part she would really be able to do justice to. Dalrymple came up with Blanche Dubois, in Tennessee Williams's *A Streetcar Named Desire*, a role that had been written for her in the first place. Though the playwright was loosely regarded as a friend – she had been touched by his recognition of her vulnerability when Williams had told a journalist, 'Tallulah is the strongest of all the hurt people I've ever known in my life,' – Tallulah had never liked his work and had steadfastly refused to watch the film because it featured 'enemies' Marlon Brando and Vivien Leigh. However, when her 'sibyl', Estelle Winwood, assured her that Blanche would be the role of her career – 'And how many times have I heard *that* one, darling?' – she agreed to attend a private screening, accompanied by Estelle, Williams, Dalrymple and a few friends. 'The film was amazing,' she said afterwards. 'Amazing that Brando never once scratched his private parts!' She then told Tennessee Williams that her Blanche would not be a carbon copy of Leigh's and added her conditions for taking on the revival. The production would open at an out-of-state theatre of her own choice for the try-outs and there would be no more than 16 performances when or if it reached New York. She then told Jean Dalrymple that she would expect one-third of all box-office receipts. Dalrymple acquiesced, knowing only too well that even in the direst production, Tallulah was big business.

Tallulah selected the Coconut Grove in Miami for the try-outs and Williams chose Herbert Machiz to direct – a young man whom Tallulah was apparently so keen to please that she gave up her beloved cigarettes and Old Grandad for a whole week while they were going through the script. But if Tallulah initially got on well with Machiz, there were times when she seemed to loathe Tennessee Williams, so much so that their respective entourages very soon endeavoured to keep them apart as much as possible.

The premiére of *A Streetcar Named Desire* was attended by the largest single gathering of homosexuals New York had ever seen, few of whom were interested in the quality of the Williams play but in cheering the woman they had dubbed 'The Queens' Queen'. Many of these young men had never seen her on the stage before, few had seen her films, save perhaps *Lifeboat*, yet they had memorized every bitchy anecdote from *The Big Show*. Virtually every line Tallulah drawled in the play was deliberately misconstrued by her or them. One, 'The girls are out tonight!' stopped the show completely and became *the* gay exclamation of the year, prompting Tallulah to announce at the end of the performance, 'Now I have Gallery Girls of both sexes, thank God!'

Tallulah also picked up one of her favourite buzz words from a gay male camp-follower. As in the days of Fat Sophie, the name of the perfume Chypre had become 'sheep', yielding to a whole range of lesbian innuendoes, so she adapted the phrase, 'beddy-byes'. One night, when she was getting happily drunk with half-a-dozen Gallery Boys, she slurred this out as 'byze', which the New York gay community quickly adopted as their secret cult term for fornication. Thus, whenever Tallulah saw a pair of her boys canoodling or even merely chatting, she would march up to them and ask loudly, 'Well, darlings! Don't you think you'd better tell me who's byzing who?'

A Streetcar Named Desire opened at the New York City Center on 15 February 1956. The critics, declaring that Blanche Dubois had not been created as 'a scapegoat for perverted humour', absolutely loathed it and severely criticized Tennessee Williams for allowing Tallulah to get away with so many one-liners, many of which bordered on the pornographic. Wolcott Gibbs, for many years one of Tallulah's most fervent allies, attacked this 'camp hero-worship' in his column in the *New Yorker*: 'There is, I suppose, no cure for this kind of vulgarity and stupidity in an audience, except possibly the brisk employment of a machine-gun.' It was a prejudiced, irresponsible statement which Tallulah openly condemned ... for whether Gibbs and his cronies approved or not, she had long belonged to that select, gay-friendly group of dramatic divas led by Dietrich, Piaf and Garland. Neither did she approve of the way in which Tennessee Williams – himself openly gay and renowned for his downtown rough-trade cruising – seized every opportunity to denounce her audiences as 'so many goddamn faggots'. They were, after all, helping him to become a rich man.

Tallulah, like these other great women, was proud of her gay fans but was never able to work out why she became such an essential part of their lives. She wrote in her autobiography:

Would I be immodest to say the Coward clientele, the Sinatra aficionados, the Lewis and Martin rooters, are more easily explained than my communicants? Sinatra singing a love-song is different than Tallulah coughing herself to death in *Camille*. He stirs a different set of glands or something. Noël's celebrants were white-tie and town-car and utterly utter. The riff and raff who idolized Lewis and Martin were swept away by slapstick violence. The delirium of *my* devotees touched off an epidemic of psychoanalysts amongst reviewers whose conflicting opinions only added to the confusion!

To please her legion of gay fans, and also to get back at the homophobes amongst the press, when *A Streetcar Named Desire* closed, Tallulah announced that she would like to star in her own Mistinguett-style revue. The great French star had died at the beginning of the year and with her had died what little had remained of the true 'feathers-and-staircase' music hall. Tallulah was no Mistinguett, as most people would have agreed, and she flatly refused to wear anything that had once been worn by a bird – or to appear as anyone but herself. She also stipulated that all the material would have to be selected by her and that again there would be no more than 16 performances. Ultimately she was approached by Richard Kollmar and James Gardiner and given free rein over a production which she announced would be called *The Ziegfeld Follies*, declaring, 'I don't give a good goddamn if the title's copyright or not. That's what I want!' It opened in Boston on 16 April 1956.

The revue was more or less a visual amalgam of *The Big Show* with the inevitable reading of Dorothy Parker, two lengthy song-and-dance routines, the subway sketch and a basketball skit which received most of the laughs. Such was its popularity that there were 16 more performances in Philadelphia but, although the Gallery Boys loved it, the critics cringed. Jerry Gehegan wrote in the *Philadelphia Daily News*, 'This is the kind of musical where you walk out whistling the sets.'

There was, however, much that the press did not know – at least not yet. Tallulah's years of chain-smoking had taken their

toll, robbing her performances of their former vigour. Her wit
was as intact and sharp as ever but occasionally she did not
possess the energy and strength to push it forward. The theatre
management were so concerned that she might not make it
through the run that they engaged an understudy – this had
only happened once before, when she had been taken ill during
The Skin of our Teeth. She was also provided with two
dressing-rooms – one next to the stage so that she would not
have to climb any steps, the other adjacent to the sweeping
staircase which she descended to join the rest of the 60-strong
cast for the finale. The photographs taken of her in this scene,
surrounded by her 'bevy of beautiful boys', are truly
remarkable and reveal that at 53 she was still one of the
loveliest women in the United States.

Hot on the heels of *The Ziegfeld Follies*, Tallulah appeared
in *Welcome Darlings!*, a virtual rehash of the former, written
by eight relative newcomers to the entertainment scene. She
also decided that this one would play in summer stock. The
director, Jay Harnick, having auditioned dozens of young
actors to play opposite her, sent his particular favourite to
Tallulah's town-house for her appraisal. His name was Jimmy
Kirkwood.

Jimmy, aged 28 when he 'exploded' into Tallulah's life, was
the son of the pioneering film stars James Kirkwood and Lila
Lee. Many years later he achieved world fame with his
phenomenally successful *A Chorus Line* but even in 1956 he
was very much the all-rounder, with television and film
appearances to his credit and a best-selling novel. At the age of
14 Jimmy had been at the centre of a scandal when he had
stumbled upon the body of the man his mother was suspected
of murdering. *There Must Be a Pony*, based on the incident, to
which Jimmy had added a powerful homosexual sub-plot, had
been immensely popular with the then-closeted American gay
community, and Tallulah had read it several times. On top of
this, her new co-star was currently appearing in *Valiant Lady*,
her favourite television soap. Their interview had been
scheduled to last just 30 minutes but, when Tallulah recognized
him, she kept him transfixed for over five hours while she

chattered non-stop about television, men, sex, her father, politics and herself, pausing only to light one cigarette after another. Confessing that she had had a fling with his father in London during the twenties, she then flopped on to the couch next to him, planted her feet in his lap and asked Jimmy if he thought she still had pretty ankles. When he said that she had, little did the young man know what he would be letting himself in for.

Inevitably, Jimmy Kirkwood became Tallulah's caddy and she often said that he was one of the few men she knew who matched up to her standards where wit, honesty, intelligence and sheer effrontery were concerned. Soon after taking him on, she asked him to name the two people he most wanted to meet in the world. He told her: Laurence Olivier and Eleanor Roosevelt. Tallulah did not know how to contact Olivier at such short notice but she did arrange for Mrs Roosevelt to drop in for tea the next afternoon. It was an event Jimmy would never forget. She arrived 15 minutes early, as Tallulah was watching another of her soap operas, *Edge of Night*. She was told to sit on the sofa next to Jimmy and keep quiet until it had finished, while Tallulah swore profusely at one of the 'baddy' characters she disliked. When the programme ended, she switched off the set and announced, 'I gotta pee!' She then dashed into the toilet which was directly opposite the sofa and used the toilet – accompanied by a running commentary – in full view of her astonished guests. When Jimmy later suggested that her behaviour might not have been altogether ladylike, Tallulah exclaimed, 'But Mrs Roosevelt knows all about bodily functions, darling. She pees too, you know!'

Tallulah's first tiff with Jimmy Kirkwood happened during the rehearsals for *Welcome Darlings!* and concerned the sets. Her contract stipulated that she should not appear in front of anything white as this would only clash with her still magnificent hair – so when she arrived at the theatre to discover that this instruction had been ignored, in a fit of rage she tore down the offending backdrop. Then, grabbing a chair she set about demolishing the sets until Jimmy carted her off screaming. By the next day she had calmed down a little but she still could not agree with him over a sketch he had written, entitled 'Reader's Digest', which she claimed no one would ever understand. The theme ran along the lines:

> America's Number One Killer: Zippers!
> Do the Duke and Duchess?
> Are American Tennis Balls Underfuzzed?
> I Bailed Out of an Eagle!
> There Is Sex After Death!

Tallulah protested vehemently about the last line, saying that it was in bad taste and would have to be removed. As she explained, 'You can plough through life, darling, breaking all the conventions, but religion and death must be respected.'

Welcome Darlings! opened at Westport, Connecticut, on 16 July 1956 and the critics were quick to point out that absolutely everyone involved in the production – actors, producers, scriptwriters, designers – were 'that way inclined' and less than half Tallulah's age. She of course was in her element to be surrounded by so much male beauty and insisted upon keeping up appearances by having Jimmy Kirkwood constantly by her side. For the first time in her life, however, she was suffering from stagefright – Jimmy said in an interview that close up, she sometimes looked old and ill. As with the last revue, she had to descend a staircase and he was worried that she might not make it, worse still that she might fall. And yet, only a moment before the curtain rose, the miracle occurred: the public were able to see the Tallulah they had known and loved for so long, smiling radiantly, brash but undeniably sincere.

The première, however, was not without incident, when Jimmy Kirkwood missed his cue and rushed on to the stage still zipping his flies. His shirt-tail caught in these and, when he faced the audience, his shirt was sticking out so suggestively that he received the biggest laugh of the evening. Jimmy managed to complete his routine but not without breaking down in the middle of it in a fit of giggles. The microphones were still connected when the curtain came down on the first act and, though the audience did not see Tallulah laying into her co-star's shins with the toe of her shoe, they heard her bellow, 'You unprofessional sonofabitchprickbastard!' followed by Jimmy's equally vociferous, 'Madam, go fuck yourself!' After this, Tallulah stomped off the stage into her dressing-room, locked herself in, grabbed her maid Rose Riley's cutting shears and hacked the larger part of her costumes to shreds. The second part of the revue then resumed as though nothing untoward had happened, going well until the finale, 'May the Good Lord Bless and Keep You', which had now become her unofficial theme song. Tallulah had agreed to greet each member of the cast with a kiss at the foot of the staircase and, as her leading man, Jimmy was naturally expected to be last. As he descended the staircase, she began walking away and the audience thought that this was all a part of the show until she suddenly stopped the music and announced, 'I'm so sorry, darlings, I almost forgot this little bastard!' Within the hour, though, Tallulah and Jimmy were back to being best friends and remained so for life. As for the offending line, it was mutually agreed that this should stay in the finale.

Several days into *Welcome Darlings!*, Tallulah and Jimmy were invited to a supper party at a country inn near Westport, hosted by Abraham Ribicoff, the Jewish governor of Connecticut. By the time the couple arrived, Tallulah was already half-stoned on bourbon and throughout the evening she kept on referring to Ribicoff's Jewishness and mispronouncing his name – the fact that it ended with an 'off' only made matters worse, of course. She then began telling the governor's wife how attractive she thought he was, cracked a few jokes about 'circumcision, pork chops and Moses', and became so abusive to Mrs Ribicoff when asked to leave that Jimmy fled to the gents' lavatory in shame. Tallulah ran after him and the pair somehow got locked in and began yelling for help. The restaurant manager, having been alerted by Mrs Ribicoff, misinterpreted this as a fracas and called the state police who, when they arrived witnessed the spectacle of Tallullah shinning down the drainpipe leading from the lavatory window pantieless, with her skirt hoisted around her waist.

After touring with *Welcome Darlings!* Tallulah was approached by Herbert Machiz to star in *Eugenia*, Randolph

Carter's adaptation of Henry James's novel, *The Europeans*. She accepted the play without even reading the script – the name itself was for her a lucky omen. Eugenia had been one of her mother's names and it belonged to the two people dearest to her in the world: her sister and Eugenia Rawls. And though she did not like Herbert Machiz, she respected him and had never held anyone but herself responsible for the fiasco that had been *A Streetcar Named Desire*. Machiz introduced her to Randolph Carter, whom she had met once before when he had worked with John Emery on *Wuthering Heights* and it was he – and Estelle Winwood again – who persuaded her that this time she really would be on to a winner. Tallulah half-believed him and chose John C Wilson to produce. Her co-stars were Tom Ellis, Scott Merrill and the French actress Thérèse Quadri, her maid from *Private Lives*.

Eugenia previewed in Philadelphia in November 1956 and this time the problems centred around Tallulah's health. Though her eyesight was getting progressively worse, vanity prevented her from wearing her spectacles in public and she kept bumping into things. In one scene where she had to slam a door, her hand went straight through the set and she broke a little finger. In another she tripped, laughed at the incident, said, 'It's the bourbon, darlings!' and spent three days in hospital with four broken ribs. Her injuries were not helped by her dependence on alcohol and drugs. She was reported to be drinking a quart of Old Grandad every day and taking up to nine Tuinals at once, besides her usual Dexedrine, Benzedrine and Dexamyl. In addition, in order to combat the agonizing pain caused by her accident, she was being prescribed morphine. Astonishingly, she only slipped up the once. This was in Baltimore, when she froze completely during a scene with Tom Ellis, keeping everyone waiting until, completely out of the blue, she uttered a line from *The Little Foxes*. With incredible skill – he had appeared in a school production of the Hellman play – Ellis improvised the next few lines and for several minutes kept the momentum going until Tallulah had pulled herself together. 'And nobody was any the wiser,' she later confessed. 'That just goes to show how crap the script must have been.'

Eugenia opened in New York at the Ambassador Theatre on 30 January 1957 and subsequently had its death-knell sounded by Walter Kerr of the *Herald Tribune*:

> There can be no question whatever that Miss Tallulah Bankhead is an irresistible force, but in *Eugenia* she has flatly, finally, and irrevocably met an immovable object ...

Tallulah did try desperately to inject some life into the role, knowing full well from experience that New York audiences were notoriously harder to please than those out in the sticks. The plot of *Eugenia* centred around an unscrupulous fortune-hunter who gets her comeuppance at the end of the play. The scene demanded that, while reassuming her mid-European grandeur, she should study her reflection in the mirror before ascending a staircase without actually saying anything but implying that her schemings were by no means over. This worked well, until she unexpectedly growled, 'I shall go around the world in a mackintosh!' The last straw, however, came on what should have the Saturday matinée performance. All the seats had been sold but 30 minutes before curtain up there was no sign of Tallulah. Backstage, there was an immediate panic. She had flatly refused to work with the understudies engaged for *The Ziegfeld Follies* and *Welcome Darlings!* and, when Randolph Carter had suggested hiring one for *Eugenia*, she threatened to rip up her contract. Now, there was a frenzied discussion as to who should go looking for her – lots were drawn and the manager of the Ambassador Theatre took a taxi to Tallulah's town-house. She had tripped and fallen again earlier in the day and the manager found her in her bath, soaking away her aches and pains in a drinks-drug-induced daze. The performance was cancelled and Randolph Carter gave orders for the play to close at once.

Some years later, Carter relived his experiences with Tallulah by writing a play about her. *The Late, Late Show* told the story of an ageing film star who compels two of her best friends to sit through innumerable screenings of her old films and whose only pleasure in life is reminiscing about her past. This was not, however, the real Tallulah who, though she clung to many memories of what had been but with absolutely no regrets, had already borrowed the phrase from President Eisenhower, 'It is better to live than vegetate.'

14

Crazy October
and a Vulgar Clown

During the spring of 1957, Tallulah received an urgent call from Major Donald Neville-Willing, the owner of London's snobbish Café de Paris. How would she like to bring her cabaret show to the city of her first triumphs? Tallulah immediately telephoned Marlene Dietrich – her friend or foe, depending on her mood – and sought her advice. Marlene had recently enjoyed two enormously successful seasons at the establishment and, though she was the archetypal all-round entertainer whereas Tallulah's singing voice in particular left a great deal to be desired, Marlene assured her that the 'gimmick' would work. She added that before Neville-Willing had signed her up, his first choice had been Greta Garbo, who had turned his offer down when told that the stage was in such close proximity to the audience that they would have been able to see up her nostrils. Tallulah's response to this was, 'If they pay me the same as they were going to pay Garbo, they can look up anything I've got.'

Once she had signed the contract, Tallulah arranged to be interviewed by Alan Brien of the London *Evening Standard*, then in New York. The journalist arrived *chez* Tallulah at six in the evening – like Jimmy Kirkwood, anticipating no more than a 30-minute 'consultation'. Seven hours later he was still there being entertained and slowly exhausted by this indefatigable siren who, he declared, held a conversation the way a firemen held his hose. Brien's description of 'the most fascinating monologue in theatrical history' was itself a remarkable piece of journalism:

> This knock-you-down filibuster was not entirely continuous. She danced the Charleston, sang 'Bye-Bye Blackbird', read from the Bible, acted out a sketch by Dorothy Parker. There was a break ... to watch a television quiz show in which she answered all the questions. She chain-smoked her English cork-tipped cigarettes, chain-drank American whisky and ginger ale, chain-talked her stream of consciousness soliloquy ... as restless as a cat on a hot-tin roof, tiger-footing around the room in her red pyjamas, hauling down snapshots and copies of her autobiography to prove each remark she made. It would have been easier to list the things she wasn't talking about ... during the evening she became so animated that she might have been invented by Walt Disney. She high-kicked six inches above her head. She sang in a haunting, tear-spilling voice like a smouldering mink. Her grin was a necklace of pearls. She leapt in the air like a whirling dervish. She rolled across the carpet and beat her hands in ecstasy ... she is a sphinx with few secrets. 'I'm as pure as the driven slush, and I wouldn't have minded illegitimate children, but I had relatives in politics.' But she has one deadly secret ... despite all her pretence of impropriety, I believe that she is an addict of domesticity. She is a housewife forced to masquerade as a femme-fatale.

Tallulah's fans were surprised to find her looking subdued when she arrived at London's Heathrow on 20 May 1957, wearing a dark dress, her mink stole, and a large old-fashioned picture hat. 'It's to cover my grey hairs, darlings!' she told everyone. She refused to be professionally photographed, saying that she was tired and wanted to look her best for her press conference at the Ritz, where she had booked her old suite. 'I've got a new double chin,' she announced. Then, climbing on to the roof of a car and crouching in the most unladylike manner, she urged her fans to snap her with, 'Try me from this angle, darlings. I look much better!' She was still wearing the hat four hours later when she faced the press, telling one photographer, 'Photograph down, darling. That's how they made Shirley Temple look beautiful. They used to shoot her through gauze, but they shoot me through *linoleum!*'

Tallulah was asked if she would be meeting any old friends, and she replied, 'I'm afraid some of them have gone and popped their clogs and I shan't know who's left, darling, until they start wheeling 'em in.' She denied, however, that Major Neville-Willing was paying her £18,000 for her six-week engagement, and laughed, 'Even your Tallulah isn't worth quite that much!'

Tallulah opened at the Café de Paris on 27 May in what she herself promoted as 'a subtle blend of sophisticated comedy, song and chatter' – in effect, the same blend as she had offered in Las Vegas. She was accompanied at the piano by Ted Graham and by the alternating orchestras of Arthur Coppersmith and Harry Roy. The humour was high camp, the audiences predominantly gay, as they had been with Marlene Dietrich. She sang a few songs, recounted the usual Dorothy Parker poem, warned everyone to watch out for the 'snowstorms' while she was dancing the black-bottom because she did not have her panties on, and told risqué jokes which some critics thought she should have kept to herself. Six weeks later, speaking to a reporter in the airport lounge, she confessed, 'The Café de Paris was divine, darling. But I have to say that it was a one-off. I only did it for the money.' The thousands of admirers who had paid through the nose to see her in cabaret, however, knew differently.

On her return to New York, there was a great deal of radio and television, more often than not with Tallulah talking about Tallulah. She appeared twice in *The Arthur Murray Party*, a then popular celebrity dance competition on NBC-TV. She danced with Rod Alexander, and won both times. On *The Polly Bergen Show* she warbled 'Give Me the Simple Life' and there was a guest spot in *The Lucy and Desi Show*. There were also two television plays – *The Hole Card*, with Isobel Elson, and Jameson Brewer's *Eyes of a Stranger*, directed by Ray Milland and co-starring the dashing Gavin Gordon who had 'seduced' Marlene Dietrich in *The Scarlet Empress* but who showed no interest whatsoever in Tallulah, who did her best to seduce him.

Early in 1958, Tallulah's friend Jean Dalrymple, who had been appointed Co-ordinator of the American Performing Arts Programme for that year's Brussels World Fair, announced in the *Herald Tribune* that Tallulah had again been offered the part of Amanda Wingfield in *The Glass Menagerie*. Apparently, the announcement was made without Tallulah's knowledge but, for her, one stab at Amanda had been enough. There was a brief summer-circuit tour with George Batson's *House on the Rocks*, a comedy-mystery which she dismissed as 'a dead duck' and, while this was running, she was sent the script of *Crazy October*, which James Leo Herlihy had adapted from his own short story, 'The Sleep of Baby Filbertson'. Tallulah rejected it at once, telling the playwright over the telephone, 'I can't do it, darling. It's just another of those downbeat, down-trodden, degenerate Southern *thaangs!*'

Herlihy, however, was not the kind of man to give up easily. 'Tallulah Bankhead is the greatest actress alive,' he told the press with the utmost sincerity, then set about engaging the rest of the cast for *Crazy October*, in the hope that they might persuade her to change her mind. Joan Blondell, who played the waitress, told a newspaper that she had accepted the part only because she had wanted to experience 'the profound joy' of working alongside Tallulah. This touched her, though not so much as Herlihy's good fortune in securing Estelle Winwood. Anything her best friend did had to be good, and Tallulah signed the contract straight away. Herlihy then played another blinder when he suggested that before the try-outs she should enter a drugs-drink clinic for treatment. The brief respite did her some good and after her discharge she spent several weeks at Herlihy's home in Key West. While here she was interviewed by a woman reporter who had recently lost her hearing. Tallulah demanded her address and several days later sent the young woman a dog which had been especially trained for the hard of hearing. She also visited a local home for underprivileged children and bought everyone bicycles and toys. Again she told the press that she had always regretted never having had children of her own.

Down-beat *Crazy October* certainly was, and full of camp

black humour. Tallulah played Daisy Filbertson, the landlady of a dilapidated West Virginia inn who stomps around wearing curlers and rolled-down men's socks and who is paid $1,500 by an elderly, eccentric widow (Winwood) to cremate her husband, only to bury him in a parking lot instead. The play was awarded a budget of £100,000 and Tallulah's very exacting demands – $1,500 a week, 15 per cent of the box office, approval of the entire company from the director down to the technicians, first-class travel when the show was touring and the services of a paid, full-time maid – were met without hesitation. Two additional clauses stipulated that she should be in complete control of the lights, including the now little-used footlights and that she should also exercise the right to actually miss a performance, should she be asked to appear in a television show, for a $6,000 forfeiture which would be paid to the producer. The missed performance of *Eugenia* still rankled but no theatrical entrepreneur could deny that Tallulah Bankhead was anything but a megastar with tremendous pulling power, even in bad plays with short runs.

Crazy October opened in New Haven and because of the hype instigated by Estelle Winwood a send-off party gathered outside New York's Grand Central Station. Tallulah did not disappoint. She arrived smack in the middle of the rush hour, mink-clad and with minutes to spare before the train was due to leave, accompanied by her maid Rose Riley, Herlihy, and two small dogs which snarled at the press. She appeared to be drunk but was actually suffering from the effects of being roused from a drug-induced sleep – and when she opened her mink to pose for photographs, she was naked underneath. She was no less troublesome at the dress rehearsal. She arrived drunk, refused to walk on to the stage until most of the props and an essential staircase had been repositioned, then stormed out of the theatre when someone reminded her that it was time to watch her favourite soap opera. She was sober when the curtain rose on the première, a 'problem' which she rectified by rushing into the wings after each scene and downing a tumbler of neat bourbon.

The play moved on to Washington, then Detroit, and if most of the critics hated or merely misunderstood it, Tallulah's fans loved it. In Los Angeles, she saw her old pal Montgomery Clift sitting in the front row. 'Come back after the show, darling,' she improvised. 'I haven't had a decent girls' night out in months.' The riotous evening concluded with a visit to Winwood's favourite, exceedingly expensive, restaurant. Monty, who was able to drink anyone under the table, stumbled about the room filching pieces of food from the other diners' plates, then spitting them back again into the ashtrays. Tallulah managed to calm him down and all was well until Estelle Winwood introduced him to the hunky waiter – quite unnecessarily, for the pair had already exchanged telephone numbers – with, 'This is Mr Clift, the famous actor. He sucks cocks, you know!' ... to which Tallulah retorted, in her best Alabama drawl, 'Is that so? He never sucked mine, darling!'

While in Los Angeles, Tallulah also acquired another factotum. Ted Hook was a red-headed, handsome, butch-looking dancer in his mid-twenties who had first met Tallulah in Las Vegas when he had worked in the chorus at the Sands Hotel. In Los Angeles, on 30 October, he saw her on television in *The Jack Parr Show* and rang every hotel in the city until he was connected to her suite at the Knickerbocker Hotel. Ted did not expect the call to get past her maid – what he did not know was that the pair had had a row, causing Rose Riley to storm out in a huff and leave Tallulah to fend for herself. He was so stunned when she picked up the phone that he asked her out to dinner. Tallulah compromised by inviting him to dine with her at the Knickerbocker and, within the hour, she had appointed him as her caddy. ' "A hundred a week, all the food and booze you can consume, your cleaning bill and a room of your own – but you buy all your goddamn cigarettes!" were her only terms,' Ted reflected, explaining that his new boss had then set him a simple task – sharpening her Victory Red lipstick, which had to be kept on ice for 30 minutes before being dipped in bourbon, ready to use. Ted passed the test and moved into her house the next day. Rose Riley was fired, though with typical generosity Tallulah kept her on the payroll for ten more years.

When Ted Hook entered Tallulah's life, such was her mania for being fussed over that, according to Estelle Winwood, she was incapable of surviving for more than a few hours without someone waiting on her hand and foot. She also had another foible, which involved Ted running her bath every afternoon, at four on the dot, then dousing her with a bucket of ice cubes to tone up her skin, thus, she hoped, preventing it from getting wrinkled. She still gave interviews and held audiences in the bathroom, or while she was sitting on the toilet, and according to Ted Hook, if her guest was a man he would always be greeted with, 'Keep your eyes *up*, darling. My ass looks like an accordion.' She had also begun sleeping in baby-blue cashmere sweaters and one of Ted's duties was to change these every week on account of the cigarette burns. She also slept with the radio on, full blast, the only way, she said, that she could sleep at all. If Ted switched the radio off, Tallulah awoke and made everyone's life miserable.

Another of Tallulah's foibles concerned her lipstick. It was said that though she used Victory Red all her life, she never once used up a stick. They were usually misplaced, left in taxis, given away as keepsakes, or thrown at people. During Ted Hook's employ, she was invited to appear on a television show sponsored by Revlon cosmetics. With a great deal of media hype, a representative from the firm turned up on her doorstep with an enormous box of make-up, courtesy of one of the directors, Charles Revson. He was halfway through his well-rehearsed spiel when Tallulah, looking breathtakingly lovely, bawled, 'Please tell Mr Revson to take his make-up and shove it where the sun don't shine. I'm an Elizabeth Arden girl, I've always been an Elizabeth Arden girl, and God willing I intend to remain an Elizabeth Arden girl.'

During the *Crazy October* tour, Tallulah got on well with Joan Blondell – unusually so perhaps, considering how she had treated some of her female co-stars in the past. It may well be that the younger actress actually took the time to get to know her by forcibly but tactfully standing up to her. 'She reminded me of a female John Barrymore – stoned out of her mind half the time but an absolutely wonderful person,' she later said. Joan Blondell was also one of the many people who praised Tallulah for her great generosity. When the play opened at the

Geary Theatre in San Francisco in the middle of December 1958, Tallulah handed out tiny notices upon which she had printed: THERE WILL BE NO FUCKING CHRISTMAS THIS YEAR – I DESPISE CHRISTMAS. Joan Blondell ignored the instruction and put up a small Christmas tree in her dressing-room and the rest of the cast waited for Tallulah to explode. No such thing happened. She threatened to fire Ted Hook for failing to remind her that it was Christmas, then gave him $1,000 to spend on presents and bottles of drink for every member of the company. On Christmas Eve, after taking numerous curtain calls, she announced that there was going to be a 'last-minute' collection for the Actors' Benevolent Fund – buckets were then passed around the audience and thousands of dollars were raised for her favourite charity. Out of gratitude, she executed a somewhat tipsy Charleston. Then, after singing 'May the Good Lord Bless and Keep You', she gave a short speech which ended, 'Merry Christmas, darlings. I hope it'll be my last.' The performance was one of the last she gave of *Crazy October*. It closed when the company were in San Francisco.

At the beginning of 1959, Tallulah was offered an astonishing $100,000 for a series of ten guest appearances on the *Ed Sullivan Show*. The first of these was on 19 April, when she read Dorothy Parker's 'The Waltz' and launched into the subway sketch which had made audiences roar in Las Vegas. It was also her last, for though she was a huge success, Tallulah hated the way Sullivan rushed from one section of the show to the next with apparent disregard for the artistes' need for time to catch their breath. 'It was like being shot out of a cannon,' she said, pocketing her cheque and telling the head of CBS-TV what to do with the rest. On 27 May she gave probably her most unusual interview of recent years, to Shirley Eder of NBC Radio's *Monitor*, from her private room at the Flower Fifth Avenue Hospital, after sustaining a fall at her home.

Exactly how this had happened may only be guessed. Most of the newspapers carried conflicting stories and Tallulah seemed more concerned for 'a mysterious houseguest with hepatitis' than she was for herself. The later police report clarified the matter somewhat: 'At 12.30 am one Tallulah Bankhead, age 56, at residence 230 East 62nd Street ... fell over a vase and cut her left forearm. Subject refused medical aid of Beth-David ambulance.' The wound required five stitches and that Tallulah was still drunk when admitted to the hospital remains undisputed. The *New York Times* began its story with the headline:

TALLULAH HOSPITALIZED ...
HOSPITAL TALLULAH-IZED!
Tallulah has entered the hospital for 'a general check-up', and some of the other patients there are positive that the doctors aren't going to find anything wrong with the lady's lungs. One patient said yesterday, 'From the hammering and noise going on in that room, she's getting everything she's hollering for!'

One of the more scurrilous tabloids perhaps came to the logical conclusion that, given her 'riotous and downright immoral' way of life, Tallulah had also received treatment for venereal disease and that syphilis may have been contributing to her failing eyesight. She dispelled this theory, as only she could, by calling a press conference and emphasizing that no photographers would be allowed into her room. There was a sound reason for this. After inserting her finger into her vagina and holding it aloft for all to see, she smeared it across her eyes and announced, 'You see, darlings, it doesn't make you go blind!'

Tallulah emerged from whatever treatment she had been given, unsteady on her feet but raring to go. She was offered a new play whose very title almost caused her to have a relapse: *Oh Dad, Poor Dad, Mamma's Hung You in the Closet and I'm Feeling So Sad!* When asked why she had rejected it, she replied, 'It's vulgar. I was raised in the South, so it would be impossible for me to be common. Send it to Shelley Winters. She's cornered the market in tarts and whores.'

She did accept the job as narrator in the film *The Boy Who Owned a Melephant*, adapted from a story by Malvin Wald and starring her godson, Brockman Seawell. The film opened at the New York Palace on 6 October and subsequently won a Gold Leaf at the Venice International Children's Festival.

At the end of 1959, Tallulah launched a ferocious attack against racism in an interview with Alan Morrison of *Ebony*. Accompanying the feature, which appeared in the January 1960 issue of the magazine, she insisted upon being photographed embracing the singer Nat King Cole. 'My greatest regret is that Lady Day couldn't be here to witness this,' she said, reflecting on Billie Holiday's recent death. She then criticized the black community itself for 'singling out the South as the whipping boy on the race issue', declaring that racism was not a regional scourge but a national one and concluding that she had been utterly in favour of the 1954 Brown *v* Topeka Board of Education Supreme Court decision mandating the desegregation of schools.

Needless to say, such 'anti-social comments' had much to do with Tallulah being offered virtually no work at all until the beginning of 1961, when a joint birthday party was organized for her and Carol Channing to which Morton da Costa – now an influential theatrical agent – was invited. Ted Hook pleaded with him to find Tallulah work, but da Costa refused to have anything to do with her, telling Hook, 'I had to fight to get away from Tallulah, before. If I get involved again, she'll never let me go.' This much was true, though da Costa did compromise by going to see Tennessee Williams, who offered her a revival of *Sweet Bird of Youth* only to be told, 'Go peddle your filth elsewhere.' The role of the aged, drug-addicted film star was by now a little too close to the truth.

On a more serious note, she and her actor friend Tony Randall joined in with the current political rallies, first supporting Adlai Stevenson, then John F Kennedy in the campaign against Richard Nixon. In November 1960, when bad weather delayed Kennedy's visit to a rally in Teaneck, New Jersey, she and Randall kept an audience of 17,000 amused for five hours in sub-zero temperatures while, one by one, the other artistes deserted their cause. For the first time in her life, Tallulah ran out of things to say, so she encouraged the crowd to join her in community singing.

Physically and mentally, however, she was getting progressively weaker now that she had so little to occupy her time, and there were renewed problems with her insomnia. There was another near-fatal incident when, after taking too many sleeping pills, she finally dropped off, setting fire to her dog, Dolores, for the second time. Ted Hook tried to help by arranging for her to spend some time with Dola Cavendish in British Columbia, but her saving grace did not come until the end of 1960 when she was offered *Midgie Purvis*, the brainchild of Mary Chase, the creator of *Harvey* and *Mrs McThing*, two whimsical pieces which had had a wide family appeal.

Midgie Purvis told the story of a 50-year-old woman who, rather than attempt to make herself look younger, transforms herself into an octagenarian so that she can hire herself out as a baby-sitting granny and have fun with her charges: there was a scene where she had to slide down the banister and croon 'Yes, We Have No Bananas!' and Burgess Meredith and Robert Whitehead, friends of long standing who were chosen to produce the play, were terrified of handling her in a theatrical situation in case anything go wrong with the stunt. Mary Chase aggravated everyone with her inability to get some of the scenes right – fickle beyond belief, she changed whole chunks of dialogue on the spur of the moment and even Tallulah, with her phenomenal memory, was unable to register them in her mind before they were changed again. Aided by Ted Hook and a private nurse, she had taken great pains to diminish her intake of opiates and alcohol and was temporarily 'thriving' on an unconventional but strict diet of ice-cream soda and shellfish. Therefore the least she expected after making such a monumental sacrifice was discipline and integrity from her team. When she saw that this was not to be forthcoming, she became so aggressive towards everyone that the otherwise genial Burgess Meredith did his utmost to persuade her to drop out of the production, if only for the sake of their friendship. Tallulah stuck it out and the play opened at the Martin Beck Theater on 1 February 1961 to mixed reviews. Howard Taubman called Midgie 'a vulgar clown ... a product of showbusiness', hinting once more that whatever she did,

Tallulah could only ever be Tallulah. Walter Kerr admonished,
'Half the time you won't know where the people have come
from, or where they are going, but in a spooky and entirely
impertinent way they always get there.' John Chapman of the
Daily News enthused,

> As a dramatic structure, *Midgie Purvis* is rickety now and again,
> but I for one do not intend to make picky complaints about a
> slow spot here and there. Putting playwright Mary Chase and
> actress Tallulah Bankhead together is an inspiration, like
> inventing the Martini. Her performance is a joy to behold and
> hear, for it bubbles with the comic spirit and falls in perfectly
> with the playwright's witty notions.

Tallulah was nominated for a Tony for playing Midgie
Purvis, though this did not make it any more popular with the
box office. The première went well, and she took countless
curtain calls. From then on, it was all downhill. Mary Chase
persisted in interfering too much in the production, amending
lines night after night, Tallulah ranted, Burgess Meredith and
Robert Whitehead grew more and more despondent and, after
21 performances, the curtain came down for good.

The closure of *Midgie Purvis* was followed by several months
of deep, almost psychotic, depression. Tallulah, who loved
nothing more than showing off in public, began secluding
herself in her home or hotel room for days on end, refusing to
be seen save by her closest friends. There was an exception,
when Gordon M Eby of the *Huntsville Times* flew to Baltimore
to interview her at the Belvedere Hotel. Even then she would
not see him until midnight, by which time she had downed
enough bourbon to make herself 'presentable'. Eby, however,
saw through her charade:

> Whatever Tallulah was (or was not) or what she had been (or
> could never be) or what she might have been (and never was) she
> WAS a personality. She was an actress, a Southern belle, an
> author, a comedienne – but she was these AFTERWARDS. First
> she was a personality. The Frankenstein of the Foul Mouth,
> low-cut necklines and deep-throated epithets, she made herself

only a reflection of the REAL Tallulah, and it was a mighty poor and inadequate one at that. But this one-sided monstrosity was the image she preferred the public and her private acquaintances to see and know. She said as much to me, and I am sure she liked this public image better than any other. No other celebrity I have met SEEMED quite the enigma Tallulah wanted me to think she was, but whether this was a wise policy or not, the redoubtable Miss B had taken a course she would not (or could not) abandon.

During this period of depression, Tallulah became abjectly fascinated by death and the occult, reading dozens of books on the subject and even borrowing a crystal ball from a mystic. One of her first 'sightings', she claimed, was of a tiny puppet being manipulated by three people. Even more curious was the irony that a few days later, when she sent a friend out to buy cigarettes, he was mugged by three hoodlums. She also claimed to have received a visitation from her mother – henceforth she would carry Ada's photograph around with her, placing it next to her bed or on the table in her dressing-room. She confessed some years later in a radio interview, 'I never knew my mother, but her presence influenced every major decision I made from that day forth. That's why I dropped to my knees, unfailingly each evening before curtain rise, to beg her and God to spare me from making a fool of myself.'

Tallulah was almost recovered when she received a call from her sister Eugenia, now living in Tangier with a younger lover – a call not inquiring after her health, but asking for money to start up her own business. Tallulah had never forgiven Eugenia for 'swanning off in search of adventure', leaving her son, Billy, with Louisa Carpenter. She refused to part with a cent and intimated to Donald Seawell that she no longer looked upon Eugenia as a member of her family.

Shortly after this episode, Tallulah again dropped off to sleep with a lighted cigarette in her hand. This time the consequences were dire. The burn, between her two smoking fingers, left a deep fissure that would not heal and was so bad that she narrowly missed having the fingers amputated. To kill the pain, she took more opiates and these caused hallucinations. Several

nights in succession she called friends in a blind panic, thinking
that 'fiends' were in her apartment trying to kill her. One night
she became so hysterical that the police had to break down the
door to her bedroom – she had jammed a heavy dressing table
against it. She was also entering her sixtieth year and obsessed
with the fact that she may have been losing her looks. Even so,
she was still showing complete strangers her 'bazoobs', still
maintaining that she had never had a facelift and on one
occasion giving herself a blinding headache by plucking all the
grey hairs from her scalp – only to be told by a television
producer that on a black-and-white screen she still looked
'Monroe-blonde'. She did, however, show off her legs as much
as she could because they were still shapely and firm. To
combat her double chin she began walking with her head held
high and this is noticeable when one watches television footage
of her at the time. Only her hands actually looked old, so she
took to wearing gloves, sometimes even in bed. Her doctor,
when told that she was spending several hours each night
staring at her reflection in the mirror, begged her to see a
psychiatrist, or at least enter a clinic for treatment. Tallulah
would not hear of this, vowing, 'My career will kill or cure me,
darling.'

Tallulah's problems began causing problems within her
household. Robert Williams, her chauffeur, found it impossible
to stay under the same roof 24 hours a day. There was a
succession of hirings and firings – a cook who attempted to
follow her employer's example by answering the door naked, a
maid whom Tallulah caught smoking hashish. She told a
reporter, no doubt truthfully, 'I didn't object to her smoking
dope but at least she could have offered some of it to me.' Ted
Hook, her faithful caddy, left to become a dancer-choreo-
grapher with Jerome Cargill, though with some reluctance.
Tallulah had urged, 'Get yourself a career of your own, darling,
and stop playing nursemaid to a neurotic old bag.' She
contacted Cargill and told him that if he knew what was good
for him, he would pay Ted a better salary than they had first
agreed upon. When Ted asked her how he might ever repay the
favour, she told him to find her another maid-companion like

the much-missed Edie Smith. After dozens of interviews – Tallulah's only stipulation was that the new employee should be black – Ted engaged a small, seemingly strait-laced elderly woman named Emma Anthony with whom Tallulah got on like a house on fire. Such was her awe of Emma that she refrained from swearing in her company and spelled out her various insults – until Emma's patience was tried once too often, and she spelled back at a star-studded charity bash, 'Tallulah, please f-u-c-k off, will you?' Tallulah also had a big argument with Robert Williams, who stormed out of the house claiming that she had called him a 'black son-of-a-bitch', and declaring that he would never speak to her again. Tallulah sent out a search party of caddies and the chauffeur was discovered sulking in a motel. She went to see him and confessed, 'I only called you a son-of-a-bitch, darling. Ah *knows* you're black.' Robert returned to the fold.

At around the time of Emma Anthony's appointment, Tallulah's breathing problems grew decidedly worse, so much so that she could not climb stairs unaided. She sold her town-house, making a huge profit, and moved to a thirteenth-floor apartment at 447 East 57th Street. Dozens of friends turned up to help her pack. Thousands of unopened letters, some dating back to the twenties, were found in trunks in the basement. Most were fan letters from Gallery Girls but there were some uncashed cheques, which were stolen by some of these people she had trusted for years, along with most of her silver. Tallulah found out about the thefts a few weeks after the move but, though urged to do so by her lawyer, Donald Seawell, she refused to prosecute anyone.

Once she had settled into her new home, Tallulah agreed to give an in-depth interview to Al Morgan of the recently founded *Show* magazine, on condition that the finished profile be spread over four issues and that she should be highly paid for the privilege of speaking frankly about her personal life. Unlike most of her earlier interviews, she stayed seated the whole time and Morgan was so touched by her obvious deterioration that he wrote only the good things about her.

Tallulah looked ill on 5 May 1962 when she played Lillian

Throgmorton in Michael Dynes's television play, *A Man for Oona*.

A few weeks later, she played Mary Hilliard in *Here Today*, a comedy by George Oppenheimer which was so successful that it played in both summer and winter stock over the next two years. Her only objection came when the director told her that Estelle Winwood would be her co-star. 'If I'm going to be working with my oldest, dearest friend, we get equal billing or neither of us does the play,' she declared. Tallulah liked the play only because Estelle was in it and because she made a new friend in the production company's wardrobe mistress, Harriet Heal, an ex-dancer who, for the last 18 years, had waited on Marilyn Monroe. She was astonished that there had been another actress totally incapable of looking after herself – Monroe had even paid Harriet to autograph her photographs and letters to fans. Shortly afterwards, however, when Monroe died, Tallulah offered Harriet a shoulder to cry on. Some years later, Harriet remembered that of all the people she had worked for – including Eve Arden, Vivien Leigh and Eartha Kitt – Tallulah had been by far the kindest and most generous.

Tallulah probably regretted, during the spring of 1963, turning down the offer to star opposite her arch-enemy Bette Davis in *Whatever Happened To Baby Jane?* particularly when she learned that the part had gone to her friend Joan Crawford. Working with Davis, of course, would have been one trauma willing to have been endured by few. The on-set rivalry between the two had been bad enough, with Crawford being kicked so hard by Davis in one scene that her scalp had required three stitches. Crawford had retaliated by concealing a weightlifter's lead belt under her costume for the 'lifting' scene; the other actress had pulled a muscle in her back and spent the rest of the shoot in agony. What Tallulah might have done to the woman who had scored success after success filming the roles she had created on the stage is anybody's guess.

On 18 May, Tallulah paid her first (and last) visit to the town of her birth, Huntsville, for the dedication of Bankhead Hall, at Redstone Arsenal, named like the town's Bankhead Parkway on Monte Sano Mountain in memory of her father. The officiator, Colonel MacPherson, announced, 'In Alabama's history there is no name more famous than Bankhead.' Tallulah, standing next to him on the platform, muttered, 'I know that, darling.' With her was her friend, President Kennedy and, when the pair were mobbed by hundreds of screaming, mostly male fans at the tiny airport, she turned to him and said, 'The girls are out again, Jack!' In a joint press conference a few minutes later, she spoke of her enthusiasm for the town's civilian space programme and, though everyone was hoping that she would keep things clean for the president's sake, it did not take her long to get down to the wisecracks, particularly when Kennedy asked her if he could get her something to drink. 'Fix me a frozen daiquiri, darling,' she barked. 'And whilst you are there, get one for yourself. They do wonders for the gizzard.' Downing three of these in as many minutes, she was then presented with a watercolour of the town by Colonel MacPherson and Mrs Armstrong, who was terrified of speaking to her lest she utter some obscenity. She did – as the Arsenal band marched past, she pointed to the strapping, handsome young soldier playing the tuba and pronounced, 'Oh, my. I wish he'd blow *me* like that!'

Nancy Nilsson, the then president of Huntsville's Little Theater, relived every exciting moment of Tallulah's visit three decades later when she told me:

> I was a long and ardent fan of Miss B, so when I heard that she was to attend a grand reception that evening, I was ecstatic! I went to the florist and got two dozen red roses, and, together with Alan Moore of the *Huntsville Times*, went off to welcome her at the airport. Our mayor, 'Speck' Searchy, was there with only one dozen, and asked me not to give them to her at the airport – didn't want his bunch to look shabby. So, Alan and I went to the Russel Erskine Hotel – I had my little speech all made up, and she came into the lobby escorted by a very young, very handsome fellow she called Kip. Oh, he was pretty! I introduced myself and started to hand her the flowers, and she said huskily, 'I'm beat, darling, and dying for a drink. Just come up!' In her room was a complimentary bottle of champagne, and she bawled, 'God, I hate champagne! Can you get me some

bourbon?' I called a bell-hop. He could only get me one pint and it cost a bundle, but she was glad to get it and insisted Alan and I stay with her and drink her champagne. We talked about Huntsville for an hour, until Kip insisted she get some rest for the gala. We hadn't been invited, but she said, 'You're the only people I know in this place. Meet me at the door!' When we arrived, the entrance was reserved for limos only, yet all the people waiting to see her just parted like that old River Nile. When she arrived with Kip, she called, 'Come on, darlings!' and we scooped under the ropes and followed her into the hall, where she had arranged a table for us, close to hers. All evening she strived to stay awake during the long, boring speeches. She was tipsy but every now and then she waved and as she was leaving she threw us a kiss. That was the last I ever saw of her ...

In August 1963, Tallulah received an impassioned call from Tennessee Williams, who was supervising the shooting of his *Night of the Iguana* in Puerto Vallarta with Richard Burton and Ava Gardner. The playwright asked her if she would play the part of Flora Goforth in *The Milk Train Doesn't Stop Here Any More*. She already knew that though the play had not actually been written for her, the central character had been based on her – Williams had 'confiscated' it after she had upset him by telling reporters, after seeing the film version of his *The Battle of Angels*, 'They have *ruined* an absolutely lousy play!' Subsequently, *Milk Train* had been tried out on three different actresses, the most promising production having been premièred at the Spoleto Drama Festival in Italy, with Hermione Baddeley, the sister-in-law of Glen Byam Shaw, Tallulah's old flame from the thirties. It had opened and closed within the same week at the end of 1962, killed off by the most abominable reviews. Tallulah read through the script and immediately knew why Baddeley had failed, exclaiming, 'A promiscuous, pill-ravaged rip, born in a Georgia swamp? That could only possibly be me!'

Tallulah accepted the play, not because she had – or would ever – changed her opinion about Tennessee Williams's work, but because the production team, the distinguished David Merrick Foundation, had engaged Tony Richardson to direct.

The young Englishman, then married to Vanessa Redgrave and enjoying a terrific success with the film *Tom Jones*, had already directed two plays for Merrick on Broadway: *Arturo Ui* and *Luther*. Ned Rorem, one of America's most innovative and controversial young pianist-composers, was commissioned to supply the music, and the cast included Marian Seldes, Ruth Ford and Tab Hunter.

On the eve of the first rehearsal, Tallulah invited the entire company to a party at her apartment. This was her usual way of softening everyone up before getting down to the serious business of war. To test their patience, she allowed her dog, Dolores, to run amok – jumping on laps, nipping ankles, yapping nonstop and doing 'whoopsies' on her pile of newspapers in a corner of the room. Tallulah got on famously with Marian Seldes, could not work out Tony Richardson, and despite his affable good looks and boyish charm, declared that Tab Hunter possessed far too much of the Brando-Cobb Method style for his own good. 'I'm absolutely certain that we'll get on like spitting cats,' she told a friend.

Tab Hunter, whom Tallulah would never cease to remind that he had been born plain Arthur Gelien, was 32 years old, yet still very much the teen-idol. Much of his success had been attributed to his clean-cut image and impeccable manners – which did not remain quite so perfect once he began working with Tallulah on 19 November 1963 at the Lunt-Fontanne Theater, for Hunter proved that he could out-curse anyone, including his leading lady. To a certain extent this earned him her respect. She enjoyed seeing him lose his temper but became bored with his incessant stories about his team of horses, which he had arranged to travel around with him during the run of the play. When Hunter remarked at a press conference that he had recently spent some time in Egypt filming *The Golden Arrow*, a tale about horses, magic carpets and dashing heroism in the East, Tallulah spat out, 'They should have fucking well kept you there, darling!'

Tallulah was rehearsing a scene with Tab Hunter a few days later when news was brought to the Lunt-Fontanne of President Kennedy's assassination. She collapsed and had to be taken home and given a sedative. Rehearsals for the next three days were shelved – Tallulah had shut herself in her apartment, seeing no one but her doctor, who prescribed Vitamin B injections. She sent a message of condolence to the president's widow which concluded, 'Jack Kennedy's murder was one of the two most horrid moments of my life. The other was when I found out there was no Santa Claus.'

Most of the problems during *The Milk Train Doesn't Stop Here Any More* were between Tallulah and her director, who was unafraid of admitting that he had never wanted to work with her in the first place. When she began extolling past triumphs and failures, Richardson told her that he was only interested in discussing the current production. And if Tallulah approved of Hunter's overt bisexuality, she did not care for this sort of thing where her directors were concerned, particularly as the one was persistently eyeing up the other and this was getting in the way of work. There was also a fierce argument over Tallulah's curtain call. In plays, she usually liked to be doing something – arranging flowers, or pouring drinks as Sarah Bernhardt had often done – to make it appear that she had been caught unawares. Richardson found this method outdated – Tallulah refused to compromise and the call was left in. The director then tried to teach her a lesson by refusing to advise her how to play a scene, always coming up with the same excuse, 'You're the actress, not me.' By the première, she was only speaking to him to appear civil. She was also in tremendous pain because of the cigarette burn to her fingers. The wound could not be bandaged for fear that, without the air getting to it, it would turn gangrenous. Tallulah covered it with a large chiffon handkerchief, which she knotted about her wrist and used as a prop.

The setting for *The Milk Train Doesn't Stop Here Any More* was confusing. The interior-exterior props were separated by abstract lighting, described by Tennessee Williams as 'the mountain sea-sky's suffusing with Italy's Divina Costiera', and Ned Rorem's musical score was equally bizarre. The story bore shades of the playwright's earlier *The Roman Spring of Mrs Stone*, which had earned Lotte Lenya an Oscar nomination: the wealthy, insecure older woman versus the young, insensitive opportunist. Flora Goforth is a dying, drug-ravaged former music-hall star who is spending her last days on the Italian Riviera, dictating her memoirs. She falls in love with a handsome gigolo (Hunter) who has fashioned a career out of consoling rich, moribund ladies, earning himself the name, 'Angel of Death'. Williams wrote:

> The death of Miss Flora Goforth is essentially the death of a clown. There is hardly a bit of nobility, nor even of dignity, in her fiercely resistant approach to life's most awful adventure ... dying. But, you will find it very possible to pity this female clown even while her absurd pretensions and her panicky last effort to hide from her final destruction make you laugh at her.

The play opened in Baltimore shortly before the Christmas of 1963. It had been well rehearsed, its problems ironed out, Tab Hunter had attempted (and failed) to make himself look less of an eternal teenager by growing a beard, and the acting all round was first class. Even so, while Tallulah was speaking some of her most poignant lines, her voice was drowned by the slamming of seats as the audience began walking out. There were further complications when, a few days into the Baltimore run, Tony Richardson left for London to audition the cast for his production of *The Seagull*. This had been part of his deal with the David Merrick Foundation and arrangements had already been made for Richardson to fly back to New York in time for the New York première. Tallulah accused him of deserting his company in its hour of need and vowed never to speak to him again. She was as good as her word. The play opened at the Brooks Atkinson Theater on 1 January 1964 and the photograph of Tallulah that adorned the cover of that month's *Playbill* magazine was the most beautiful that had been taken of her in recent years. For the first time ever, she filled an auditorium because the public – not her regular audience of galleryites and devotees but the same breed of morbidly curious individuals who would later swamp Judy Garland's final London season – simply wanted to see her fall flat on her face. Rumours had spread like wildfire from press circles in

Baltimore that she had appeared drunk on the stage, fluffing and mismanaging her lines. The critics were there with sharpened pens and one six-word review – 'Miss Bankhead was hoarse and unhappy' – was sufficient for David Merrick to close the play after just five performances, although the stupefying effect of President Kennedy's death on the American nation had not helped ticket sales. Nobody was more pleased than Tallulah, who once more told reporters that she had always loathed working on the stage, a statement that prompted Tennessee Williams to write in the *New York Times*, 'Tallulah loves the theatre with so much of her heart that, in order to protect her heart, she has to say that she hates it. But we know better when we see her on the stage.' What she did not know was that she would never play Broadway again.

As Tallulah's breathing difficulties intensified, her doctors diagnosed emphysema and ordered her to stop smoking. Had she followed their advice, she probably would have recovered enough to lead a reasonably normal life. She did not, and attempted to make up for the sheer folly of getting through 150 Kents a day by taking oxygen, between puffs, from a portable cylinder. She received news on the grapevine that the Elizabeth Taylor-Richard Burton villa in Puerto Vallarta was about to be put up for sale and rang Glenn Anders. Now 78, Anders had retired to Guadalajara in Mexico but Tallulah's was a genuine *cri de coeur*: she would buy the villa, give up her career save for the occasional selective film role or television-show guest slot and he would move in with her. Acting on the spur of the moment – aware that his own failing health would never withstand the rigours of being under the same roof as Tallulah for too long – he told her that the Mexican climate was indescribably bad for emphysema sufferers and that two local women had died from the disease that very week. It must have been a terrible thing to lie so blatantly to a woman who had spent her entire life being remarkably honest. What is more, Tallulah knew that her former lover was lying. She compromised by going to stay with her old friend Dola Cavendish in British Columbia. It was here, during the summer of 1964, that among the dozens of scripts forwarded weekly from New York she read *Fanatic,* a Gothic horror story based on Anne Blaisell's novel, *Nightmare.*

15

Hey, Everybody!
Tallulah's Back!

Under normal circumstances, Tallulah would never have agreed to play Mrs Trefoile, the hideous old religious fanatic who has become deranged after the death of her only son. Her attitude had changed, however, after witnessing the astonishing success of *Whatever Happened to Baby Jane?* Several other former Hollywood actresses, including Shelley Winters, had jumped on to the horror bandwagon with much acclaim. Dola Cavendish also insisted that making the film would do Tallulah good – not to mention the $50,000 fee, the usual ten per cent of the profits and the fact that she would be working in England, possibly for the very last time. As a safety precaution, Dola arranged for her attractive niece, Laura Mitchell, to accompany her. Laura was a wise choice: in her late forties, she was regarded by many as the spitting image of the younger Tallulah.

Fanatic was to be directed by Silvio Narizzano and Tallulah's co-stars were Stefanie Powers, Donald Sutherland and Peter Vaughan. Tallulah expected at least one of these people to meet her when she flew into Heathrow in the middle of October – all she had was a small group of fans from way back and a liveried Rolls-Royce to drive her to the Ritz. Kenneth Carten was waiting for her there. He had not seen her for a number of years and rushed to embrace Laura Mitchell instead. Tallulah laughed off the incident, though secretly she was deeply hurt. Ascending the steps to the hotel, while trying to hold her hat on and wave to onlookers at the same time, she caught one of her high heels in the rubber mat and sprawled backwards. A hotel employee rushed to her aid but she told him to get lost. The press and everyone else who witnessed the event were ready to swear that she had been drinking but for once she was stone cold sober. One of the better quality newspapers reported, in her very own words, 'Never in all her 61 years of ups and downs had anything so positively ghastly befallen Tallulah – but no one could dispute that Tallu took her tumble with a dramatic flair!'

London was able to observe a quieter, more reserved and disciplined Tallulah. There was a dinner party with the music-hall star Dorothy Dickson, a tearful reunion with her former maid, Elizabeth Lock, now in her eighties, and just the one press conference. When asked if she was hoping to catch up with old friends in England, she cracked, 'I've tried, darling, but they're all dead and they didn't leave forwarding addresses!' When asked why she used the term 'darling' so much, she mused, 'All my life I've been terrible at remembering names. Once, I introduced a friend of mine as Martini – her real name was Olive.' Then, asked why she had turned down an offer to attend Judy Garland's latest London season, she responded, 'Because she's a nervous wreck, darling. Why else?'

There was a problem with Tallulah's insurance, instigated by her over-fondness for talking about herself. The film company, Columbia Pictures, demanded the mandatory insurance policy for everyone appearing in *Fanatic*, and when the agent asked Tallulah for any history of serious ailments, she took over an hour to fill him in with her every illness from colds and spots to pneumonia, that she had had since the age of five. The agent reported back to the moguls at Columbia, 'This lady doesn't need an insurance policy, but a coffin.' Subsequently, Silvio Narizzano was told to replace her with someone who was less of a risk but rather than throw a tantrum – Tallulah was too ill and weak for too many of these – she told the director that she would be willing for Columbia to hold her fee as a guarantee of her completing the picture. She then engaged a private doctor to visit her suite each morning to administer a vitamin injection and she stopped drinking – at least for the duration of the shoot. Under the circumstances, she was acting unwisely. Though not entirely dependent on alcohol and opiates, being without their stimulation caused her more problems than she could have imagined. Her face became so swollen that speaking became near impossible and Silvio Narizzano was told to halt the production until she was feeling a little better. Her doctor prescribed penicillin and ordered her not to work. Tallulah screamed that she was a professional, that as such she had always suffered for her art. She tripled her medication and two days later filming began.

For once, Tallulah got on well with her 'team', spending most of her free time with Silvio Narizzano and his family, telling stories of her adventures and beating everyone at poker. She surprised everyone – herself included – by liking Stefanie Powers, who portrayed Patricia, the dead son's fiancée whom Mrs Trefoile tries to murder. The production team had worried about clashes of personality, bearing in mind that the young actress was stunningly beautiful and Tallulah no longer so. She herself had expressed her disapproval over one scene where she had to slap Stefanie across the face. The director instructed her to 'be realistic', and Tallulah hit her so hard that she almost knocked her out, after which she told the press, without meaning to sound unduly malevolent, 'Well, it'll do her complexion good!' In one of the closing scenes of the film, where she had to drag the unconscious Patricia down a flight of stairs, she refused to use the stunt double and had to be given oxygen.

Halfway through the shooting schedule, however, Tallulah did turn nasty. This was when Columbia announced that the title of the film would be changed to *Die! Die! My Darling!* She accused the company of 'taking the piss' out of her most frequently used adage. For the benefit of her British fans, the original title was retained but it had to be changed for the American market. The rest of the shoot might have been miserable, had Tallulah not suddenly succumbed to an attack of gambling fever – not poker this time, but horse-racing. For five weeks she studied the form guides, and spent one hour each morning in 'deep conference' with one of the male wardrobe assistants who placed £2 on her behalf at every meeting with an 80 per cent success rate. She told everyone of a previous visit to Britain, many years before, when she had enjoyed a passionate affair with the debonair jockey, Steve Donahue. She added, 'I always used to know when Steve was going to win because he would stand in the paddock holding his whip in his right hand. On such a jaunt, I once won a thousand pounds, and I can assure you of one thing, darling. Steve certainly knew how to ride!'

Upon the completion of the film, Tallulah was personally driven to Heathrow by Silvio Narizzano – in a Rolls-Royce with HEL 777 registration plates. The director was rewarded with a tiny gold medallion inscribed with an image of the devil.

Tallulah spent the Christmas of 1964 with Dola Cavendish in British Columbia. She was stopped at the customs by an official and when asked if she was *the* Tallulah Bankhead, replied sarcastically, 'I'm what's left of her, darling!' When asked to open her luggage for inspection, quick as a flash she retorted, 'You don't have to bother searching my bags, darling. There's nothing in them but liquor and drugs.' The man took her seriously and detained her for over an hour.

Tallulah returned to her New York apartment and after a brief respite appeared on television in *The Andy Williams Show* with the Beach Boys. *Die! Die! My Darling!* was premièred at 24 New York cinemas on 19 May but Tallulah attended a private screening with James Herlihy and Jimmy Kirkwood. The film's make-up department had overdone trying to make her look old and haggard, coiling her hair into a bun and dyeing it deep grey. As if to make a point, she signed one of the stills for her friend, Cal Schumann, 'Who dat? Not me? Oh, well! Tallulah.' worst of all, the camera had zoomed in for several relentlessly cruel shots of her artificially wizened face and when the lights came up she told the audience, 'I want to apologize to all of you for my appearance on the screen – looking older than God's wet-nurse!' Later, she was devastated by the dreadful reviews for the film, most of them attacking her appearance and almost all of them confusing the actress with the part. Only one was honest. Tallulah was so pleased by it that she pasted it into her scrapbook. Written by Dora Jane Hamblin for *Life* magazine, it concluded:

> The whole enterprise may have been partly designed to make Tallulah look ridiculous. If so, the idea has back-fired. Her superb acting is the saving grace of the film. She may be launched, at 60 or 65, on a new career. Hey, everybody! Tallulah's back!

Whether the film was successful or not was immaterial to her entourage, who genuinely believed that Tallulah's career now had taken a turn for the better and that more roles of the Trefoile ilk would come her way. They did, and she turned every single one of them down. She had telephoned Dola Cavendish every day since the Christmas of 1964, since learning that her friend had been diagnosed as suffering from cirrhosis of the liver. As cigarettes had taken their toll on Tallulah's health, so had Dola destroyed herself with gin. In March 1966 she had a stroke and a few days later she died.

Tallulah shut herself off from the world, emerging from her apartment only to appear on the occasional television show. She was 'mystery' guest on *What's My Line?* and she starred with Jack Jones and Connie Francis on *The Mike Douglas Show*. She also provided the voice for the Sea Witch in Arthur Rankin's film version of *The Daydreamer*, based on four short stories by Hans Christian Andersen. She became even more depressed when she learned that Dola Cavendish had bequeathed her several pieces of extremely valuable jewellery. Because the duties for importing them into the United States were so high, she was advised to go to Canada and put them into auction there. This, she declared, would be worse than committing treason. The jewellery stayed put.

Tallulah's saving grace was the Black and White Ball, hosted by Truman Capote at the New York Plaza, to which he invited 540 of his closest friends and acquaintances. The *New York Times* considered the party so important that it printed the guest list in its entirety and some celebrities who had not been invited – notably Dorothy Parker – actually left New York to make it appear that they had been overlooked owing to their absence. Tallulah took several weeks preparing for the event, though she had decided from the outset to wear the priceless sapphire and diamond ring given to her three decades before by John Hay Whitney and kept most of the time in her 'tragedy fund' – a cache of jewels, valued in excess of $60,000, held in an anonymous New York bank vault. She then contacted Capote and informed him that she was broke and could not afford to pay for a new dress. A compromise was reached between the pair: Tallulah was given a concessionary ticket which she exchanged with her couturier for a gown that ordinarily would have set her back hundreds of dollars. Then, by word of mouth, Tallulah drummed up trade for the designer, who received commissions from some of the other guests.

Shortly before the Black and White Ball, Tallulah made a wager with a reporter that no one would speak to her all evening, even though she did her best to antagonize certain people. She arrived clutching a bottle of champagne and wearing a white mink and cat-mask – not that anything could disguise her once she opened her famous mouth – and when the party was in full swing she donned a sash inscribed BETTE DAVIS. She also lost her wager. Throughout the evening, friends crossed continually to her table, including Lillian Hellman. The pair had not spoken since their row over the Finnish refugees at the time of *The Little Foxes*, yet they now fell into each other's arms like long-lost sisters. Tallulah told the journalist covering the bash, 'Lillian and I never had a cross word, darling. It was all the fault of *Time* magazine.' Later on in the evening, she was asked to dance by Frank Sinatra and Norman Mailer but declined on account of her illness. She needed her strength, she said, to smoke and drink.

At the Plaza, Tallulah was reacquainted with Jesse Levy, a self-confessed playboy who was then aged 45, whom she had first met some years before at one of Louisa Carpenter's parties. When the Capote extravaganza broke up at around two in the morning, Levy was asked back to her apartment for a nightcap. Within the hour, impressed by his solid frame and rugged good looks, she had asked him to caddy for her. Levy's response was that he would be delighted to fetch and carry for her – all she had to do was add a nought to whatever salary she had been about to offer. Tallulah was feeling so lonely by now that she would have agreed to almost anything. When asked by her friends why she had employed a caddy some two decades older than most of his predecessors, she replied that in view of her age and increasing infirmity, she needed a man with strength and one who had proved himself time and time again. Levy had served with the American Navy during the Second World War and had since been discharged from Korea as a Lieutenant-Commander. What she did not add was that this man never tried to stop her from drinking, smoking and popping pills – in other words, from slowly killing herself.

Also in 1966, Tallulah was approached by Roddy McDowall and asked to contribute to his book, *Double Exposure*, a concept within which famous stars were invited to write about their favourite people. James Stewart wrote some very kind things about Marlene Dietrich and, in a future edition of the book, the ballet dancer Mikhail Barishnikov would go over the top describing his alter-ego, Fred Astaire. Writing about her 'sibyl', Estelle Winwood, Tallulah kept it simple:

> Estelle is my oldest, closest friend who has never failed me. She is granite in a crisis. A world with more Winwoods would be a more desirable place to fret and fume.

At around the same time, she was propositioned by Bill Dozier, the producer of the *Batman* television series, who asked her to play the villainous Black Widow. At first she refused, until Estelle Winwood – and the $20,000 fee – convinced her that she would touch upon a whole new generation of admirers. She told the press upon signing the contract, 'I've stooped not to conquer, and I'm going to do *Batman*!' And when Bill Dozier informed her that her portrayal of the Black Widow would have to be camp, in keeping with comic-strip tradition, she quipped, 'Don't talk to me about camp, darling. I invented the word.' She and Jesse Levy were then flown out to Hollywood and installed in a two-roomed suite at the plush Beverly Hillcrest for ten days.

Tallulah's schedule was a tough one. She who, for years upon years, had never so much as moved a muscle before mid-afternoon, was compelled to report for work at the Desilu studios at six every morning, and this and her rapidly failing health put her in some of the worst moods anyone had ever seen. Bill Dozier was so frightened of her that he put Jesse Levy on salary as an intermediator, so that the production team might be warned in advance what kind of state she was in. There were the lighter moments, of course, usually for the benefit of the press or the handful of admirers who were allowed on the shooting lot. During the first dress rehearsal, when she was trying on her tight-fitting Balenciaga trouser suit, she winced and said to Adam West, who was playing Batman, 'Well, there goes one ball, darling!' Her role also demanded that she climb in and out of a motorcycle sidecar several times and run around a lot. She told the other actors and the producer to forget that she had emphysema and that she was doing what she had to do, for the sake of her art. She never complained once about being short of breath and away from the set she did not refrain from throwing parties, though with the exception of a dinner with Bill Dozier and his wife, and another with her friend George Cukor, she did most of her socializing in her hotel suite with a cigarette in one hand and an oxygen mask in the other. Because she felt old and ill most of the time – nothing of which comes across in the finished episodes of *Batman*, quite the reverse – she was pleased when the time came for her to return to New York. She had booked a seat next to Cary Grant but she slept throughout the flight and had to be carried from the aircraft by Robert Williams. Her feet and legs had swollen through misuse of barbiturates and she was in tremendous pain.

No sooner had she recovered from her ordeal than she was sent a copy of *Lena*, the recently published and for its time controversial autobiogrphy of Lena Horne. The singer had severely criticized a number of Southern stars, notably Miriam Hopkins, for their alleged racism, and she wrote of Tallulah,

I had the feeling she was a lady ... a genuine dyed-in-the-wool
Southerner who really thought she was protective of Negroes:
misguided, but essentially kind. When she talked about how
cute the little piccaninnies were and discussed the non-Negro-
ness of my features, she was being honestly herself ...

Tallulah was livid and publicly called Lena Horne 'a lying
bitch' for even suggesting that she, who had spent the happiest
years of her childhood in the black community, could have used
a word like 'piccaninny' and be branded a racist. In fact, she
would very soon find herself faced with a reverse situation for
being supportive of her black friends.

After resting for several weeks, and seeing almost no one,
Tallulah was asked to guest on *The Smothers Brothers Show*.
She agreed, with the usual conditions: first-class hotel
accommodation and travelling expenses, private hairdresser
and secretary and all for as little in-studio activity as possible.
Her demands were met with little hesitation. Her peers, like
herself, knew only too well that she was living on borrowed
time and Tallulah herself reiterated this on 24 November, prior
to leaving New York, by changing her will. Three lawyers and a
secretary were summoned to her apartment; the amendments
were drastic, particularly so far as her sister was concerned.
Tallulah had still not forgiven her for the Tangier incident.

In Hollywood, Tallulah was reunited with a 47-year-old bar
pianist named Fred Hall, an otherwise insignificant man from
San Diego whom she had first met in 1941 when she had been
touring the military installations and he had been about to serve
overseas. Hall had been terrified of getting killed and Tallulah
had spat in his eye for luck. He had survived the war, since
which time he had written to her every week, without fail.
Tallulah was more depressed in Hollywood than she had been
for years but when Hall asked to see her he was granted an
entire evening and succeeded in cheering her up. She saw no one
else until 9 October, when she attended Marlene Dietrich's
one-woman show on Broadway after receiving a personal
invitation from the star herself – otherwise she would not have
gone. She was driven to the Lunt-Fontanne Theater with

Maureen O'Sullivan, and caused a riot of excitement when she stepped out of the limousine to be cheered by hundreds of adoring fans. Afterwards she attended the private party at the Rainbow Room.

It took Tallulah five days to film less than 30 minutes of television footage for *The Smothers Brothers Show*; she completely ignored her agent Milton Goldman's advice to 'just sit around, talk, and look good'. During her first sketch, she played Mata Hari and sang 'My Funny Valentine'. She then narrated a monologue about gun control and quipped, 'If one out of every four Americans is carrying a gun, darlings, that means one of the Lennon Sisters must be packing a rod!' A great controversy raged, however, when Tallulah insisted upon introducing a group of young black singers called The Temptations. This was cut from the finished transmission, which went out on 17 December – the official excuse was that Tallulah had overrun her allotted time on the show by talking too much. Her rendition of 'My Funny Valentine' was also cut, in order to make way for a number from Cass Elliot, the singer with the Mamas and the Papas. Tallulah hit the roof, branding her 'that idiot fat woman' but she was particularly vindictive towards her mortal enemy, George Wallace, for 'supporting racist views'. She vowed that she would never appear on the television again but, within a few weeks, she had changed her mind when offered a spot on *The Merv Griffin Show*.

Tallulah had always had a soft spot for Griffin, since working with him in cabaret in Las Vegas. She found him warm and sincere and she trusted him implicitly. She had appeared in two of his shows immediately after *Batman* but the most painful excursion for her was the one that went out on 23 January 1968, eight days before her sixty-fifth birthday. Griffin sent a car to collect her and even instructed the driver to carry her every step of the way from her room to the car. She was so ill that it took her fully ten minutes to shuffle the five yards from the backstage area to her seat and, while Griffin overran his script praising her with every superlative in the book, the cameraman was given the signal to steer clear of Tallulah, who was literally fighting to get her breath back. Eventually, she was

handed a tumbler of water – it was in fact neat gin – and once
she had downed this she was ready to continue. This time there
would be no singing. She spoke about soap operas, her
favourite politicians, bridge, illness, and loneliness. When Merv
Griffin asked her, as the credits were rolling, why she had so
obviously put herself through the mill to do the show, she
replied, 'I wanted to prove to all my fans that I'm not dead,
darling.'

On 14 May, Tallulah appeared alongside Paul McCartney
and John Lennon on *The Tonight Show*, hosted by Joe
Garagiola. She told the famous pair from Liverpool that the
real love of her life had always been baseball, then went into a
long, laboured speech which clearly caused her some distress:
'My godson adores all your songs, darlings, but I don't think I
understand all of them. Too much social significance, you
know! I like a song I can hum because I can't always remember
all the words – in all the right places, I mean!' These were the
last words her fans ever heard her speak.

At the end of June, Tallulah was lounging on the couch in her
living room, deeply engrossed in one of her soap operas, when
the ceiling fell in. Astonishingly, though several large chunks of
plaster landed on her, she was unhurt. Jesse Levy telephoned
her sister, who at 67 had curbed her globetrotting to spend
more time at her lakeside cottage in Rock Hall, Maryland.
Eugenia owned a second cottage, quite near by, which she
always used to put up guests, and Levy was instructed to bring
Tallulah at once. However, because Tallulah was terrified of
getting stuck in a traffic jam, she refused to budge from her
apartment until the holiday traffic had abated. Thus the pair
did not arrive in Rock Hall until 6 July. Tallulah should have
been happy. Tamara Geva, with whom she had got on
unusually well since John Emery's death in 1964, was a
neighbour, and Louisa Carpenter owned a large estate. She
invited Tallulah and Levy to go shooting with her. The offer
was declined, of course, and much of the three-month stay was
passed playing bridge, dining with Tamara and going at it
hammer and tongs with Eugenia. A frequent visitor to Rock
Hall was Cindy – William Brockman's wife brought her two

children, Mary Eugenia, aged four, and Tallulah Brockman, aged one. The older Tallulah pretended to be horrified when told that she had a namesake, and declared, 'The bitch'd better have blue eyes!' She did, and Tallulah adored her.

When the time came for Jesse Levy to drive her back to New York, Tallulah revealed her most heartfelt ambition. She said to Eugenia, 'I don't care any more. Each night when I go to bed, I pray to God that I won't wake up in the morning.' New York was in the clutches of an Asian flu epidemic and Tallulah caught it almost at once. Jesse Levy summoned her doctor, who arranged for her to be admitted to St Luke's Hospital, where pneumonia was diagnosed. For a while she seemed to rally: there were reports of her screaming at the doctors and other patients, or merely complaining about the service.

The following day, Eugenia flew in from Rock Hall, but by now Tallulah was dying. Her breathing failed and she was put on to a ventilator – fighting against this, she pulled out the intravenous tube and immediately lapsed into a coma from which she did not emerge. During the night of 12 December 1968, she died. Her last audible words had been, 'Codeine, bourbon.'

Epilogue

Tallulah's will surprised many, and shocked a few. She, who had often claimed she was hard up, was now revealed to have been worth in excess of $2 million.

No preference was given for 'long service' though faithful retainers such as Robert Williams and the Underdowns from her London years were not forgotten, and Edie Smith was bequeathed $10,000 and a priceless cache of jewellery. Jesse Levy, who had only acquired importance during the last few years of her life, inherited one quarter of her estate, $10,000, and the Baldwin grand piano with which he had brightened her nights long after men had ceased to be any use to her. Estelle Winwood was also left $10,000, along with the diamond and sapphire pendant that she had admired. She would survive her friend by some two decades, living to be over a hundred.

Eugenia Bankhead, with whom Tallulah had hardly ever seen eye to eye, lost out on her inheritance owing to her indiscretions in the recent past – she was bequeathed just $5,000, an old mink and a monthly annuity of $250. The one woman whom Tallulah had loved and respected above all others, Eugenia Rawls Seawell, inherited with her children one half of the estate, a Renoir and several pieces of very valuable jewellery. The remaining quarter of the estate went to her sister Eugenia's two grandchildren, Mary and Tally. Kenneth Carten and Philip Hall each received $10,000. Tallulah had wanted to bequeath her Augustus John to her most trusted friend, Jock Whitney, but never got around to adding the clause to her will. Whitney purchased it for an undisclosed amount, then donated it to the

National Portrait Gallery at the Smithsonian Institution.

Eugenia Bankhead – she had reverted to her maiden name after her seventh divorce – gave permission for a post mortem. Though Tallulah's liver had hardly been affected by half a century of bourbon, her lungs were 70 per cent ravaged with emphysema, a condition that her doctor claimed would almost certainly have been reversed, had she given up smoking. Her body was then taken to Rock Hall for the funeral on 14 December, the arrangements for which were made by Louisa Carpenter and Robert Williams. The service at the tiny St Paul's Episcopal Church was officiated at by the Rev Alfred Nobel Redding. Tallulah's coffin was lined with baby blue silk and she had been dressed in her favourite bedwrap complete with a multitude of cigarette burns. Before the lid was closed, Louisa Carpenter slipped in the rabbit's foot given to her many years before by her father. The coffin was then drenched in hundreds of white chrysanthemums ... and as it was being carried into the churchyard, in a gesture which probably would have amused Tallulah, a flock of wild geese swooped noisily overhead.

Leading the 40 or so mourners were Eugenia (who 11 years later would be laid next to her sister) and her family, the Seawells and Estelle Winwood – the only showbusiness personality who could make it to the funeral and the only one Tallulah would have wanted there. None of her relatives from Jasper was there – they were still bearing a grudge because Tallulah had not attended Will's burial. And though these people had always spoken kindly of her during her lifetime – afraid of doing otherwise, according to one close friend, for fear of her exposing too many family secrets – it would not take them long to begin criticizing her now, particularly as she had had the last laugh by cutting them out of her will ... though they have since repaid her by never once visiting her grave.

Tallulah had often remarked, 'I don't care what they say about me after I'm dead, so long as they say something!' The tributes were legion and continue three decades after her passing. None, however, was quite so touching or sincere as those proffered by her fellow Alabamans. Nancy Nilsson, whose proudest possession is the autographed photograph given to her by Tallulah in May 1963, which still hangs on her wall to this day, spoke of her first visit to Tallulah's grave, which remains almost offensively plain, bearing just her name and dates:

> I remembered she said that what she wanted written on her tombstone was 'Press On'. I took out my lipstick and just before writing those words on that plain, cold granite but Dex, my husband, suggested perhaps the local folk might not appreciate it. I wanted to do it anyway, but didn't. I did, however, speak to her and said, 'Press on, Lady. Press on!'

The ultimate homage was bestowed on Tallulah by an anonymous scribe from the *Huntsville Times*, the day after her death, and should serve as this most remarkable woman's epitaph:

> Her piercing epithets were directed only at persons big enough to withstand them without injury. She had no patience with cruelty, pretence or hypocrisy. Acutely sensitive to disloyalty herself, she was intensely loyal to the causes she thought noble and generous to those who earned her friendship. These were instincts inherited from a family noted for a practical idealism in public life. They were not ladylike mannerisms learned at her finishing school. So, whoever is composing her eulogy should avoid any reference to Tallulah the Lady – that could evoke a raucously contemptuous snort from the wings. It is as Tallulah the Gentlewoman that she should take her last bow.

Appendix I
The Films of
Tallulah Bankhead

The Wishful Girl   Empire Mutual, 1918
Directors: Del Henderson, John B O'Brien. Producer: Edna
Goodrich. Tallulah won her part in the play after sending her
photograph to *Picture Play* magazine.

When Men Betray   Sterling Films, 1918
Producer/Director: Ivan Abramson. Based on short story by
Clark Jefferson Winston.

Thirty a Week   Goldwyn Pictures, 1918
Producer: Samuel goldwyn. Screenplay: Thompson Buchanan.
With Tom Moore.

The Virtuous Vamp   Gladstone Productions, 1919
Director: John Emerson. Producer: Joseph M Schenk. Tallulah
was only an extra. The stars of the film were Constance
Talmadge and Conway Tearle.

His House in Order   Ideal Films, 1928
Based upon the play by Sir Arthur Wing Pinero. When the
original star Gladys Cooper was replaced by Tallulah, her
co-star Gerald du Maurier dropped out and was replaced by
Ian Hunter.

Tarnished Lady   Paramount, 1931

Director: George Cukor. Screenplay: Donald Ogden Stewart. Also starred Clive Brook, Phoebe Foster, Osgood Perkins, Alexander Kirkland, Elizabeth Patterson.

My Sin   Paramount, 1931
Director: George Abbott. Screenplay: Adelaide Heilbron, Owen Davis. Also starred: Fredric March, Ann Sutherland, Scott Kolk, Harry Davenport, Margaret Adams, Lily Cahill.

The Cheat   Paramount, 1931
Director: George Abbott. Storyline: Hector Turnbull. Also starred: Irving Pichel, Ann Andrews, Henry Warwick, Jay Fassett, Harvey Stevens, William Ingersoll, Hanaki Yoshiwara, Robert Strange.

Thunder Below   Paramount 1932
Director: Richard Wallace. Screenplay: Sidney Buchman, Josephine Lovett, based on the book by Thomas Rourke. Also starred: Charles Bickford, Edward van Sloan, Paul Lukas, Eugene Pallette, Ralph Forbes, James Finlayson, Mona Rico, Leslie Fenton, Gaby Rivas.

Make Me a Star   Paramount, 1932
Director: William Beaudine. Screenplay: Sam Mintz, Arthur Kober, Walter DeLion. Starred Zasu Pitts, Joan Blondell, Stuart Erwin, Ben Turpin and others. Tallulah's name was omitted from the list of credits.

The Devil and the Deep   Paramount, 1932
Director: Marion Gering. Storyline: Harry Harvey. Also starred: Charles Laughton, Gary Cooper, Cary Grant, Arthur Hoyt, Juliette Compton, Paul Porcasi, Henry Kolker, Dorothy Christy.

Faithless   M G M, 1932
Director: Harry Beaumont. Storyline: Mildred Cram. Also

starred: Robert Montgomery, Louise Closser Hale, Maurice Murphy, Hugh Herbert, Anna Appel.

Stage-Door Canteen   United Artists, 1943
Director: Frank Borzage. Producer: Sol Lesser. This version was different from the one starring and centring around a fictional meeting between a GI and Joan Leslie, and featured Tallulah, Ina Claire, Katharine Hepburn, Katherine Cornell, Ethel Merman, Paul Muni, Yehudi Menuhin, Judith Anderson, Humphrey Bogart, Merle Oberon, Gypsy Rose Lee, George Raft and others.

Lifeboat   20th Century-Fox, 1944
Director: Alfred Hitchcock. Producer: Kenneth MacGovan. Screenplay: Jo Swerling, based on novel by John Steinbeck. Also starred: John Hodiak, William Bendix, Canada Lee, Hume Cronyn, Walter Slezak, Mary Anderson, Henry Hull, Heather Angel.

A Royal Scandal   20th Century-Fox, 1945
Director: Otto Preminger. Producer: Ernst Lubitsch. Screenplay: Edwin Justice Mayer, adapted by Bruno Frank from *The Czarina*, a play by Lajos Biro and Melchior Lengyel. Also starred: William Eythe, Anne Baxter, Charles Coburn, Vincent Price, Mischa Auer, Sig Ruman, Vladimir Sokoloff. Eva Gabor appeared in some prints.

Main Street to Broadway   M G M, 1953
Producer: Lester Cowan. Screenplay: Samson Raphaelson. Director: Tay Garnett. Tallulah played herself. The cast included: Ethel and Lionel Barrymore, Agnes Moorehead, Shirley Booth, Helen Hayes, Cornel Wilde, Mary Martin, Rex Harrison, Lilli Palmer.

The Boy Who Owned a Melephant   Universal-International,
                                                        1959
Producers/Script: Saul Swimmer, Tony Anthony. Tallulah narrated the story which starred Brockman Seawell, her godson. The film won the Gold Leaf Award at the Venice

International Children's Film Festival.

Fanatic (Die! Die! My Darling!)   Columbia, 1965
Director: Silvio Narizzano. Producer: Anthony Hinds. Screenplay: Richard Matheson, from the novel *Nightmare* by Anne Blaisdell. Also starred: Stefanie Powers, Peter Vaughan, Donald Sutherland, Yootha Joyce, Maurice Kaufman.

The Daydreamer   Embassy Pictures, 1966
Director: Jules Bass. Producer/Script: Arthur Rankin Jr, based on four stories by Hans Christian Andersen. Tallulah was the voice of the Sea Witch. Other voices included: Hayley Mills, Ed Wynn, Boris Karloff, Sessue Hayakawa, Burl Ives, Victor Borge.

Appendix II
The Stage, Radio and TV Plays
of Tallulah Bankhead

The Squab Farm   13 March 1918
                                              Bijou Theater, New York
Written by Frederic and Fanny Hatton. Produced by Jake and
Lee Shubert. Directed by J C Huffman. Try-outs: New Haven.
With Alma Tell, Gladys Sinclair, Harry Davenport, Helen
Barnes, Lowell Sherman, William L Gibson, Raymond
Bloomer, G Oliver Smith, Marie Centlivre. 45 performances in
New York.

39 East   31 March 1919
                                        Broadhurst Theater, New York
Written and directed by Rachel Crothers. Produced by Jake and
Lee shubert. With Sidney Blackmer, Henry Hull, Lucia Moore,
John Morris, Alison Skipworth. Tallulah replaced Constance
Binney on her weekends off. 6 performances.

Footloose   10 May 1919
                                        Greenwich Theater, New York
Written by Zoë Akins, adapted from Herman Merivale's and F
C Grove's 'Forget-Me-Not'. Directed and produced by George
C Tyler. With Norman Trevor, Emily Stevens, John Webster,
Lillian Brennard, Elizabeth Risdon, Robert Casadesus. 32
performances.

Nice People   2 March 1921
                              Klaw Theater, New York
Written and directed by Rachel Crothers. Produced by Sam
Harris. With Rod la Roque, Francine Larrimore, Katherine
Cornell, Henry Hull, Hugh Huntley, Merle Maddern, Charles
Gibney. 120 performances.

Everyday   16 November 1921
                             Bijou Theater, New York
Written and directed by Rachel Crothers. Produced by Mary
Kirkpatrick. With Henry Hull, Lucille Watson, Minnie Dupree,
Mary Donnelly. 30 performances.

Danger   22 December 1922
                        39th Street Theater, New York
Written by Cosmo Hamilton. Produced by Carle Carleton.
Tallulah replaced Kathlene MacDonnell. With Leslie Howard,
H B Warner, Ruth Hammond, Gilda Leary, Stapleton Kent,
Know Orde, Marie Goff. 79 performances.

No, Sirree!   30 April 1922
                        49th Street Theater, New York
A 'one-off, anonymous entertainment' produced by The
Algonquin Round Table, with sketches/performances by
Tallulah (in 'He Who Gets Flapped'), Alexander Woollcott,
Dorothy Parker, Robert E Sherwood, Ring Lardner, Robert
Benchley, George S Kaufman, Marc Connelly, etc. Music by
Jascha Heifetz.

Her Temporary Husband   31 August 1922
                             Frazee Theater, New York
Written by Edward A Paulton. Directed and produced by H
Frazee. With Henry Mortimer, Ann Andrews, Selena Royle,
William Courtenay. 92 performances.

The Exciters   22 September 1922
                       Times Square Theater, New York
Written by Martin Brown. Directed and produced by Archie

and Edgar Selwyn. With Aline MacMahon, Chester Morris, Enid Markey, Allen Dinehart, Robert Hyman, Thais Lawton, Florence Finn, Echlin Gayer. 43 performances.

The Dancers   15 February 1923
                                  Wyndham's Theatre, London
Written by Hubert Parsons (Sir Gerald du Maurier, Viola Tree). Directed and produced by Sir Gerald du Maurier. With him, Nigel Bruce, Audrey Carten, Lilian Braithwaite. 344 performances.

Conchita   19 March 1924
                                   Queen's Theatre, London
Written/directed by Edward Knoblock. Produced by Jeffry Lowden. 37 performances.

This Marriage   7 May 1924
                                   Comedy Theatre, London
Written by Eliot Crawshay. Directed by J E Vedrenne and José G Levy. Produced by E Holman Clark. With Herbert Marshall, Cathleen Nesbitt, Thomas Reynolds, A Bromley Davenport, Auriol Lee. 53 performances.

The Creaking Chair   22 July 1924
                                   Comedy Theatre, London
Produced/directed/starring C Aubrey Smith. With Nigel Bruce. 235 performances.

Fallen Angels   21 April 1925
                                    Globe Theatre, London
Written/directed/produced by Noël Coward. Tallulah replaced Margaret Bannerman. With Edna Best. 158 performances.

The Green Hat   2 September 1925
                                   Adelphi Theatre, London
Written by Michael Arlen. Produced by Gerald Hopkins Jr. With Leonard Upton, Robert Horton. 128 performances.

Scotch Mist 26 January 1926
St Martin's Theatre, London
Written/produced by Sir Patrick Hastings. With Godfrey
Tearle. 117 performances.

They Knew What They Wanted 18 May 1926
St Martin's Theatre, London
Written by Sidney Howard. Directed/produced by Basil Dean.
With Glenn Anders, Sam Livesay. 108 performances.

The Gold Diggers 14 December 1926
Lyric Theatre, London
Written by Avery Hopwood. Produced by William Mollison in
association with Jack Waller and Herbert Clayton. With
Madge Aubrey, Jobyna Howland, Ian Hunter, Joan Barry,
Sidney Seaward, Dorothy St Elmo, Marjorie Brooks, Hugh
Williams, Ruth Terry, Fred Kerr, Joan Clarkson, David Wilton,
Charles Carson, John Perry. 180 performances.

Always Apologize 5 April 1927
Café de Paris, London
A 'one-off gala entertainment' for the benefit of King's College
Hospital, London, written by Audrey and Waverley Carten.

Great Lovers of Romance 6 May 1927
New Theatre, London
A one-off performance written/produced/staged by Olga Lynn
for the benefit of the Leicestershire Nursing Association.
Tallulah played Cleopatra.

The Garden of Eden 30 May 1927
Lyric Theatre, London
Written by Bernauer & Oesterreicher, adapted by Avery
Hopwood. Directed/produced by Herbert Clayton and Jack
Waller. With Hugh Williams, George Bellamy, Rex Caldwell,
Eric Maturin, Marcelle Roche, Arthur Ross, Eva Moore,
Robert English, Barbara Gott, Arthur Holman, Annie Esmond.
232 performances.

Blackmail   28 February 1928
                                        Globe Theatre, London
Written by Charles Bennett. Directed/produced by Raymond
Massey and A H Woods, in association with Sir Alfred Butt.
With Frank Vosper, Alexander Onslow, Amy Veness, Julian
Hamilton, Henrietta Watson, Alfred Clark, Reginald Gardiner,
James Rennie. 42 performances.

Mud and Treacle   9 May 1928
                                        Globe Theatre, London
Written/produced by Frederick Lonsdale.

Her Cardboard Lover   21 August 1928
                                        Lyric Theatre, London
Written by Jacques Deval and P G Wodehouse. Produced by
Jack Middleton. With Leslie Howard, Elizabeth Arkell, Jack
Melford. 173 performances followed by tour, commencing
Glasgow 15 April 1929.

He's Mine   29 October 1928
                                        Lyric Theatre, London
Adapted/produced by William Mollison from a French farce.
With Helen Haye, Frederick Volpe, George Howe, Allan
Aynesworth. 98 performances.

The Lady of the Camellias   5 March 1930
                                      Garrick Theatre, London
Written by Alexandre Dumas. Directed/produced by Nigel
Playfair in association with the Daniel Mayer Company (Ernest
W Parr, William Macqueen-Pope, T E Adams, Anthony
Eustrel). Music by Alfred Reynolds. Sets/costumes by Mrs
Gordon Craig, Mrs Lovat Fraser, George Sheringham. With
Glen Byam Shaw, Joan Matheson, Terence de Marney, Cecil
Humphreys, Marcus Barron, D A Clarke-Smith, Winifred
Evans, Violet Marquesita, Renée de Vaux, Angus L MacLeod,
C V France, Joan Sutherland, H Scott Russell, Ellen Pollock,
Harold Warrender, Richard Goolden. 136 performances.

Let Us Be Gay 18 August 1930
Lyric Theatre, London
Written/produced by Rachel Crothers, assisted by Gilbert Miller. Try-outs: Birmingham. With Helen Haye, Joan Matheson, Bellenden Powell, Arthur Margetson, Sybil Carlisle, Ernest Haines, Walter Fitzgerald, Francis Lister, Ronald Ward, Cecily Byrne, Eric Cowley. 128 performances in London.

Forsaking All Others 1 March 1933
Times Square Theater, New York
Written by Frank Morgan Cavett and Edward Barry Roberts. Produced by Tallulah, with Archie Selwyn. Directed by Thomas Mitchell/H Wagstaff Gribble/Frank Morgan Cavett/Arthur J Beckhard. Costumes by Hattie Carnegie. Sets by Donald Oenslanger. With Fred Keating, Ilka Chase, Henry Fonda, Cora Witherspoon, Barbara O'Neil. Tryouts in Boston, Providence, Wilmington, Washington. 110 performances in New York.

Dark Victory 9 November 1934
Plymouth Theater, New York
Written by George Brewer Jr and Bertram Bloch. Directed by Robert Milton. Produced by Alexander McKaig. With Earl Larimore, Dwight Fiske, Helen Strickland, Ann Andrews, Frederick Leister, Myra Hampton, Lewis Dayton, Mildred Wall. 51 performances.

Rain 12 February 1935
Music Box Theater, New York
Written by John Colton and Clemence Randolph, based on story by William Somerset Maugham. Directed by Sam Forrest. Produced by Sam H Harris. With Kent Thurber, Ethel Wilson, Granville Bates, Ethel Intropodi, Herbert Ransom, Nicholas Joy, Emma Wilcox, Jack McKee. Try-outs: Philadelphia. 47 performances in New York.

Something Gay 29 April 1935
Morosco Theater, New York
Written by Adelaide Heilbron. Directed by Thomas Mitchell.

Produced by Jake and Lee Shubert. Sets by Donald Oenslanger. With Walter Pidgeon, Kent Thurber, Hugh Sinclair, Nancy Ryan, Percy Ames, Roy Gordon, Elizabeth Dewing. Try-outs: Boston. 56 performances in New York.

Reflected Glory   21 September 1936
                                    Morosco Theater, New York
Written/directed by George Kelly. Produced by Lee Shubert. Sets by Norman Rock. With Clay Clement, Ann Andrews, Robert Bordoni, Alden Chase, S T Bratton, Philip Reed, William Brisbane. Try-outs: San Francisco, Los Angeles. 127 performances in New York followed by cross-country tour.

Twelfth Night   30 August 1937
                                    CBS Radio: Radio Playhouse production
A single performance with Estelle Winwood, Orson Welles, Sir Cedric Hardwicke, Conway Tearle, Helen Menken.

Antony and Cleopatra   10 November 1937
                                    Mansfield Theater, New York
Adapted from Shakespeare by William Strunk Jr. Directed by Reginald Bach. Produced by Tallulah/Rowland Stebbins (under the name of Lawrence Rivers). Costumes/Sets by Cecil Beaton and Joe Mielziner. With John Emery, Regina Wallace, Conway Tearle, Stephen Fox, Thomas Chalmers, Fania Marinoff. Try-outs: Pittsburgh. 5 performances in New York, with musical score by Virgil Thomson.

The Circle   18 April 1938
                                    Playhouse Theater, New York
Written by William Somerset Maugham. Directed by Bretaigne Windust. Produced by William A Brady. Sets by Donald Oenslanger. Costumes by Hattie Carnegie. With John Emery, Bramwell Fletcher, Dennis Hoey, Cecil Humphreys, May Marshall, Audrey Ridgewell. 72 performances.

I Am Different   August 1938
                                    Los Angeles

Written by Zoë Akins, translated from the play by Lily Hatvany. Produced by Lee Shubert. With Glenn Anders, John Emery, Fritzi Scheff, Margaret Sedden, Ara Gerald. The play began touring in Los Angeles in the August, and closed 26/11/1938 in Washington.

The Little Foxes   15 February 1939
                                      National Theater, New York
Written by Lillian Hellman. Directed/produced by Herman Shumlin. Sets by Howard Bay. Costumes by Aline Bernstein. With a several times changed cast including Eugenia Rawls, Patricia Collinge, Florence Williams, Carl Benton Reid, Dan Duryea, John Marriott, Abbie Mitchell, Lee Baker, Frank Conroy, Charles Dingle. There were 408 performances. The national company began its tour in Washington on 5/2/1940, played 12 cities, and closed in Detroit on 15/2/1940. After *The Second Mrs Tanqueray* it reopened in Princeton on 14/9/1940, and toured until 5/4/1941, when it closed in Philadelphia.

The Second Mrs Tanqueray   1 July 1940
                                   Maplewood Playhouse, New Jersey
Written by Sir Arthur Wing Pinero. Directed by Romney Brent. Produced by Leo Bulgakov, Cheryl Crawford, Proctor Jones. Sets by Albert Ward. Costumes by Madame Karinska. With Stephan Cole, Colin Keith-Johnston, Eugenia Rawls, Edmund George, Madeleine Clive, Leonore Harris, James MacColl, Jess Barker, Ralph Kellard. Summer stock followed by dates in Amherst, Taunton, Harrison, Stockridge, Dennis, White Plains, Cedarhurst, Marblehead.

The Talley Method   18 April 1941
                                   CBS Radio: The Campbell Playhouse
No other details.

Her Cardboard Lover   July 1941
A revival of the aforementioned London production, directed by John C Wilson and produced by Cheryl Crawford. Costumes by Hattie Carnegie. Make-up/hair by Elizabeth

Arden. With Stephan Cole, Fred Keating, Harry Ellerbe, Sandy Campbell, Viola Frayne. The play opened in Westport, and played dates in Brighton, Maplewood, Marblehead, Ogonquit, White Plains, Cedarhurst.

The Little Foxes 10 October 1941
CBS Radio: The Philip Morris Playhouse
A single performance, with the original Broadway cast.

Clash By Night 27 December 1941
Belasco Theater, New York
Written by Clifford Odets. Directed by Lee Strasberg. Produced by Billy Rose. With Lee J cobb, Robert Ryan, Katherine Locke, Stephan Cole, Art Smith, William Nunn, Joseph Schildkraut, John F Hamilton, Joseph Shamuck, Harold Grau. Try-outs: Philadelphia, Detroit, Baltimore. 49 performances in New York.

Suspicion 3 February 1942
CBS Radio: The Philip Morris Playhouse
Written by Dorothy L Sayers. No other details.

The Skin of Our Teeth 18 November 1942
Plymouth Theater, New York
Written by Thornton Wilder. Directed by Elia Kazan. Produced by Michael Myerberg. Costumes by Mary Percy Schenck. With Fredric March, Montgomery Clift, Florence Eldridge, Stanley Prager, E G Marshall, Florence Reed, Frances Heflin, André Ratoucheff. The try-outs were in New Haven, Baltimore, Philadelphia, Washington, with 229 performances by Tallulah in New York before she left the production.

I Served On Bataan 2 May 1943
NBC Radio: That They Might Live
A war drama. No other details. Repeated on 29/2/1944.

These Are Our Men 16 January 1945
NBC Radio: The War Bond Show
A war drama, as above, with Walter Huston.

Foolish Notion　　　　　　　　　　　　　　13 March 1945
　　　　　　　　　　　　Martin Beck Theater, New York
Written by Philip Barry. Directed by John C Wilson. Produced
by Armina Marshall, Theresa Helburn, Lawrence Langner. Sets
by Joe Mielziner. Costumes by Mainbocher. With Donald
Cook, Henry Hull, John Emery, Aubrey Mather, Mildred
Dunnock, Barbara Kent, Joan Shepherd. Try-outs in New
Haven, Boston, Baltimore, Washington, followed by 104
performances in New York, and lengthy tour.

A Salute to The U.S. Cruiser Helena　　　　14 August 1945
　　　　　　　　　　　　NBC Radio: The Navy Hour
A war drama. No other details.

The Story of Helen Zabriskie　　　　　　　　26 June 1946
　　　　　　　　　　CBS Radio: Radio Reader's Digest
No other details.

The Eagle Has Two Heads　　　　　　　　19 March 1947
　　　　　　　　　　　　Plymouth Theater, New York
Adapted by Ronald Duncan from Jean Cocteau's 'La Mort
Écoute Aux Portes'. Directed/produced by John C Wilson. Sets
by Donald Oenslanger. Costumes by Aline Bernstein. with
Marlon Brando, Colin Keith-Johnston (both replaced), Helmut
Dantine, Eleanor Wilson, Kendall Clark, Cherokee Thornton.
Try-outs (as 'Eagle Rampant'): Hartford, Washington, Boston,
Providence, Baltimore, Philadelphia, Toronto, Pittsburgh,
Montreal, Cleveland, Detroit, Buffalo. 29 performances in New
York.

Private Lives　　　　　　　　　　　　　4 October 1948
　　　　　　　　　　　　Plymouth Theater, New York
Written by Noël Coward. Directed/produced by John C
Wilson. Sets by Charles Elson. Costumes by Mainbocher. With
William Langord, Donald Cook, Barbara Baxley, Thérèse
Ouadri. There were very extensive tours before and after the
Broadway run of 248 performances, totalling 204 weeks
en-theatre. It finally closed on 3 June 1950 in Passaic. There

were several directors besides Wilson, including Martin Manulis and Bob Henderson, and several cast changes (Buff Cobb, Eugenia Rawls, Phil Arthur and others).

Lifeboat   16 November 1950
          NBC Radio: Screen Director's Playhouse
Written by Jack Ruben, adapted from the Steinbeck novel which had formed a basis for the film. Directed by Alfred Hitchcock, Bill Karn. Produced by Howard Wiley. With Jeff Chandler, Henry Rowland, Ann Diamond, William Wilms, Sheldon Leonard, Barbara Eiler, Bob Glen.

Dark Victory   15 February 1951
          NBC Radio: Screen Director's Playhouse
Directed by Edmund Goulding. With David Brian.

Humoresque   19 April 1951
          NBC Radio: Screen Director's Playhouse
Written by Fannie Hurst. Directed by Jean Negulesco. With Stephen Cochran.

Anta Album   6 May 1951
                                          Ziegfeld Theater, New York

A single performance devised/produced by Jean Dalrymple, Robert C Schnitzer, Ben Krantz, Herman Shapiro for the American National Theater & Academy. Tallulah was Mistress of Ceremonies. Guest performers included Hedda Hopper, Gloria Swanson, Phil Baker, Shirley Booth, Geraldine Page.

All About Eve   16 November 1952
          NBC Radio: Theater Guild Of The Air
Tallulah, resenting the fact that the part had been given to her enemy Bette Davis, played herself (alias Margo Channing). With Beatrice Pearson, Kevin McCarthy.

Hedda Gabler   5 January 1954
                           ABC-TV: The United States Steel Hour

Written by Henrik Ibsen. Produced by the Theater Guild. With
Eugenia Rawls, Luther Adler, Alan Hewitt, John Baragrey.

Dear Charles   15 September 1954
                                        Morosco Theater, New York
Adapted from Sauvagon and Jackson's 'Les Enfants d'Edouard'
by Alan Melville. Directed by Edmund Baylies (following
Arthur Penn). Produced by Robert Aldrich, Richard Myers.
Costumes by Gene Coffin. Sets by Donald Oenslanger. with Fred
Keating, Nora Howard, Grace Raynor, Tom Raynor, Robert
Coote, Larry Robinson, Peter Pell, William Roerick, Werner
Klemperer, Hugh Reilly, Alice Pearce, Mary Webster. 155
performances.

A Streetcar Named Desire   15 February 1956
                                            City Center, New York
Written by Tennessee Williams. Directed by Herbert Machiz.
Produced by Jean Dalrymple. Sets based on original designs by
Joe Mielziner. With Francis Heflin, Rudy Bond, Jean Ellyn,
Bruno Damon, Gerald O'Laughlin, Sandy Campbell. Try-outs:
Miami, Palm Beach. 16 performances in New York.

Ziegfeld Follies
Produced by James Gardiner, Richard Kollmar. Musical
direction by Jack Cole. The revue opened in Boston on 16/4/56
and after 16 performances there were a further 16 in
Philadelphia, where it closed. The Broadway run commencing
26/5/56 was cancelled. The cast of 61 included Elliott Reid,
Mort Marshall, Herbert Banks, David Burns.

Welcome Darlings!   16 July 1956
                                        Westport Theater, Connecticut
Written by Jerry Herman, Dean Fuller, Jay Harnick, Paul
Keyes, Hugh Martin, Timothy Gray, Marshall Barer, Jerry de
Bono. Produced by Philip Langner, Peter Turgeon. Musical
direction Peter Howard, Ted Graham. Sets by Marvin Reiss.
Costumes by Mandel, McIntosh, Brooks, Manhattan. With
Jimmy Kirkwood, Don McKay, Gwen Harmon, the Martins,

Sheila Smith, Don Crichton, Preshy Marker, Bob Bakanic. After Westport, the revue played along the Eastern seaboard.

Eugenia   30 January 1957
                                          Ambassador Theater, New York
Adapted by Randolph Carter from Henry James's *The Europeans*. Directed by Herbert Machiz. Produced by John C Wilson. Costumes by Miles White. With Tom Ellis, Scott Merrill, Irma Hurley, Anne Meacham, June Hunt, Robert Duke, Reynolds Evans, Jay Barney, Thérèse Quadri, 12 performances.

The Hole Card   8 November 1957
                                     CBS-TV: The Schlitz Playhouse of Stars
with John Bryant, Ottola Nesmith, Isobel Elsom, Jesslyn Fox, George O'Hanlon. Repeated 18 July 1958.

Eyes of a Stranger   8 December 1957
                               CBS-TV: The General Electric Theater
Written by Jameson Brewer. Directed by Ray Milland. Produced by William Frye. With Gavin Gordon, Cynthia Leighton, Joan Warner, Richard Denning, Dan Tobin.

House on the Rocks
Written by George Batson. The play toured the summer circuit, taking in Kennebunkport, Harrisburg, Binghampton, Laconia-Gilford, Nyack, but failed to make Broadway.

Crazy October
Written/directed by James Herlihy. Produced by Walter Starcke. Sets by Ben Edwards. Costumes by Alvin Colt. The play began its tour in New Haven, then took in Washington, Detroit, Los Angeles, and closed in San Francisco. With Estelle Winwood, Joan Blondell, Collin Wilcox, Jack Weston, J Frank Lucas, Fred Beir.

Midgie Purvis   1 February 1961
                                    Martin Beck Theater, New York

Written by Mary Chase. Directed by Burgess Meredith. Produced by Robert Whitehead, Roger L Stevens, in association with Lawrence Carr, Robert Fryer, John Herman. Sets by Ben Edwards. Costumes by Guy Kent. With Alice Pearce, William Redfield, Jean Bruno, John Cecil Home, Nydia Westman, Kip McCardle, Russell Hardle, Paul Mace. 21 performances.

A Man For Oona   5 May 1962
                    CBS-TV: the United States Steel Hour
Written by Michael Dynes. Directed by Tom Donovan. Produced by George Kondolf. With Murray Matheson, Nancy Carroll, Christine Pickles, Patrick Horgan, Astrid Wilstrud, Yoshi Naka, Patrick Horgan, Lucie Lancaster, Walton Butterfield.

Here Today
Written by George Oppenheimer. the play toured in summer/winter stock in 1962/3/4, achieving most of its success in Skowhegan, Ivoryton, Mountainhome, Ogunquit, Fitchburg, Dennis, Falmouth. With Estelle Winwood.

The Milk Train Doesn't Stop Here Any More   1 January 1964
                    Brooks Atkinson Theater, New York
Written by Tennessee Williams. Directed by Tony Richardson. Produced by the David Merrick Foundation. Music by Ned Rorem. Sets by Rouben-Ter-Arutunian. Costumes by Kirinska. With Tab Hunter, Ralph Roberts, Marian Seldes, Ruth Ford, Bobby Dean Hooks, Konrad Matthaei. 5 performances.

Batman   15-16 March 1967
                                                    ABC-TV
Tallulah appeared as The Black Widow in two episodes of this popular series: 'The Black Widow Strikes Again' and 'Caught In The Spider's Web'. With Adam West and Burt Ward.

Index